THE WINOOSKI

Rivers of America Books

ALREADY PUBLISHED ARE:

THE ALLEGHENY by Frederick Way, Jr.
THE ARKANSAS by Clyde Brion Davis
THE BRANDYWINE by Henry Seidel Canby
THE CHAGRES by John Easter Minter
THE CHARLES by Arthur Bernon Tourtellot
THE CHICAGO by Harry Hansen
THE COLORADO by Frank Waters
THE COLUMBIA by Stewart H. Holbrook
THE CONNECTICUT by Walter Hard
THE DELAWARE by Harry Emerson Wildes
THE EVERGLADES by Marjory Stoneman Douglas
THE FRASER by Bruce Hutchinson
THE FRENCH BROAD by Wilma Dykeman
THE GILA by Edwin Corle
THE HOUSATONIC by Chard Powers Smith
THE HUDSON by Carl Carmer
THE HUMBOLDT by Dale L. Morgan
THE ILLINOIS by James Gray
THE JAMES (New Revised Edition, 1945) by Blair Niles
THE KAW by Floyd Benjamin Streeter
KENNEBEC by Robert P. Tristram Coffin
THE KENTUCKY by T. D. Clark
LOWER MISSISSIPPI by Hodding Carter
THE MACKENZIE by Leslie Roberts

THE MERRIMACK by Raymond P. Holden
THE MISSOURI by Stanley Vestal
THE MOHAWK by Codman Hislop
THE MONONGAHELA by Richard Bissell
THE OHIO by R. E. Banta
THE POTOMAC by Frederick Gutheim
POWDER RIVER by Struthers Burt
RIVER OF THE CAROLINAS: The Santee
by Henry Savage
RIVERS OF THE EASTERN SHORE by Hulbert Footner
THE SACRAMENTO by Julian Dana
THE ST. JOHNS by Branch Cabell and A. J. Hanna
THE ST. LAWRENCE by Henry Beston
THE SALINAS by Anne B. Fisher
SALT RIVERS OF THE MASSACHUSETTS SHORE by Henry F. Howe
THE SANGAMON by Edgar Lee Masters
THE SASKATCHEWAN by Marjorie Wilkins Campbell
THE SAVANNAH by Thomas L. Stokes
THE SHENANDOAH by Julia Davis
THE SUSQUEHANNA by Carl Carmer
SUWANNEE RIVER by Cecile Hulse Matschat
THE TENNESSEE: The New River, Civil War to TVA
by Donald Davidson
THE TENNESSEE: The Old River, Frontier to Secession
by Donald Davidson
TWIN RIVERS: The Raritan and the Passaic
by Harry Emerson Wildes
UPPER MISSISSIPPI (New Revised Edition, 1944)
by Walter Havighurst
THE WABASH by William Ex. Wilson
THE WINOOSKI by Ralph Nading Hill
THE WISCONSIN by August Derleth
THE YAZOO RIVER by Frank E. Smith
SONGS OF THE RIVERS OF AMERICA edited by Carl Carmer

Rivers

OF AMERICA

EDITED BY

HERVEY ALLEN AND CARL CARMER

AS PLANNED AND STARTED BY

CONSTANCE LINDSAY SKINNER

The Winooski

HEARTWAY OF VERMONT

WITHDRAWN

BY

RALPH NADING HILL

ILLUSTRATED BY

GEORGE DALY

New York   *Toronto*

RINEHART & COMPANY, INC.

First Printing, April 1949
Second Printing, June 1959

To my family — all four generations

And there's fish in our streamlets and rivers, which take
Their course from the hills to our broad-bosomed lake;
Through rock-arched Winooski the salmon leaps free,
And the portly shad follows all fresh from the sea.

John Greenleaf Whittier

CONTENTS

CHAPTER

I	Old Rocks and Water	3
II	Go Forth, John Williams	9
III	Indian Summer	14
IV	Land of the Onion	20
V	A River of Their Own	28
VI	Terror Without Homicide	33
VII	Gout, Graft and Gumption	40
VIII	British Lake—A British River?	44
IX	Let Fools Contest	55
X	"His Ex'cy is at a Loss . . ."	63
XI	"Nothing But Hurry-Canes"	74
XII	One-Eyed Tom	78
XIII	Darkness at Noon	82
XIV	To a Man of Spirit	91
XV	Apparently Without Pain	107
XVI	Morning on a Warpath	113
XVII	Late Ice and First Growth Men	118
XVIII	Taking the Snake	127
XIX	Victory is a Duty	133
XX	Pray for Yourselves	139
XXI	Tom Davenport's Machine	146
XXII	The Cabot Enigma	150
XXIII	Judgment Day	153
XXIV	The Iron Ligament	156
XXV	The Empire of Justin Morgan	162
XXVI	When the Moon Rises	166

XXVII	Free Love in November	171
XXVIII	The Fortunes of Millstone Hill	175
XXIX	And the Waters Prevailed	185
XXX	Montpelier-On-The-Onion	203
XXXI	The Queen City	214
XXXII	For the Genius of the Students	223
XXXIII	In its True Colors	235
XXXIV	Voices of the Valley	238
XXXV	Echoes and Overtones	245
XXXVI	Downstream	259
	Acknowledgments	280
	Bibliographical Note	282
	Bibliography	283
	Index	295

THE WINOOSKI

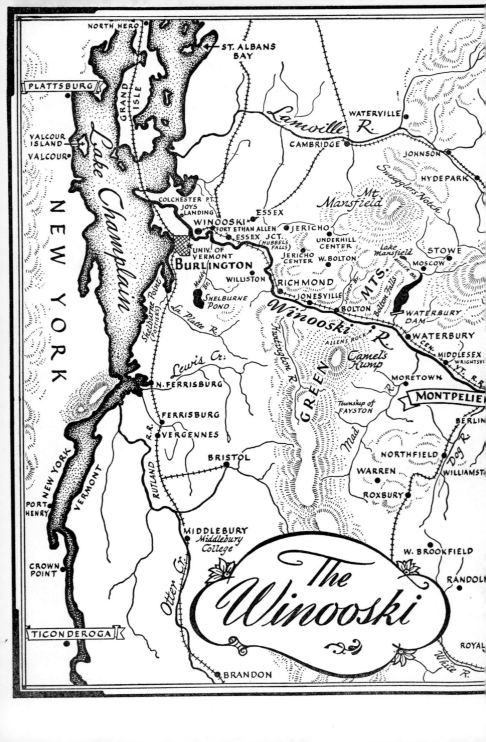

1

OLD ROCKS AND WATER

*Y*OU wouldn't call a river that drains a thousand square miles very big, yet seeing as how we in Vermont don't own even a square inch of the Connecticut, the Winooski is our largest river. I am not apologizing for its scant, meandering ninety miles. Today ninety thousand people, over one-fourth the inhabitants of Vermont, live in the valley that the Winooski has carved out of the Green Mountains. Yesterday, before the axes of these people's ancestors first echoed on the lowlands in the late 1700's, there were centuries when the Onion Land River—Winooskie-Took as Indians called it, was their special water highway between *Caniaderi-Guarunte,* "the-lake-that-is-the-gate-to-the-country," and *Quinatucquet,* "the-long-tidal-river."

For hundreds if not thousands of summers before white men saw New England, wine-skinned Algonquins canoed on the water trail of the Winooskie-Took, flowing northwest across Vermont through the wilderness of ridges and woods to the blue basin of Lake Champlain. The Indians cleared acres of timber on the flatlands near the river mouth, and seeded their corn and beans. In the silent water of the bayous and inland where the river runs deep through narrow gorges, they fished on summer days, and in the evening waited with their arrows where the animals came down to drink.

During the American stone age the river may have run red with the blood of Indian against Indian. Some say the region of northwestern Vermont was a battleground between the Iroquois and Algonquins, but when white men came the Iroquois admitted

3

that the northeast cornerstone of their vast empire was *Regio,* a barren pyramid of shale which rises out of Lake Champlain, a few miles south of the river mouth. Thus it was the Algonquins that white men found in possession of the Vermont side of Champlain and the area north to the St. Lawrence, outlet of the lake.

When the British settled southern New England and began their conquest of the northern woods, the Winooski became a vital war trail over which Algonquin scalping parties of the St. Francis and Abnaki passed on their way to southeastern New England. The Winooski flows in the lower reaches of an area above which the French first raised their flag, and then the English, a land that has reverberated to the cannon of contending armies—a country which did not achieve its destiny until the last years of the eighteenth century.

The first pale-skins who came to live on the Winooski made an immense land company of its fertile acres. With their band of flamboyant frontiersmen, they—Ethan and Ira Allen—organized the hodge-podge of new settlers and created a sovereign republic out of what had been a no man's land—a kind of county Palatine between three designing colonies, New York, New Hampshire and Massachusetts. These rawboned opportunists did much to influence the course of the American Revolution in the North. Chiefly through their efforts western New England's mountain republic became the fourteenth state in the Union.

Over the years the Winooski has watched Vermont's capital grow on its banks and Vermont's largest city emerge from what was once a pine plateau near its mouth. Today the river's water wheels light up an entire valley. The Montreal-Boston trains, the concrete highways, and overhead, the planes, hug the path the Winooski has sliced through the mountains. At all times the river and its tributaries have an ample supply of swimming holes on hand, picnic spots, shady pools where bass lie and deep gorges where the water is as spry as the trout.

Springing from the hills of eastern Vermont, the river, flowing west, ignores the quiet Connecticut, only a few miles farther east. As it gathers tributaries in its journey to Lake Champlain, the Winooski never grows great in breadth. It remains to the end of its moody course a mountain river. Sometimes, as it passes ' through ridge-locked valleys and white-steepled towns, its motion is hardly perceptible; again it flows with great force. Often it is shallow, occasionally very deep. Depending upon the sky, or the forests or fields or steep ledges through which it flows, its waters are blue or gray, black or green. On the flats near Lake Champlain, below the series of falls by which the river descends from the Green Mountains, small boats may navigate.

The Winooski's record is millions of years older than the brief history of the people who have come to live near it. Thirty-nine miles inland from Lake Champlain, the river shows you how it has sawed through a range of mountains nearly a mile high, and exposed the worn-off stumps of even more ancient mountains, perhaps five hundred million years old. Gigantic contortions of the earth's crust thrust up the first range of Green Mountains. When the older ranges were new, only the Adirondacks, opposite them, stood above the sea. The water, ice and wind of unintelligible years dwarfed the old range. During what geologists call the Appalachian Revolution two hundred million years ago, another vast disturbance folded the earth's crust and raised new Green Mountains to a great and jagged height. The Winooski may be older than these mountains; it may have etched its precipitous water gap at the same rate that the peaks arose. Perhaps the irregular bow of the uplifting mountains gave birth to the river. Whatever its origin, geologists do not doubt that the river is tremendously old.

If you stand at the Narrows in Bolton and look up over four thousand feet at green ranges which press in from either side and down sheer rock walls seventy feet to the river, it is hard to conceive how the Winooski could ever have done it. The answer lies partly in the fact that the river is patient. Five thousand years are nothing, the way it counts time. Even if the river is only as old as the Green Mountains, it has been millions of years creating its low valley between the high peaks—a valley which three invading ages of ice failed to destroy.

The last ice sheet, the Pleistocene, inched into Vermont from Canada about a million years ago, sweeping everything before it except the highest peaks, which it scoured and scratched, rounding their faces. Though the entire Winooski valley was buried with the rest of Vermont, the immense white sheet was moving to its destruction under the hot tongues of a greater force—the sun. As the ice withdrew, it left Lake Champlain in an old river trough between the Green and Adirondack ranges. The lake was so high, geologists say, that for a time the Winooski, by devious channels, received the waters of other backed-up northern Vermont streams and reversed its flow into the Connecticut River. Gradually, with the lowering level of Lake Champlain, then but an arm of the Gulf of St. Lawrence, and the upward tilting of land relieved of ice, the river once more returned to its outlet to the west. During the thousands of years that it carried the last water and sediment from the ice sheet, the river was deepening its vast V through the Green Mountains and building a rich plain to the west. By slow stages, the sea retreated. The Winooski was at length in undisputed possession of its valley.

2

Henry Hudson had sailed from Amsterdam, but he had not yet ventured into the broad river stretching south from Champlain to the sea. The bowsprit of the *Mayflower* would not point west for eleven years. In Canada, Algonquin Indians were convincing Samuel de Champlain that he ought to see the land of lofty mountains, green valleys, and the lake which they bordered to the southwest. Painted in such appealing pastels, this land, Champlain presently decided, would bear exploring, and in the name of Henry IV he was the man to do it.

In order to go with the Algonquins Champlain had to agree to help them fight the Iroquois, who, they said, had encroached on their lands. Champlain did not wish to mix the bow and arrow with the surveyor's compass, but he joined their war games and feasts after which, on June 18, 1609, he started from Quebec with eleven Frenchmen and a band of Indians. The endless vista of blue water and long green islands, which stretched ahead as he entered the lake on a bright early July day, excited Champlain. A panorama of grander proportions awaited him many kilometers farther when the strange flotilla reached the widest part of the lake. Champlain saw on both sides of the broad water chains of forested mountains extending into the distance. To the right were the Adirondacks, to the left, the Green Mountains, shimmering in the summer sun.

Between the two highest mountains to the east lay a deep valley which, more than the mountains, was a friend to the red man. Still more important was the spirit of that valley, which, Champlain learned from his guides, was the water that reached to the mountains.

3

In the valley of the Winooskie-Took roamed Chief Gray Lock and his Abnaki people. The "castle" of Gray Lock's own tribe was to the north on the Missisquoi, but all the land of northwestern Vermont was the hunting ground of the Algonquins. Here ran the fox and the moose. Here in the water the salmon and beaver swam. In the sky flew the gull and the golden eagle. And here in the many valleys of the lake country grew the pine and fat maple.

While Woksis, the mighty hunter, was out one day in search of game, his diligent squaw, Moqua, busied herself by embroidering him some moccasins. For the evening meal of her lord she boiled some moose meat in the sweet water from the maple tree just by the wigwam. Becoming interested in the bear pattern she was working, she forgot the moose meat and the sweet water boiled away to a thick brown syrup. When Woksis returned he found such a dainty morsel ready for his supper as he had never tasted before. He eagerly devoured the viand, licked the kettle clean, and went out to tell his tribe that Kose-Kus-beh, a heaven-sent instructor, had taught Moqua how to make a delicious food by boiling the juice of the maple, and the discovery soon became known among all the Indians.

In the land of the Algonquins Woksis and all other great hunters stood strong before their people, for they knew how to live in the forest, to track the bear and the panther, to kill them with their arrows, and to bring them back to their tribesmen in the village. Sometimes, if the snow lay thick in the forests, or in summer if the rain did not come to the corn, the squash, and the pompions tended by the squaws along the lowlands of the Winooskie-Took, there was not enough food. Yet what the mightiest hunters could obtain was shared. An Abnaki hunter had no property of his own except the game he killed in time of plenty, nor did he desire any. He did not create the trout in the stream nor the deer in the forest. But all the braves of the many tribes of the Abnaki knew that this land of high mountains and rushing streams was theirs, and they must at times fight with all their strength and wisdom to keep it.

So it was among the Abnaki that a brave stood even stronger among his people as a mighty warrior than as a great hunter. The strength of the tribe was in their straight bodies, for stone forts were unknown to the Indians. It was to prepare for times of danger that the Abnaki boy learned to read the many signs of the forest, to track down his enemy, to strike savagely.

All the Abnaki tribes knew that never had there been greater danger to the Indians of the Winooskie-Took and the Missisquoi. Among the young braves now was the time for great deeds. The white man from the north, had been welcomed into the land of the Abnaki, for had not the first one coming up the lake drawn his thunder stick against the Iroquois and driven them away? But the people of Gray Lock, one of the wisest of Abnaki chiefs, hated the friends of the Iroquois, the English palefaces from the south. It was these white men who had driven their St. Francis cousins from Maine. Now it was said by those who lived on the Great River beyond the Winooskie-Took that these same palefaces were coming from the south and east into the hunting ground of the Abnaki.

2

GO FORTH, JOHN WILLIAMS

 $\mathcal{J}$ T was not quite daybreak in Deerfield, Massachusetts, on a cold morning in 1704, as cold, they say, "as the north side of a Jenooery gravestone by starlight." Against the palisades of the northernmost English settlement on the Connecticut, the forest pressed hard. Inside, the English people of the village were asleep in their forty-one stout frame houses. As the drifts beyond the stockade caught the first light from the east, nothing distinguished this February day from any other, except that the guard was asleep.

Suddenly, from the fringe of the woods hundreds of dark forms appeared. In a moment they dropped from the drifts into the enclosure. A few minutes later Silence Hoit from her dormer window saw the Deerfield sky red with flame. She saw too, "painted savages, savage white faces, and the waving sword of a French officer."

The Reverend John Williams saw two Indians running toward his house. He grabbed his pistol. The Indians gained entrance despite the strong door; then John Williams, in his nightshirt, aimed and pulled the trigger. His clumsy flintlock missed fire. The Indians motioned to Williams to get dressed, tying him so he could do no more. From her bed they pulled Eunice Williams who shortly before had given birth to a child. They killed the baby, another helpless child, and the female servant. Allowing the Williamses only time to dress, the Indians prodded them and their five remaining children out into the cold. Here about one hundred

9

English, French, and Indians were dying. What little resistance there had been had gone out of the people of Deerfield. Their dead were everywhere and their homes burning. A hundred and twelve of them, men, women and children were herded up the mountain west of the river where their captors could obtain a splendid view of their smoldering handiwork. Then began one of the longest forced marches in the history of the colonies.

The first victim of the trek when it had hardly begun was another child, too young to carry on. The Frenchmen had sobered in revulsion at the actions of their redskin Canadian brethren, but they knew that the fate of each prisoner rested wholly with his Indian captor, who exercised life or death judgment. This, among the St. Francis tribe and all the Algonquins, was an old Indian custom. And yet Eunice Williams, daughter of the Reverend John, was carried carefully by Whistling Serpent.

At the location of the first night's camp snow was removed and wigwams made over beds of green boughs. Tying down the Reverend John and the rest of the men, the Indians got drunk on a cache of liquor they had found in Deerfield. In this condition they killed Williams's Negro servant, the second victim of the march. In the morning it was found that a prisoner had escaped. Hertel de Rouville, the Frenchman in charge of the expedition, sent for Williams and asked him to advise the prisoners that if any more escaped they would all be burned.

The line of march for half of the company was north along the Connecticut, northwest across Vermont to Lake Champlain, then north to Canada, a total distance of three hundred miles. De Rouville and his Indian allies were anxious to make the best time possible, for it was almost spring. If the ice should go out of the rivers, it would be necessary to build canoes to travel their swollen waters and the journey would be more hazardous.

On the second day the Indians allowed John Williams to aid and console his wife, Eunice, who was plodding along painfully. She said her strength was ebbing. She felt that he must soon expect to part with her and she hoped that God would preserve his life and those of his children. They forced Williams to say good-bye to the "desire of his eyes, and the companion of his many joys and sorrows." He was placed in the front ranks and kept there until, nearly exhausted when he came to the top of a mountain, he was allowed to rest. His captor would not let him help his wife. As the prisoners straggled by, they said that she had slipped in a swift stream below and was now too weak to go on. At the foot of the mountain which the pastor had just climbed, the Indian master of Mrs. Williams grasped his tomahawk and killed her with one blow. Hearing of this, the Reverend John wept—while the savages mocked him for want of manhood in shedding tears.

That same day the Indians tomahawked a baby and a girl of eleven, and that night an Indian captain consulted with Williams's master about scalping him; but this was not done. A few days later a Mrs. Mary Brooks, falling on the ice, suffered a miscarriage. She came to Williams saying she thanked God that they had allowed her to see him, for, she said, "I know they will kill me today." They did.

As they struggled to the west through the deep snow which lay along their path through the Green Mountains, the Indians constructed hand sleighs for the transportation of the Indian wounded and the children. The spring thaw was at hand, so greater speed was imperative. Even in those first days of March it was necessary to wade mile after mile in ankle-deep water. John Williams felt that he and a number of those who were left could not hold out much longer.

On the evening of March 8, ten days from Deerfield, Williams's master pointed at his captive's chest the pistol with which the parson had tried to defend himself on the morning of the raid. The Indian said he was about to shoot him, for Williams had tried to do the same to him, but he did not shoot. Later, a little girl of four was killed because the snow was so deep that Macqua, her Indian, could not carry her in his knapsack. For other reasons, still others were killed. John Williams did not know what fate was suffered by those of his children who had gone north to Canada by way of the Connecticut with the other half of the expedition, but one of those with him, aged four, narrowly escaped death several times.

On the following Sunday, which the parson had every reason to expect was his last (for he was starving), he prayed as always, encouraging his fellow sufferers. The services for these wretched people were crude. There have certainly never been any more devout. The Indians were hunting, and on the evening of this Sabbath, March 12, Williams's captor told him they had killed five moose. Three days were spent roasting and drying the meat, and although his master passed the time making snowshoes for the parson so that he might travel more easily, the days to come were among the worst. Many prisoners had to carry the moose meat in their packs, a tremendous strain on their emaciated bodies. The minister's Indian took pity on him, relieving him of his pack, which he drew on a sledge along the widening stream. Even so, it seemed to John Williams that the bones of his legs were dislocated. At night he would take off his shoes and wring blood out of his stockings. On the banks of the Winooski he found oak leaves that had somehow persevered through the winter. These he applied to his sores, which healed enough to enable him to carry on. Some of the prisoners, starving under improvident masters, subsisted for days on roots such as those of the wild onion that grew along the banks of the river. Williams's captor, increasingly kind to him, shared what moose meat he had.

It was now the middle of March. No longer captives of winter, streams on the mountainsides were small cataracts. The ice over the Winooski groaned at night. One morning before dawn Williams's master shook him, saying that he must arise, pray to God, and eat his breakfast, for they had a great journey to perform that day. So swollen and painful were his feet that the parson found he could not get up. The Indian pointed to his tomahawk—

he would plunge it into his brain and scalp him. Williams replied that he supposed he would but he could not travel fast on account of his bruises. As the ice reflected the first light, the Indian sent Williams shuffling ahead alone. There was an end to human endurance. In an hour, aching in every fiber of his body, he knew that he had reached it. Then something happened which he was at a loss to explain—the way was easier. His Indian and the others would soon catch up, but he would need no prodding now. He ate some pieces of the frozen moose meat in his pocket and started ahead with new energy. Perhaps the spirits of the mountains and of the river were saying, "Go forth, John Williams, you and your people."

For two days they traveled from dawn until after dark. During that time Williams reckoned they had covered forty-five miles in their race to Lake Champlain. The thick ice there might not go out for a fortnight, and the remainder of the journey to civilization in Canada could be made with relative ease and safety.

The mountain terrain on both sides of the river was becoming less precipitous. Soon they found themselves tramping through flat country, twisting and turning with the bayous of the broadening Winooski. The ice, however, still held firm. Finally they came to wide lowlands where the Indians raised their corn and beans. A few miles farther the ice of the river merged with that of Lake Champlain where, twelve miles away on the western shore, rose the Adirondacks. The spirits of the Indians and French were good. Here until spring, however, they chose to bury a prize which only with the utmost exertion they had hauled over the crusted beds of the Connecticut, the White, and the Winooski rivers. It was the bell from the Deerfield church, whose haunting tone had called these people to worship in the glad days before. And now it was, since time began, the first bell to ring in the valley of the Winooski.

3

INDIAN SUMMER

$\mathcal{O}$LIVER Cromwell was dead. So also in the England of the early 1700's were his ideas about free men unfettered by lords and kings. In 1714, fat George I of the House of Hanover came to the throne, bringing with him from Germany a retinue of concubines and flatterers. In France the 72-year reign of Louis XIV, with its crystal and gold leaf, was ending. Soon his grandson, Lecherous Louis, in the company of his mistresses, would provide the aristocracy with new and exciting devices of intrigue and corruption. Under these rulers Europe was, as in the past, at war, but for the first time its squabbling echoed in the forests of North America. In New England, France and Britain were sparring for a showdown since both George and Louis, "The Beloved," dreamed the familiar dream of empire. The Gateway Country promised riches beyond the heavy timber that pressed to the shores of Lake Champlain. Already, the British and French were amassing fortunes in furs, the former trading with the Iroquois, the latter with the Algonquins.

On Lake Champlain and in the Winooski valley the French had divided the land into large strips called seigneuries, the seigneur owing homage to Louis XIV and the tenant owing homage to the seigneur. On the Atlantic seaboard the English were doing the same except that their land strips were "grants" and the settlers bought the land, with the exception of the trees for the navy of George I. The Winooski and its valley were granted to a family of French aristocrats named de La Perière, one of whom became governor of Montreal in 1752. The trees in the area were re-

14

served for the masts of Louis's navy, and the shore line on Champlain for his forts and batteries.

In all of this, of course, the red man who had lived on the land for centuries and whose land it was, if priority proves anything, became involved. The Abnaki believed, as did other Algonquins, that the French were friends because they had helped to fight the Iroquois. To the south the Iroquois believed the English were friends because they had helped to fight the Algonquins.

One of the most formidable obstacles frustrating British desires for the wilderness of Vermont was Chief Gray Lock and his tribe of Abnaki Indians. Gray Lock had been a Waranoke chieftain. Many moons before, he had lived in Iroquois country, but he was a fierce defender of the lands of his adopted tribe—the Abnaki. It was not that Gray Lock merely prevented encroachment on his lands. He became aggressive. Though he may have had nothing directly to do with the attack of his St. Francis cousins on Deerfield, his Abnaki villagers made countless raids on English settlements to the south, scalping men working in the fields and whisking women away to the north. It therefore became a matter of survival for the English to root the chief out of his lair and exterminate him. For the men who tried it was no simple assignment to navigate streams and climb slippery northern mountains where they might catch sight of the wisp of smoke marking an Indian encampment.

Captain Benjamin Wright began his Indian fighting career in May, 1704, when he moved up the Connecticut with ten men, turned west along the White and Winooski rivers, and reconnoitered along Lake Champlain. Gray Lock was not to be seen. Wright's small force did capture six canoes and destroy four redskins, while on the return trip they surprised a party of French and Indians on the Winooski with attendant gun and bow-and-arrow play, taking as a prize one Abnaki scalp. The victors returned from these expeditions as shaken and demoralized as the vanquished. Dr. Thomas Hastings of Hatfield, Massachusetts, said of one of Wright's expeditions: "Saw most of ye men when they went forth; they were lusty and in good plight, effective men; saw them when they returned, and they were much emaciated, and their feet so swelled and galled that they could scarce travel on their feet—for some they were necessitated to hire horses. Some one or more applied to me to dress their feet and were under my care for a week or more, in bathing and emplastering before they were anything tolerably recruited."

Captain Thomas Wells of Deerfield (to whose fellow townsmen the sight of Gray Lock's tribe and their chief's gray hair was terrifyingly familiar, in the years after the massacre) was another scout who attempted to eradicate the crafty chief—while the villagers built secret panels and underground passages in fear of retaliation. Wells and twenty men set out in March, 1725, on one of his numerous sorties to the north. They not only failed to bag Gray Lock, but lost three men on the return trip when a canoe overturned. The governor of Massachusetts heard of Wells's failure and asked Benjamin Wright to make still another expedition to try to find and destroy Gray Lock's legendary "castle."

From Northfield Wright took what has been called the "trunk line," following the Connecticut, White and Winooski to Lake Champlain. Leaving a branch of the Winooski, "We marched . . . west north west to the top of a vast high mountain which we called Mount Discovery [probably Camel's Hump] where we had a fair prospect of ye lake." Making their camp at Winooski Falls, they spent several days brushbeating near the river mouth, but no trace of Gray Lock or his elusive band could they find. The reason was that Gray Lock, with 150 Indians, watched Captain Wright's every movement, following close at his heels, and even harassed towns along his line of march as he returned to Massachusetts.

Even when Governor Vaudreuil of Canada died in 1725 and the tide of Indian resistance against the English was ebbing, Gray Lock, his village and his "castle"—wherever they were—

remained unraided even by such as Robert Rogers. In the valleys
of the Missisquoi and Winooskie-Took his tall warriors still
fashioned their arrow points on the outcroppings of flint; their
dusky squaws still raised their papooses; and the tribesmen continued to hold their wise and eloquent conclaves to determine the
course of their struggle with the English, or the disposition of
prisoners they repeatedly took.

When warriors, ornamented and greasy, returned from successful forays against the English with collected scalps strung on
their bows, the old men, women and children formed two lines

through which they forced the prisoners to run the gantlet to the village. To have a swift, young pair of legs was an advantage but the body of an old, slow prisoner was lacerated with bruises and stripes. The victors then treated their captives with civility, even kindness, sharing the best food they had. The assembled villagers next listened to each detail of the expedition, mourning their losses with shrieks of anguish, but changing their sorrow to joy as the feast, chants, and dancing began. Men prisoners whether Indian or white, were urged to enter families of fallen heroes, where if accepted, they were accorded the privileges of the tribe. If not accepted, they were often burned at the stake. The condemned unflinchingly resisted slow death by hot irons and coals, knife stabs, and verbal torment reflecting on their bravery and integrity. Under these circumstances they could not cry out—to do so marked them as eternal cowards. For Indians tranquilly surviving such torture, bygones were bygones. They could look forward to the same sort of life they had always led. For whites there was monumental adjustment, yet many were like little Eunice Williams, one of the ninety-one survivors of the Deerfield march, who was not ransomed or returned but chose to marry a St. Francis Indian and live the life of the tribe.

So famous and so feared had Gray Lock become that Massachusetts named its highest mountain after him. In the fall of 1726 the British Indian commissioner at Albany tried to get into the mighty chief's good graces by inviting him down to receive presents and expressions of goodwill. The chieftain, who had lived through several wars, all leading to the eclipse of Algonquin prestige, but who had, nevertheless, completed fifty years as a successful enemy of British colonial efforts in the north, would hardly be led into such a trap. He, of course, never came. Record of him then disappeared.

In the deep woods along the lake and streams he must have known it was time to join his ancestors and yet the mighty chief had no fear. Among departed spirits his place was one of sure immortality. But along the trails of the Winooskie-Took and Missisquoi, the Indian sun was sinking. The weird chant of the Abnaki was growing fainter among the lofty pines. One day it would disappear, and yet in memory it must forever remain, for

Their name is on your waters,
You may not wash it out.

4

LAND OF THE ONION

$\mathcal{T}$HE boils on Ira Allen's leg would not heal. "I resolved to be my own physician," he wrote. "I applied a milk curd, turned with alum. I sent and got some old beech leaves, the bark of male elm and the bark of basswood roots—pulverized them between stones—steeped them in cold spring water and applied them to my leg." All night he sat up, applying first one and then the other. By morning he noticed some improvement. It piqued him to think he couldn't hurry nature along. A young man of twenty-two had no time to waste with boils. Yet even if he could not practice in the woods with his surveyor's instruments, he could study his crude French maps.

It seemed to him that a man could fulfill every ambition in this country to the north, so rich and various it seemed. He must see it. As soon as his health improved he got on his horse and rode to Bennington. There his brother, Ethan, poured gallons of verbal cold water on visionary land projects. Ira galloped south. In Salisbury, Connecticut, Heman Allen was more receptive. The country to the north looked good and, anyway, who could be better trusted with a loan of a few pounds than one's brother, however young?

Tough, sandy-haired Remember Baker, who had always taken on anything with the earmarks of adventure, also readily entered into partnership with his cousin. Remember agreed to advance the necessary stores and to hire men to assist in the expedition, with the understanding that he would be paid back in full later. Ira still faced the most delicate promotion of the entire

20

scheme, which he determined to handle in this manner: he would buy a sizable chunk of land in his chosen country from the Connecticut speculators who owned it. Then he would announce that he was leaving immediately on an expedition to survey the lands he had just purchased. Would they, too, like to have their lands surveyed—at a reasonable fee? The Connecticut proprietors would indeed, and commissioned him for the job.

In September, 1772, Ira and cousin Remember, with their small party, started north, shortly reaching Skenesborough, the southernmost point of Lake Champlain. Here Allen and Baker, with five other men, embarked in a small boat and passed several days rowing through choppy seas seventy miles to the mouth of the Winooski. The Indian name had been discarded for its English translation, Onion-Land, and it was up Onion River to the Falls that they now proceeded. Here Ira had agreed to meet Baker, who had landed a few miles to the south to check the woods for trouble. And it was at the Falls that he found a camp with provisions which "induced me to suppose that a New York surveyor was in the woods." He quitted the camp carefully, leaving no telltale signs, but posted one of his men to watch for Baker. He then went back down the river two miles to the intervale, where he made a camp. It was near a large pitch-pine tree opposite an island below the Falls. This was "the first day I ever set foot on the fertile soil of Onion River. . . . I went up the open meadow where the blue joint grass was thick till in sight of a large and lovely elm . . . promising myself one day to be the owner of that beautiful meadow."

Ira's sentinel apparently did not suffer from insomnia. When Baker arrived at the Falls, having an extreme appetite, he started in at once to savor the food which someone—Ira, he might have supposed—had been good enough to leave. By the time the sentinel had told Baker that the food he'd been eating was not from the Allen-Baker larder, it was impossible to restore the camp to its former status. When Baker rejoined Allen, they posted another sentinel to report on any further developments at the upper camp.

Captain Stevens, a New York surveyor, did return to his camp at the Falls. Upon discovering that perhaps Indians had been there, he escaped with most of his men before Ira's sentinel could report. Stevens, however, left two men to guard the camp, whom Baker and Allen promptly made prisoners. Ira and Remember stayed until dark, when they took the surveyor's boat, his provisions, and the two men and shoved off for their own camp downriver. As they started they saw two boats coming upriver in the twilight. Before the identity or numbers of their occupants could be distinguished, the boats turned quickly and made off into the night. Allen posted a lookout, but it was not until before sunrise that he again saw two boats coming upstream, which turned out to be bark canoes carrying Stevens, four of his men, and ten Indians. This spectacle was not one which the seven-man party on the bank could view with optimism. Ira had a case of pistols, one of the men had a gun, and Remember had his sword. Quickly arming his men with axes and clubs, Ira arranged them strategically about two rods from the riverbank, and tied the two prisoners on a pole behind them.

The first man out of the canoes was Stevens, who advanced up the bank with an ax in his hand and pistols in his pocket. He made for Baker, brandishing the ax. Instead of resisting, Baker opened his shirt, bared his chest, and encouraged Stevens to start chopping—if he dared.

"Why are my men tied?" demanded Stevens.

"It's my pleasure," Baker said. Stevens looked around. He could see down the barrel of the one gun Allen's men had. Perhaps he would spare Baker—for the moment, at least. He drew a scalping knife and started for the place where the men were tied but had taken only a few steps when Allen pulled his pistol.

"Take one step further or touch the pistols in your pocket," Ira warned, "and your portion is death." Stevens blanched. At the bank his men were getting ready to launch an attack. Allen turned his head to one of his men, Vanornam, who could speak Indian. "Tell the Indians they and we are brothers. They are welcome to hunt on our lands when they please. Tell them this is a land quarrel that's no concern of theirs." In the colorful tongue that Vanornam had learned when a prisoner of the Indians, he started to speak. The Indians hesitated, held a brief conference, then jumped into their canoes and paddled away. The coup made prisoners of Stevens and his men. He capitulated.

"Would you," asked Stevens of Allen, gathering evidence he thought he could use later, "have fired if I hadn't stopped?" Allen pointed his pistol to a mark smaller than a dollar on a pole thirty feet away.

"Suppose," he said, "that pole was your body, and that mark was your heart." He fired. The bullet struck half an inch under the mark. Allen had still not answered Stevens's question. He had no desire to be tried by the Supreme Court of New York for murder or outlawry. At the same time, these were the New Hampshire Grants. He had bought this land from men who had been granted charters for it by the royal governor of New Hampshire, Benning Wentworth. New Yorkers had no business on the Onion River—or in any part of the Grants.

Stevens's men, his boat, and stores were returned to him. Then in strong, deadly earnest language, Allen told him to get out and never to come back to the Grants again—under pain of death.

With Stevens out of the way, Ira and Remember moved their camp to the Falls, hid their lake boat under brush in a cove, and hunted for a tree which would make a good canoe. As they went to work with axes, John Whiston, one of their men, slashed his shin exposing the bone for two inches. Since a portage over the Falls was ahead, and a 20-mile trip upriver to the area to be surveyed for the Connecticut proprietors, this accident was a small disaster. Whiston hobbled around the Falls and had to be carried most of the way in the canoe. A short distance above the Falls

they found rapids, but by taking out Whiston and part of the supplies they pulled the canoe by. Above this place they found a very
strong current at a gorge which Allen described as a "hedious
place. The river . . . was here reduced to eighty feet, with rocks
perpendicular eighty feet high, which in a cloudy day made a solemn appearance." By means of poles they were able to negotiate
the gorge, the top of which they found opened into a "pleasant
country." There appeared to be little current here, yet some mysterious force suddenly turned back their canoe. They tried a second time and the same thing occurred. On the third attempt,
Allen walked along the shore on the south side, guiding the canoe
with a line. Two and a half feet underwater at the mysterious
spot he found a rock over which ran a strong but quiet current.
Below this rock bar he estimated the water to be seventy feet, perhaps more.

Upriver at Hubbel's Falls they had to leave the canoe, carrying their equipment and provisions on their backs for nearly two
miles. In Essex at a spot on the Onion later known as "the canoe
place," they hacked out another canoe with axes and proceeded
upstream to a point opposite Jericho, where they erected their
camp. Whiston's leg was painfully swollen. Allen concocted his
lotion for boils—a poultice from the bark of basswood roots, male
elm, and old beech leaves, which reduced the swelling in one night.
Remember found some balsam and fir which they placed on lint
in the bottom of the wound and after six days Whiston was much
better.

They here explored a "tremendous mountain range . . .
covered with evergreens . . . On the high pinnacle of a mountain, we discovered a tall black spruce tree, with two separate
branches near the top." This, lanky Remember and his young
cousin climbed with equal facility to a point where they could look
out for miles over a "great country."

They were running their surveyor's lines steadily. Allen
found that one of the parcels of land he had purchased was part

of a mountain with no farm land at all, which "gave Baker an opportunity to pass many hard jokes on me." They also found before many days that they were running short of provisions and that snow flurries had whitened the high colors of a mountain autumn. Allen sent Vanornam and another man to the Onion to catch fish. They were gone just one day, returning with as many trout already cleaned as they could carry. The trout offered delectable if only temporary relief; their larder had dwindled to a three-day supply. They therefore determined to start south at once for Pittsford on a cross-country tramp without benefit of river navigation. Baker departed downstream for the Falls to return their boat to Crown Point by way of the lake, while Ira with four men tramped to the riverbank on the lowland near the later site of Waterbury, ready to cross the Onion and start their trek over the mountains the next morning. It was snowing but they found an old bark camp which they made use of for the night.

The first hazard that presented itself the following morning was the snow, deep enough to make travel difficult. The second was the cold. The third was a disagreement which had broken out among the men as to the right direction to Pittsford. Allen suggested that each man lay a stick on the ground in the direction he thought they should go. The majority direction would rule. The men's sticks all pointed in slightly different directions while, by means of a compass and dead reckoning, Allen and Vanornam placed their sticks in the same direction.

It was first necessary to cross the river. To do this they made two rafts. Allen and Vanornam started off in the first one, poling out into midstream. The current was stronger than they'd anticipated, so strong that the raft had almost broken up twice by the time they were halfway. There, it became obvious that it would no longer hold more than one, so Vanornam jumped into the water and returned to the shore from which they had come. The current was carrying Allen downstream where the raft now began to sink in deep water. He had to jump, wading chest-high. When he gained the bank, he was at a place forty rods below the other men but he resolutely started back upstream, saying nothing, and when he reached a point which his raft trip revealed could be forded, he plunged into the water and waded across, followed by Vanornam. Seeing this, the other men left the raft they were building and followed suit. On the opposite bank at last, they were fortunate enough to find firewood. Drying their clothes as best they could, they rationed several mouthfuls of food—their low provisions permitting no more—and started their long trek.

Leaving the valley of the Onion the men trudged over mountainous terrain to the south, traveling as far as they could before nightfall. They slept under a camp of hemlock boughs and in the morning started off with nothing to eat. Later that day they found evidence of a moose in the vicinity, which Vanornam stalked with all the skill he possessed. Catching sight of the animal, he worked up to a point within ten rods of him where he could obtain a fair broadside shot. Unfortunately, however, an incompetent in the group had, in cutting a tree, allowed it to fall on Vanornam's gun, their only hunting weapon. This had bowed the barrel, so that Vanornam missed the moose, which now crashed off into the woods. Near starved as they were, this "occasioned round oaths." They camped again under a crude hemlock shelter.

In the morning three of the men again started to argue about the direction to Pittsford. Vanornam climbed a tree but was unable to identify any familiar landmarks. Allen, relying heavily on the strength of his arms and one leg, for boils had returned to the other, climbed to the top and satisfied himself that the mountains in the distance were to the northwest of Crown Point, and that the direction of their march was correct. Vanornam managed to bag a partridge, which they boiled in a tin kettle that night, spicing it with black pepper. Divided among seven men the bird seemed only to whet their appetites, but they were in an old camp covered with bark, an adequate protection against the rain, and their spirits were better. That the crew with Allen and Baker were not all experienced woodsmen nor men of unusual discernment was exhibited that same night by one E. Sherman who, "hearing a screech owl hoot, mistook it for a woman's voice . . . He rushed out of camp into the rain to answer his female friend, which he attempted in a loud voice—which the owl answered. Sherman called aloud for us to follow him, for she had answered him—that he would not stay starving all night in hearing of a house." Sherman slipped sheepishly back a little later, the butt of the usual jokes attending such circumstances.

The men were weak and they were desperately hungry. Had they not by good fortune and good planning on the part of Allen and Vanornam reached Pittsford the following day, there might have been casualties. Ira procured some milk and had pudding made with Indian meal, allowing a small portion of this and a half pint of milk for each man. Reminding them they had just covered seventy miles on foot on one dinner and three partridges, he rationed each a small portion of mutton and turnips and cautioned his hostess that the men should have nothing more for two hours. E. Sherman, however, seized and devoured another piece of meat before Ira could remove the platter. A short time later he was missing. They found him in a sleep so profound that he failed to respond to any amount of shaking and was resuscitated only after he had been walked up and down for an hour.

There was one thing for which Allen could be thankful, in retrospect. Toward the end of the trip he stuck the knot of a tree into the boil on his knee. It "caused a severe sensation and some harsh words; but I could walk the better after it."

5

A RIVER OF THEIR OWN

*I*F Ethan Allen had stayed in the iron business in Salisbury, Connecticut, he might have won a contract to make cannon balls for Benedict Arnold's fleet. He probably never could have stuck around making shot—he liked too well to shoot it. At the age of nineteen he left the Litchfield farm where he was born in 1737, the eldest of six brothers and two sisters. He joined the French and Indian War for two weeks, but when Fort William Henry failed to remain British he came home. Early in life he fell in with Dr. Thomas Young, an effervescent radical, whose talk, full of Deism and Rights of Men, helped to determine the pattern of his political and religious thinking. He became explosive in his talk and actions and intolerant of the established order—a restlessness that was nowhere more apparent than in his home life. His marriage in 1762 to a staid woman seven years his senior was notable for the fact that he never did like her very well.

French and Algonquin dreams of empire in Canada and New England had dissolved with their defeat of 1763, when all the northern lands became British. Unpopular in Connecticut because of his swearing and bizarre religious views, Ethan was constantly on the move during the next years. He tramped around the Grants, bought his first rights there, and identified himself among the people as a loud and dependable voice among the settlers from New Hampshire and Connecticut in their land war with New York. When defending two Yankee farmers in Albany in 1770 (after refusing a bribe to desert their cause), Ethan was warned by martial-minded Yorkers that "might often makes right." Bristling, Ethan menaced them with the celebrated remark, "The gods of the hills are not the gods of the valleys." Asked by New York lawyers what that meant he said, "If you accompany me to the hills of Bennington, the sense will be made clear."

Ethan's future was determined the day Ira returned from Onion River in 1772. Ira pictured what he and Baker had seen on the Onion—water power, farm land, timber, a navigable lake, and navigation to the Falls. To Ira's persuasive propaganda, served up to appeal to a great woodsman, a man of adventure who had no business being shackled to iron mines or farms in settled communities—Ethan submitted. The plan was simply that the brothers pool their resources to buy the entire valley of Onion River.

But first Ira had to get rid of the mountain he had bought by mistake from the Connecticut speculators. Avoiding talk which would reveal the real character of the land, Ira took the brother of one of the proprietors (an "ignorant fellow") aside and quietly tried to buy his rights to his part of the mountain. The man said he didn't dare to sell them without consulting his brothers. Since Ira was secretly attempting to buy the rest of the mountain, the brothers figured it must be valuable, so they urged him to sell the whole thing back to them—which he did, and obtained £90 for the survey besides. The Allens laughed heartily over this, agreeing that Ira was a sharp trader.

By scouting through the woods, Ethan and Ira learned every valley and hill to the north—knowledge that in the years to come proved its worth time and again.

"Ira," Ethan said one day, "they say that you are the greatest woodsman in the Grants. I don't believe it because I know a man who can beat you, at least in traveling in the woods." Though probably suspicious of what was coming, Ira nevertheless asked who.

"It is myself, sir."

There was of course no honorable way out of this except a contest. Two mornings later at sunrise they started out from the northernmost house of the settlement of Rutland. They were to race forty miles to a point south of the banks of the Onion. The man who arrived first and in better condition would be the winner. They covered the whole distance through the woods in one day with only a short rest at noon. By sundown they were "essentially fagged," neither admitting it—and they called it a draw. Ira later confessed that had he not indulged in what he called "finnesse," he would have lost. He knew the country well. When they were approaching a swamp he would go around, while Ethan would plunge in straight ahead tearing through brambles by main strength. Ira would meanwhile be on the other side enjoying a fifteen minutes' rest. He did this repeatedly, which "served the double purpose of fatiguing him and resting me, so as to equalize our chances of victory in this terrible jaunt." Ira admitted that on equal terms Ethan, though thirteen years his senior, would outclass him. Others declared there was little difference between the brothers when it came to nerve and stamina.

On one of Ira's Onion River surveying trips he came with a group of men to the Narrows, whose precipitous cliffs were among those he had previously described as "hedious." They ate lunch on the high ledge above the Falls. Afterwards someone proposed that as a test of nerves each of the group try to stand on the edge and look straight down at the river. A dozen men tried it, all weakening and glad to withdraw from such a shattering experience. Ira got up, walked to the edge, placed his toes an inch or two over it, looked straight down into the water with no sign of fear or hesitation—then after several moments turned and strode back. Since that day the cliff at that part of Bolton Narrows has been known as Allen's Rock.

Ethan probably liked Ira better than any of his other brothers. Perhaps he saw in Ira much that he admired in himself. His physique was more perfect if not so large boned, his brain as active, his judgment as mature and his tongue, if not so deadly, was more facile. Throughout their career they complemented each other. It was usually Ira who made the snowballs, Ethan who threw them—and each was happy with his part of the operation.

By 1773 four of the Allen brothers, Ira, Ethan, Heman, and Zimri, and Remember Baker had formed a partnership to purchase much of Onion River and to develop it. They bought most of the lands they wanted, but there were some strips near the mouth of the Onion they had to get of owners who lived in White Plains, New York. A Yankee's name in New York was already mud, and the Allens, who had previously sided with New Hampshire claimants (because most of their own lands had been bought from New Hampshire and they had no intention of paying for New York charters to them) were in particular disfavor. Ethan, Ira, and Remember fortified themselves with a case of pistols and, dressed like British officers, started for White Plains making "no small parade." Part of the plot was that brother Heman would travel near to but not with the party as an itinerant merchant (which he really was).

When they reached White Plains they put up at a Mr. Burling's tavern with no suspicion on the part of the proprietor as to who they were. Burling owned most of the lands they wanted. One evening when Heman entered the tavern, the "British officers" made a great ruckus, questioning the character of this lowly placed Yankee merchant. Burling, quite disturbed by this, also treated Heman with scorn, and it was only when he purchased a round of drinks that the incognito-Allen was allowed to join the group, while his brothers bit their lips to keep straight faces. It was a three-curtain performance. During their visit at Burling's they bought most of his Onion River lands and those of his associates.

On the morning they were to leave, with the charters firmly in hand, they announced who they were, even informing a peddler on his way to New York that they were the Allens—the Allens on whose heads were New York bounties because they had chased Stevens, the New York surveyor, off Onion River. The peddler streaked to New York to report to the governor and Council, who took immediate steps to raise a force of light horsemen. By that time the Green Mountain Boys were back over the border in Yankee territory.

6

TERROR WITHOUT HOMICIDE

"*L*ATELY purchased by Allen and Baker, a large tract of land on both sides of mouth of Onion River and fronting westerly on Lake Champlain, containing about 45,000 acres, and sundry lesser parcels of land further up said river."

The ad in the Hartford, Connecticut, *Courant* in June, 1773, described such advantages as the abundance of fish and game and the "salubrious climate," declaring that there was no land between New York and Canada as good, and wound up with: "Whoever inclines to be a purchaser may apply to Ethan Allen, Zimri, and Ira Allen on premises, or to Heman and Levi Allen in Salisbury."

Ethan and Ira were building a blockhouse on the north side of Onion River Falls. Made of stout logs it had thirty-two port-holes. The second story jutted out over the first so that they could shoot straight down on attackers, and the roof was detachable so that it could be lifted off and thrown over if the Indians should ignite it with flaming arrows. The blockhouse was completely small-arms proof. Its name: Fort Frederick. Remember Baker with his family arrived and set up housekeeping in the fort, with Ira as a boarder. They made clearings for farm lands and mills around the Falls and cut a 70-mile road to Castleton. Ira passed his spare time surveying and acquiring additional parcels of land.

One day rain forced a group of men who had been fishing at the Falls into the fort, where Remember "kept sperets for

33

sale." Over a bowl of punch they began to rib Ira for his purchase south of the Falls—of the terraced pine plains that faced
the lake. There was no good reason, they said, for buying such
uneven land. Ira said that for a double-bowl of punch he would
give his reason.

"A dry pine plain is easy digging," Ira began over his double-
bowl. "If, as suggested by some, the spirits of the deceased con-
verse with each other, it would be convenient passing from tomb
to tomb in that light earth." Before they had decided that this
was unsatisfactory reasoning Ira had drained his double-bowl.

When the younger Allen was on a surveying trip upriver,
Ethan and Remember decided to unload the worthless pine-cov-
ered sand banks on a Massachusetts land speculator who happened along. They made a fat profit and couldn't wait to tell Ira.

"Baker and I have gotten you out of a foolish scrape," the
colonel-commandant announced on Ira's return. Then he described how he had sold the miserable sandbanks by the lake for
£11, five more than Ira had paid for the whole tract of which
they were a part. Ira was piqued. He got on his horse and sniffed
the trail of the speculator to Massachusetts where, after much
dickering, he succeeded in buying back the land for £16—five
more than the speculator got it for. In this way the Onion River
Land Company repurchased the site of Burlington, the largest
city in the future state of Vermont.

2

Across the lake, fifteen miles away, New York glowered.
Deputy Surveyor of Lands Benjamin Stevens had never recovered from the humiliation of being chased off Onion River the
previous September. He complained to the authorities that he
and his men had been insulted, threatened, beaten. He said Allen
and Baker had stripped him of his property, tied his man John
Dunbar, thrown him in the fire, and otherwise abused him in a
cruel manner. Furthermore, Allen and Baker had swiped four

gallons of "Jamaica sperets." Ira stoutly denied Stevens's cor-
poral punishment story, but freely admitted putting the trespasser
to flight.

A solemn pact had been made among the partners to keep
the Grants—particularly Onion River—purged of Yorkers.
Sometimes it must have seemed like trying to keep salmon and
pike from coming up the Onion to spawn. One Yorker-hunting
expedition entailed forty miles of upriver travel. An alien surveyor was supposed to be on one of the tributaries, so it was up
Stevens Branch that Ira and his men went. Here they met a foot
traveler who, when casually but carefully questioned, told them
there was a New York surveying party within ten miles of Kings-
land Center. As for himself, the man said he was on his way
downriver. The Green Mountain Boys continued a short distance
when Ira ordered a halt and an about-face. As they returned to
the Onion, the foot traveler's widely spaced tracks confirmed
Ira's suspicion that the man had reason to be in a hurry. The exact
opposite of a liar's statement usually being nearer the truth, Allen
decided that he hadn't gone downriver as he had said, but up.
From his tracks at the Onion this proved to be so. Allen then concluded that the man, as scout of the surveying party, would go as
fast as he could to warn his expedition that the Green Mountain
Boys were on the warpath.

Marching four or five miles, Allen and his men reached
Lightning Ridge above East Montpelier, where they could scan
the countryside. Scrutinizing the forest in the vicinity of future
Plainfield, they saw the faint but telltale ribbon of smoke. Swiftly
they descended the ridge, quietly threaded the woods, and made
a rush on the camp. Too late! The spy had reached there first and
the entire party, judging from the low fire, had fled for their lives
about two hours before. Ira took over the camp and provisions,
and stayed for two days to make additional explorations.

Most New Yorkers failed to get away that easily. One
William Cockburn on another occasion was tracked down by Ira,

Remember, and Seth Warner, in Bolton. He underwent Green Mountain Boy court-martial proceedings on the spot, was declared guilty, and his surveying instruments were smashed. He was also given a flying start back to New York—and the threat of a death penalty if he should return. On all such occasions the Green Mountain Boys used the terror approach—never homicide. They would sneak up into the bushes around the camp of the enemy surveyor, then charge in waving their swords, shooting pistols in the air, and yelling like a band of Indians. The enemy would disperse in horror and flee into the forest while the raiders demolished the camp. Thus mounted the New York evidence against the tyrants of the Onion. Ira and Remember both had a price on their heads but this didn't deter them or the rest of the Green Mountain Boys from their self-imposed program of vigilance.

Their expeditions were sometimes dangerous, often arduous, but always fun. In July, 1773, armed with provisions and spirits, they started out from their fort to hunt a surveyor in Waterbury. They found nothing in Waterbury, Middlesex, or Berlin. Meanwhile the wooden gallon bottle of spirits carried alternately by Baker, Allen, and their three men, fortified them against loss of enthusiasm for the search. West of Stevens Branch their dog put up a fuss. The transgressor turned out to be not a surveyor but a moose. This they tracked down and shot, stripping the carcass and hanging up the skin to dry. The marrow bones were too much of a delicacy to go to waste, so they encamped for the night and feasted on the bones. What was left of the bottle of spirits here served famously. It was, recorded Allen, "easily emptied." They took the jug, placed it ten rods away, with the head toward them. Then each man took as careful aim as was possible under the circumstances and put a ball through the neck. As for the New York surveyors, there had been some around but they got away.

Ten years previously a Colonel John Reid had been granted

IRA ALLEN

by the governor of New York seven thousand acres on both sides of Otter Creek, the Onion's neighboring stream to the south. When Reid occupied it, he chased the New Hampshire purchasers off, taking possession of all the buildings including sawmills with fourteen thousand feet of pine board. The owners, aided by Ira and Seth Warner, got together, launched an attack on Reid's settlers and drove them back to New York. Reid's steward then assembled a party and once more drove off the original settlers. This obviously was a job for the Onion River squad and the rest of the Green Mountain Boy aggregation.

Led by Ethan, Remember and Seth on August 11, 1773, they swooped down one hundred strong on Reid's Scotch squatters. They burned the huts, wrecked the mills, smashed the millstones and demolished the crops. One of the Scotchmen, James Henderson, who had the supreme misfortune of being present, reported: "Our Houses are all Brunt Down. The Grist mill is all Put Down. The Mill Stones Brock and Throns in To the Crick, the Corn is all Destroed by There Horses, and When it Was Proposed That we Should Build houses and keep Possion, they threatened to Bind some of us To a Tree and Skin us alive. Therefore we think its imposable To us To Live hear in Peace."

Ethan had not yet come to live on the Onion. As chief officer of the Green Mountain Boys, he was needed in other parts of the Grants. Though he made frequent trips there to engage with Ira and Remember in the business of the company, Onion River was still pretty far north as a base of operations. On one such trip in the summer of 1773 he asked Ira to conduct him on a tour of their properties. They took some stores in a canoe and for several days viewed the country. One night they made a fire and laid straw on the floor of an old log house on nearby Shelburne Point, *Quineska-Took* (Long Joint), which juts like a green spine into Lake Champlain. Before turning in they thought they heard rowboats in the bay. Yorkers? They dismissed the suspicion. In the night Ira happened to look toward the door. There was a man approaching silently, gun in hand. Since there was no window in the place, there was no other exit. Having used his holster as a pillow, Ira carefully reached for his pistols, at the same time drawing up his feet for a leap through the door. The man was now almost in the doorway. Ira got up on his knees and elbows with a pistol in each hand. Bracing himself, he cocked the right-hand pistol. At this, Ethan woke up and seized him. Ira then awakened. The figure in the doorway had vanished with his dream. The unsettling thought that Yorkers were now invading their sleep was responsible for insomnia on the part of the Allens for the remainder of that night.

Governor Tryon of New York boosted the rewards for the Green Mountain Boys. For the leaders it would be death without benefit of clergy. To which Ethan's acid pen swiftly responded early in 1774:

Be it known to that despotic fraternity of lawmakers and lawbreakers that we will not be . . . frightened out of our property . . . printed sentences of death will not kill us when we are at a distance, and if the executioners approach us, they will be as likely to fall victims of death as we; . . . we flatter ourselves upon occasion we can muster as good a regiment of marksmen and scalpers as America can afford; and we now give the gentlemen . . . an invitation to come and view the dexterity of our regiment; and we cannot think of a better time for that purpose than when the executioners come to kill us . . . and provided any of us or our party shall be taken, and we have not notice sufficient to relieve them, or whether we relieve them or not, we are resolved to surround such person, or persons, whether at his or their own house or houses, or anywhere that we can find him or them, and shoot such person or persons dead . . . our lives, liberties and properties are as verily precious to us, as to any of the King's subjects, and we are as loyal to his Majesty or his government, as any subjects in his province; but if the governmental authority of New York will judge in their own case, and act in opposition to that of Great Britain, and insist upon killing us, to take possession of our vineyards, come on, we are ready for a game of scalping with them; for our martial spirits glow with bitter indignation and consummate fury to blast their infernal projections.

7

GOUT, GRAFT, AND GUMPTION

THE worst that had happened up to 1775 in the skirmishing between New York and the Grants was that Remember Baker had lost his thumb. This happened when a party of New Yorkers surrounded his house in Arlington in 1772 and took Remember and his wife and children prisoners. Mrs. Baker was gashed in the swordplay at the house, and Remember got his thumb sliced off. John Whiston, the Green Mountain Boy who bared the bone of his leg with an ax on the first surveying trip up the Onion, tried to stop the Yorkers from carrying Remember off in a sleigh; but it was not until a posse of Green Mountain Boys came to the rescue that the Yorkers ran for their lives, leaving Baker free but weak from loss of blood.

The fault had not at first been that of His Majesty George III. His Excellency Benning Wentworth, the stout governor who ruled the colony of New Hampshire, had been partly to blame. When he was not stuffing with rich food and drink or taking care of his gout, Wentworth had been busy raising cash by chartering the lands to the west with no clear idea that they belonged to him. Furthermore, many of the Grants he made were to speculators. "Even in 1769 no more than fifty-one of Wentworth's one hundred and twenty-eight townships had any inhabitants other than the birds and the bees." They threw Went-

40

worth out of office. That same year (1764) the king in Council had ordered that the lands in question be transferred to New York jurisdiction, presumably because the king liked the New York idea of big estates with tenants better than the farmer-owner policy that had developed more or less in the Grants. Besides, colonization had been slipshod under New Hampshire. But the King's Council never intended that the settlers in the disputed area, who had already bought and paid for their land under New Hampshire, should be dispossessed or bothered in any way. New York, however, believed that all those who owned lands under New Hampshire should get their titles "confirmed" by New York. "Confirmation," the settlers found, involved a second payment.

New York's point of view was that a lot of land had been fraudulently granted by Wentworth, and in order to straighten out the tangle it would have to be resurveyed. The cost of this was presumably to be passed on to the settlers. Even so, to the average farmer owning one hundred acres the cost of validating his title would be only $8, or 8½ cents an acre. For big land-holders like the Allens, with holdings in 1773 of some sixty thousand acres, this cost was staggering. It is easy to understand why the sympathies of the Onion River Land Company would not rest with New York. The Allens understandably got busy circulating petitions to be sent to his Majesty, charging New York with graft and complaining of the outrage of having to pay twice for the same lands.

When his Majesty heard in this manner that New York was trying to milk for double fees lands that had already been chartered, his ministry wrote Moore, the indolent New York governor: " . . . The unreasonableness of obliging a very large tract of country to pay a second time the immense sum of thirty-three thousand pounds in fees . . . is so unjustifiable that His Majesty is not only determined to have the strictest enquiry made into the circumstances of the charge, but expects the clearest and fullest answer to every part of it." Moore supplied neither a full answer nor a clear one. He indulged in some double-talk about the Stamp Act. There was nothing in his reply about compliance with the order. Meanwhile the settlers in question declared they were still under New Hampshire because their original land charters were New Hampshire's. When New York tried to send in agents to enforce its decrees, the resistance led by Ethan, Ira, Remember and Seth proved to Yorkers that their possession of this land was on paper only.

When the King's Council meanwhile considered transferring the land back to New Hampshire owing to petitions from the settlers telling what New York had been doing, New York speculators flooded the Grants with spies who went around getting names of the settlers. Upon their return to New York, the speculators had names forged to a lengthy petition which was brought to the king by the speculators as proof of the unanimous wish of the settlers to have jurisdiction of the Grants remain with New York. This was chicanery of the foulest order, but even worse was New Hampshire's attitude. She wouldn't back her settlers, and gave in to New York.

The New York governor now started selling the lands to his friends, with the result that the Grants were alive with surveyors, and there was no sleep for the Green Mountain Boys. The only solution Ira could see was to make a third royal colony of the disputed lands. He went to visit a rich British landholder, Colonel Philip Skene, who owned a tract of land at the head of Lake Champlain, with the idea that Skene go to England, get a charter for the new colony, and make the arrangements. This, Skene started to do.

It was beginning, however, to look like civil war between Yorkers and Yankees. On March 13, 1775, the spark of Yankee revolutionary spirit against Yorkers—and against Britain—burst into flame, when a posse of pro-British Yorkers who were trying to hold court in Cumberland County shot 22-year-old William French at Westminster.

> Here William French his Body lies
> For Murder his blood for vengeance cries
> King George the third his Tory crew
> tha with a bawl his head shot threw
> For Liberty and his Countrys Good
> He lost his Life his Dearest blood.

That same month the Onion River Land Company held a hasty conference. The flames of revolution at Lexington burned high. It was war. Philip Skene and the new royal colony plan would now go down the drain. From Canada, the British would invade the colonies. Their route? Without question up Lake Champlain past the Onion River Land Company. Their $300,000 holdings in northern Vermont were in more danger of being lost to the British than to Yorkers. With Ticonderoga, the strongest bastion in New England, held by the British, Lake Champlain would be a British Lake, the Onion a British river, and the Onion River Land Company—extinct.

"Friends and fellow soldiers: You have for a number of years past been a scourge and terror to arbitrary powers. Your valor has been famed abroad, and acknowledged, as appears by the advice and orders to me from the General Assembly of Connecticut to surprise and take the garrison now before us. I now propose to advance before you, and, in person, conduct you through the wicked gate; for we must this morning either quit our pretensions to valor, or possess ourselves of this fortress in a few minutes; and, inasmuch as it is a desperate attempt, which none but the bravest of men dare undertake, I do not urge it on any contrary to his will. You that will undertake voluntarily, poise your firelocks."

Every man raised his gun.

8

BRITISH LAKE — A BRITISH RIVER?

$\mathcal{D}$URING the few minutes it took to subdue Ticonderoga and obtain surrender from Captain de la Place, Ethan had become famous. Throughout the colonies Ticonderoga was considered a sort of Gibraltar of the northern frontier. When its conqueror, wearing his fancy colonel's uniform and carrying his huge sword, appeared before the Philadelphia Continental Congress in June, 1775, he was looked upon with curiosity and much respect. George Washington had been made commander in chief only a few days before. War had not yet been formally declared. Ethan's bold coup had certainly taken the representatives by surprise. They were scared, however, and wanted to dismantle Ticonderoga at once and move the equipment south to Lake George where a defense could be made that wouldn't involve so much vulnerable northern territory. This attitude brought the wrath of all New England down on their heads. What did Congress propose to do—leave that area to the British and Indians? And if Congress dismantled Fort Ti, what, Ethan and Ira had wondered, of the Onion River Land Company which was even twenty-five miles farther north than the fort?

Ethan's immediate mission in Congress was to get the Green Mountain Boys commissioned as a regular outfit of the colonies. Since the country represented was still a strip of disputed land—neither fish nor fowl—its status was unique. To complicate the picture Ethan made the incredible suggestion that the Green Mountain Boys operate with the New York forces (for purposes of war against England). New York still had a price on his head

44

and had sentenced him to death on capture, without benefit of clergy. Nevertheless, since it was unmilitary to have guerrilla bands operating independently in time of war, Congress agreed that it would be a good idea for the Green Mountain Boys to join forces with New York.

Shortly after, Ethan and Seth were in New York City, where the New York Provincial Congress was meeting. The news that Julius Caesar was outside would probably not have startled them any more than the announcement: "Ethan Allen is at the door and desires admittance." They let him in, but instead of death without benefit of clergy Ethan got the Green Mountain Boys made an official part of the New York forces. Shortly after this, however, came probably the biggest blow Ethan ever suffered. The Green Mountain Boys chose Seth Warner as their colonel. Nobody knows why. Maybe they thought Ethan would lead them into one northwoods death trap after another in the name of the Continental Congress and the Onion River Land Company. Heman Allen was made captain; Ira and Ebenezer, first lieutenants—but Ethan was left completely out.

" . . . the old farmers . . . who do not incline to go to war . . . in their nomination of officers . . . have wholly omitted me," Ethan wrote the governor of Connecticut, "but as the commissions will come from the Continental Congress, I hope they will remember me, as I desire to remain in the service." And in the postscript: "I find myself in the favor of . . . the young Green Mountain Boys. How the old men came to reject me, I cannot conceive, as I saved them from the encroachments of New York."

Perhaps the Green Mountain Boys knew what they were doing when they chose the more cautious Seth. Ethan had the military bug, liked being a hero. Right after Ticonderoga he got the idea that he wanted to capture Montreal, which meant Canada, with a quick thrust, before the British got ready to fight. He felt he could do it with the Green Mountain Boys and any friendly Indians he could get to join up. He also felt it was not enough to hold Ticonderoga. If Onion River was to remain an Allen river—the frontier must be pushed further north. "Their design," wrote a discerning observer in the Grants at that time, "appears to me . . . to hold these places [Ticonderoga and Crown Point] and to push on to . . . the Sorel [Richelieu] and make a post there for the security of their lands on Lake Champlain and Onion River."

With this in mind, less than two weeks after Ticonderoga, when he still headed the Green Mountain Boys, Ethan had sent off a letter "to our good brother Indians of the four tribes, viz.: the Hocnawagoes, the Swagaches, the Canesdaugans and the Saint Fransawas . . ."

> I was always a friend to Indians, and have hunted with them many times, and know how to shoot and ambush like Indians, and am a great hunter. I want to have your warriors come and see me and help me fight the King's regular troops. You know they stand all along close together, rank and file, and my men fight so as Indians do, and I want your warriors to join with me and my warriors, like brothers, and ambush the regulars; if you will, I will give you money, blankets, tomahawks, knives, paint, and anything that there is in the army, just like brothers, and I will go with you into the woods to scout; and my men and your men will sleep together and eat and drink together . . . But if you our brother Indians do not fight on either side, we will still be friends and brothers; and you may come and hunt in our woods, and come with your canoes in the lake, and let us have venison at our forts on the lake, and have rum, bread, and what you want, and be like brothers.

He also had written Congress that he could take Montreal with five hundred men. Now was the time, Ethan thought, since the Canadians were watching the balance of power and would cast their lot with whichever side seemed stronger. Unfortunately, Congress didn't see it his way until later, when the British had organized, and it was then too late. As a scout during the summer Ethan had with a few men tried to ambush the British near the border. In August, 1775, General Schuyler finally gave him a job preaching politics to the French. General Carleton wrote Lord Dartmouth that the American emissaries were injuring British prestige. He of course meant Ethan, who, when it came to talking, was several emissaries wrapped up in one.

The temptation to take Montreal plagued Ethan until one day in September he decided without orders to try it with a mixed force of about one hundred men. When the people of Montreal heard that there was an American force at the gates there was a great to-do. So little was Carleton prepared for war that he was said to have been ready to leave the city with government officials. Disastrously for Ethan, however, a spy informed Carleton of Ethan's small force. Carleton then gave orders to pursue him. Ethan had arranged to join forces at the gates of Montreal with a Colonel Brown and his troops, but Colonel Brown failed to show up and Ethan found himself in the most desperate jeopardy. He nevertheless, deployed the few men as advantageously as he could. When the British attacked on the afternoon of September 25 there was a flurry of shooting but nothing decisive until the redcoats started flanking Ethan's right. At this point fifty of his Canadians gave up and took off. With only fifty men left, Ethan retreated about a mile with the British in blistering pursuit. There is little doubt that he himself would have fought to the end, but he would not sacrifice men needlessly. He surrendered.

> The officer I capitulated with, then directed me and my party to advance towards him, which was done; I handed him my sword, and in half a minute after, a savage, part of whose head was shaved, being almost naked and painted, with feathers intermixed with the hair on the other side of his head, came running to me with an incredible swiftness; he seemed to advance with more than mortal speed; as he approached near me, his hellish visage was beyond all description; snakes eyes appear innocent in comparison of his; his features extorted; malice, death, murder and the wrath of devils and damned spirits are the emblems of his countenance . . .

Ethan grabbed the British officer, and spun him like a pinwheel between himself and his attacker until they could disarm the redskin. The colonel was then brought before General Prescott. Prescott swore and shook his cane at Ethan—Ethan shook his fist at Prescott. In great wrath the general ordered thirteen of Ethan's Canadians shot immediately.

> It cut me to the heart to see the Canadians in so hard a case, in con-

sequence of their having been true to me; they were wringing their hands, saying their prayers, as I concluded, and expected immediate death. I therefore stepped between the executioners and the Canadians, opened my clothes, and told Gen. Prescott to thrust his bayonet into my breast, for I was the sole cause of the Canadians taking up arms.

The guard, in the meantime, rolling their eye-balls from the General to me, as though impatiently waiting his dread commands to sheath their bayonets in my heart; I could however plainly discern, that he was in a suspense and quandary about the matter: This gave me additional hopes of succeeding; for my design was not to die, but save the Canadians by a finesse. The general stood a minute, when he made the following reply; "I will not execute you now; but you shall grace a halter at Tyburn, God damn you."

Washington wrote Schuyler: "Colonel Allen's misfortune will, I hope, teach a lesson of prudence and subordination to others who may be too ambitious to outshine their general officers, and regardless of order and duty, rush into enterprises which have unfavorable effects to the public and are destructive to themselves."

If Ethan had had a few hundred more men, for whom he had so often begged, the story might have been different. The country might have been spared its later, and disastrous, Canadian campaign. Ethan's expedition might easily have been as spectacular as Ticonderoga . . . He might have become a brigadier general . . . Canada and the United States might have been one . . . This, of course, is speculation. As for his rash skirmish, it had precipitated him into a quagmire of misfortune, but Ethan could not control his knight-errantry. Whatever he felt, he felt more deeply than most.

2

Somewhere in 38-year-old Remember Baker's lanky frame reposed a reservoir of endurance enough for nine men. He had lived as many lives. He served as a private among the provincial troops recruited for the invasion of Canada in 1757. He was in General Abercrombie's expedition against Canada in 1758. He fought with Lord Howe when the general was killed near Ticon-

THE CAPTURE OF ETHAN ALLEN

deroga in the engagement that wiped out 300 French and captured 148 more. He served under General Amherst when the British took Ticonderoga and Crown Point. As a captain of the Green Mountain Boys he participated in nearly all their frays, with a £20 New York bounty on his head. In May, 1775, he had left his blockhouse home on the Onion to take from the British at Crown Point the fortress he had previously helped them take from the French. This he did with his usual skill, helping capture it the day after Ethan took Ticonderoga.

And now in August, 1775, detailed by General Schuyler, he was on his way to Canada as leader of the second scouting expedition sent out within a month to spy on the British. He landed at night in a Canadian bay of Lake Champlain near Isle aux Noix, where the British troops were stationed. In the morning he found a vantage point where he could observe what was happening on the island. While he was watching, some Indians stole his boat and started to St. Johns. From his observation post Remember saw them coming, hailed them good-naturedly, and asked them to please leave the boat. After all, he said, there was no war between the Indians and the Americans. When they failed to stop, Baker said he would fire unless they obeyed. One of the Indians raised his gun to fire, but Baker was quicker—he pulled the trigger. Because of a faulty flint his musket failed to go off. In the last few seconds of his life Remember Baker stuck his head out from behind the tree as he hammered his flint. At that moment a bullet from the Indian's gun passed through his head and killed him. His men, now leaderless, shot and killed two Indians and then fled. The Indians came ashore, cut off Baker's head and put it up on a pole in St. Johns, Quebec. The British bought the head so that they might bury it with his body.

A hush fell over the American troops stationed at Onion River Falls the night the news of Remember's death was told within the stout, hand-hewn logs of his blockhouse. And there was sadness throughout the Grants, not so much because he was a celebrated soldier—the first killed in the Northern Department—but because, in a rough sort of way, he was a gentleman.

3

With Baker dead and Ethan chafing in irons in the hold of a British ship, Ira now became three-fifths of the Onion River Company. He had Baker's will and his children on his hands, as well as a third of the valley of the Onion. As a lieutenant in the Green Mountain Boys, with his attention fixed on the British in Canada, Ira now joined the war. Though he was only twenty-five, his reputation as a scout and expert strategist had reached the ears of General Montgomery, who named him to his staff. There he served conspicuously in the successful campaigns against St. Johns and Montreal.

On the fateful last night of December, 1775, Montgomery had chosen Ira as one of two officers to lead an attack on Cape Diamond. He was responsible for launching rockets as a signal for the three other detachments to start the offensive on Quebec. Fate willed that Montgomery die that cold night, and that the American expedition crumble. Ira didn't stay long after that—he could see that for the raw new settlements of the Grants it was not now a question of offense, but defense.

During Ira's last weeks with the army, General Schuyler detailed him as escort to a man whom the general thought a valuable friend of the colonies. Allen's uncanny sixth sense, enabling him to look inside people, told him that the man was a British spy. He dumped his charge in the middle of the woods, leaving him to the elements. In February, '76, Ira started home from Canada—three hundred miles through forests in the dead of winter. He must, as he rode through the woods, have foreseen the retreat of a ragged army up Lake Champlain the following summer, for he was now going home to Onion River—to face the British, the Yorkers, or any other challengers, and to fight for troops to protect the northern settlements.

Before Generals Sullivan, Schuyler, and Gates at Crown Point Ira projected a line of forts strung along the Onion across Vermont to the Connecticut, to hold the northernmost rim of the frontier. According to Ira, the generals agreed that Onion River would be the best place, and Sullivan immediately ordered a detachment of troops there. Additional forces were soon sent to the Onion ostensibly to protect the people who were gathering their crops and to prevent their being carried off by Indians. The troops bivouacked at Colchester Point, where the Onion enters Lake Champlain, at the blockhouse near the Falls, and upriver at Jericho, where another blockhouse was built by a company in command of Captain Jonathan Fassett. A redheaded young radical, Lieutenant Matthew Lyon, shared the plight of Fassett and the other officers, when the enlisted men rebelled one night. Surrounded by British Indians and separated from the main body of the American forces, the Onion River troops were suicide troops, complained the spokesman of the enlisted men.

According to Matthew Lyon, who as Vermont's rebellious representative in Congress, would one day cast the deciding ballot for the election of Thomas Jefferson to the presidency:

On my return I found the soldiers more than ever anxious about their situation. They complained bitterly of the orders which bound them to the north side of Onion river, more than twenty poles wide, at that time not fordable, and but a single canoe to cross with. I endeavored to encourage them with assurances that we could withstand any number of Indians in our log house and a hovel or two which stood near; and, after a battle, if we should find the enemy too troublesome, we might retreat with honor. I urged them to their duty as soldiers and patriots. Every preparation was made to repel the attack which was expected from the enemy that night. Being fatigued and off duty, I had laid down to rest, with my fuzee in my arms. About nine o'clock in the evening I heard a violent bustle, with a cry of "Turn out! turn out!" I turned out and inquired where the enemy were discovered, and was answered, "Nowhere." The soldiers were paraded, and I found by what was said by the sergeants that they were about to march off and cross the river. I expostulated with them long and earnestly, pointing out the dishonor which such an action would reflect on their country. I urged them to stay the event of a battle, and I spoke the truth when I assured them that I preferred death in battle to the dishonor of quitting our post.

All entreaties were ineffectual; they declared they had been abused
—there was no chance for their lives there, and they marched off for the
south side of the river. A sergeant returned with some soldiers, and called
upon the officers to cross the river. As they were going to take the canoe
to the other side, they insisted on our going, and threatened violence if
we refused. The other officers, which were two captains and one lieutenant, seemed willing to go, and I did not think it my duty to resist
alone.

On the opposite bank of the river in Williston, the men declared that unless they were immediately marched south to Otter
Creek, where they might discharge the duties for which they enlisted—defense of the New Hampshire Grants—they would all
disperse and go home. The officers had half an hour to accept. If
the men would turn over to them the leaders of the mutiny, the
officers offered to accede to their terms considering the "poor,
weak situation we are in—officers without soldiers, and soldiers
without officers, in an enemy's land—savages all around us."

General Gates damned Lyon as a coward and arrested him.
The officers of the Court decided that:

Captain Jonathan Fassett, Lt. Jonathan Wright and Matthew Lyon
are guilty of deserting their post without orders, or without being attacked or forced by the enemy; and that they are also, with Lieutenant
Rufus Perry, guilty of a breach of the sixth article of war, and so adjudge
that the said [officers] be cashiered, forfeit all their pay (to be appropriated towards making good the damages sustained by the inhabitants
of the Onion River on account of their unsoldierlike retreat) . . . and
that each of them are hereby declared to be incapable of ever after holding any military commissions or employment in the [government] . . .
and that their names and crimes be published in the newspapers.

Some of the men received sentences of thirty-nine lashes on their
bare backs, with one week's imprisonment picking oakum.

Perhaps General St. Clair, the officer who reviewed the sentences, saw in Matthew Lyon's volatile nature indications that he
would one day ascend the nation's political ladder. Schuyler later
restored his rank, but the curse of the "wooden sword" followed
him the rest of his stormy career.

During that spring and summer, 1776, ominous clouds of invasion shadowed the Onion. Burgoyne was on his way up Lake

Champlain, bolstered by Indians, including an array of Abnaki, descendants of tribes such as that of old Gray Lock. Benedict Arnold had been in a frenzy of activity trying to transform the tall trees at Skenesborough into the first American fleet. Half the American forces were down with smallpox. The boom of cannon from across the Lake at Valcour, where Arnold met Burgoyne's fleet, resounded in the Onion valley, and the smoke of Arnold's burning *Royal Savage,* the United States' first flagship, lifted to the horizon. Arnold had slowed the British but not stopped them and it must have seemed to Ira that a minor miracle was necessary. "When the King heard the news of the British victory on Lake Champlain, he rushed into the Queen's apartments in great delight exclaiming that he had beaten all of the Americans"—and so it seemed in the north at least, for by 1777 Ticonderoga had once more fallen to the British. "The popular imagination had invested it with the impregnability of an enchanted castle. It was the bursting of a meteor, which by its awful peal, shook every habitation from Maine to Georgia." And now fell Crown Point and Skenesborough. Champlain was again a British lake, the Onion a British river. Settlers fled from the Allen lands, leaving their good farms to the British, the Indians, and the elements.

These were times for the stoutest hearts. If the British won, Ira suspected that the Onion River lands might not be worth the almost worthless charters Wentworth had granted. As for the people of the Grants—they didn't particularly care to fight for the independence of the newly declared United States in order to be taken over by New York as soon as the shooting was over. But Ira Allen had a plan which he thought might help the affairs of the United States—and incidentally relieve the strain on the Onion River Land Company.

9

LET FOOLS CONTEST

$\mathcal{M}$URDER, conspiracy, blasphemy, rape, bestiality, sodomy false witness, premediated arson, and malicious maiming would be the capital crimes. Adultery would be punished by thirty-nine lashes, branding the letter A on the forehead, and wearing it on the clothes. Counterfeiting would cost the guilty man his right ear. He would also be branded with a C and thrown into prison for life. A thief who stole six pounds would get thirty-nine lashes, while drunkenness, lying, or profanity would commit one to the stocks. Forty shillings would be the price for breaking the Sabbath, with five to ten lashes depending on the degree to which it was broken. The man who killed a wolf or panther would receive £8, and the closed season on deer was January 10 to June 10.

It was February, 1779. Vermont was a republic, and it had all been Ira's doing. He had started that somber summer of '76, when Burgoyne was on his way up the lake. His first task had been to mount his horse and ride all over the Grants, talking up the idea of an independent state among the leading men of various towns. This done, he circulated announcements for a convention of town delegates, the purpose being to vote a Vermont Declaration of Independence from Great Britain—and New York. Though it was in the heat of the Revolution, New York and New Hampshire had fought the idea from the start, so Ira had to follow their agents and lobbyists all over the new republic, defeating their arguments and neutralizing their activities.

During those three years, besides setting up the first convention, he had to draft the state Declaration of Independence, publicize and defend it; he had to help draft the Constitution along Pennsylvania lines, publicize and defend it—and each step carried problems as ponderous as millstones. In the third convention of July, 1777, when the delegates were finishing up work on the Constitution, the news that Ticonderoga had fallen to the British put the members in a rout. Even Ira couldn't prevent them from returning to their homes. Only a roaring thunderstorm is said to have kept them in their seats until they cleaned up the slate.

But the agenda had brought more problems. The delegates had approved Ira's suggestion of a Council of Safety whose duty it would be to think up ways and means of protecting the new republic from the hostile advances of almost everybody, including the British and all the neighboring states. When the Council of Safety—of which Ira was of course a member—would meet, the minor matter of pay for the officers who would enforce the laws of the new republic had to be dealt with. And where was the money coming from for the State Guard they proposed to raise for the defense of the homelands?

When the Council met in July, 1777, Ira paced the floor all night and in the morning came forth with the idea that the Council confiscate all the lands of the Tories, auction them off, and pay the troops. As soon as the Council agreed, Ira put the decree into effect, and that was how in fifteen days Colonel Herrick was in the field with his Rangers and how John Stark ever came to say, "There are the redcoats and they are ours, or this night Molly Stark sleeps a widow."

John Stark wrote Ira from New Hampshire asking about the best route through Vermont. Where would his supplies come from, and where would he meet with Herrick and his newly recruited Rangers, with Seth Warner and the Green Mountain Boys? Ira wrote Stark to come to Manchester, where Colonel Herrick and Vermont's men would be and where he would arrange for supplies. So it was at Manchester that Stark, Herrick, Seth Warner, and Ira met to talk strategy.

Secretly Ira sent spies to check on whether Burgoyne was getting an expedition ready to cross Vermont. The spies reported a force had been sent to Bennington under Baum. John Stark set out for Bennington with the idea of attacking Baum on August 17, but Ira's scouts meanwhile reported that Burgoyne, who characterized the Vermonters as "a gathering storm" to his left, was sending a large reinforcement to Baum. With this valuable intelligence Stark set his attack on the day before Burgoyne's reinforcements would arrive. Thus he was able to fight the British forces separately and to win over both. If he had waited one day, he would probably have lost.

Ira then busied himself with plans to cut off Burgoyne's Lake Champlain supply line to Canada, and retake the forts. Burgoyne's fiasco at Saratoga is in every history book, but what is not so well known is that if it had not been for Ira Allen's vital services prior to and during the Battle of Bennington in helping smash Burgoyne's Vermont expedition, the outcome could conceivably have been quite different.

The fortunes of the Onion River Land Company were improving. The British would now have to withdraw to Canada, leaving Champlain a United States lake. Vermont, now a blushing young republic, was quite eligible for statehood—look what her Council of Safety and its troops had done for the Common Cause! It was a record which New York would have a hard time to belittle, reflected Ira Allen, as he planned more publicity pamphlets.

2

Poor Ethan had been out of association with his friends for two years and eight months. After his capture near Montreal he had been clapped in chains on a British ship commanded by a Captain Littlejohn, who, when visiting British brass were not aboard, treated him with "lenity and honour." When Littlejohn got in a dispute with one of his own officers, he invited Ethan to serve as friend and counselor. "If it is consistent with my situation," declared Ethan, accepting, "I will do myself the honour."

Later he was transferred to a man-of-war under a Captain Smith and confined to irons in the inkiest section of the ship. Soon, however, Smith had Ethan's irons removed and invited him to dine. Emerging from the hold, Ethan remarked that he would probably never be able to repay the compliment, to which Smith replied: "Gentlemen do not know when they may render essential services to one another." Smith may have known of one essential service Ethan could perform right away. A number of prisoners on board and apparently some of the crew were planning to murder Smith and take over the ship. When the prisoners reported their secret to Ethan, he told them that if they murdered the captain they would have to murder him. He then urged them to forget their plot, that he would be as faithful to them as he had been to Smith. It would seem that Ethan was possibly selling his honor for a seat at the captain's table. If he had joined the mutineers, however, he would certainly have had his freedom, which to him was worth more than anything.

Captains of other ships on which he was imprisoned were less humane. For forty days he was chained on one ship in darkness so complete that he couldn't see the other prisoners. He had fever, diarrhea, and was covered with body lice. Only the deadly gruel fed to prisoners kept him from starvation. For a time he was held in a prison in Halifax. Later he was sent to Ireland, where in the Cove of Cork the people exhibited their historic respect and kindness to revolutionaries. They showered him with presents, which the captain later took away.

Finally on May 3, 1778, the British exchanged him for a Colonel Campbell. Ethan, apparently not at all chastened by his wretched experience, wrote: " . . . as I advanced into the country [I] received the acclamations of a grateful people." Though he'd done nothing at all in the war since he took Ticonderoga, he went to Valley Forge, where he paid his respects to General Washington. "There is an original something in him," Washington wrote to the president of the Continental Congress, "that commands attention." Ethan also visited Congress, and once more impressed the representatives, who voted him a brevet colonelcy in the Continental Army and pay for the entire period of his imprisonment. His obscure traveling partner going north was Burgoyne's nemesis— General Gates. When he reached New England he thought he'd stop off at his old home town, Salisbury, Connecticut. There he learned that Heman had contracted pneumonia at the Battle of Bennington and recently died. Another brother, Zimri, had died the previous year, and, with Baker dead, only Ethan and Ira remained of the original five partners of the Onion River Land Company.

Continuing north, he received the ovations of the populace as he entered Vermont. Some say he promoted the celebrations himself, but Vermont did seem glad to have the resounding swashbuckler back home. Ira, now treasurer of the republic as well as surveyor general, was delighted; Ethan would of course take over at once as commander in chief of the republic's militia. With Tom Chittenden, a close friend and protégé, as governor, and other intimates scattered statewide in the government, the Allens controlled the political, legal, financial, and military branches of the republic, a record which even machine politicians of today must pause to admire.

Ira was in a quicksand of responsibility, however. New and perilous problems confronted Vermont. It seemed that there were sixteen towns on the Connecticut River which desired to secede from New Hampshire and join Vermont. The Allens looked with jaundiced eyes on this. Their first ambition was to see Vermont become the fourteenth state of the Union; then all their titles on Onion River would at last be free of the designs of the "united claiming states." If they should take on New Hampshire's sixteen towns, New Hampshire would be a bitter enemy in Congress and fight to the last ditch Vermont's entrance into the Union. The sixteen towns on the Connecticut under the generalship of President Eleazar Wheelock of Dartmouth College in Hanover, New Hampshire, seceded nevertheless, and applied to Vermont for admission, which the new republic's assembly reluctantly granted in June, 1778. Perhaps this would not be so bad after all, the Allens decided. They now had a bargaining point. If New Hampshire would help Vermont become a state, Vermont would promise to get rid of the sixteen towns. Ira wrote the governor of New Hampshire that what the Dartmouth College group really had in mind was a separate state on the Connecticut River with headquarters at or near Hanover. A slightly charred pot was calling the kettle black when Ira wrote that the college men who "claime the antient jurisdiction of New Hampshire" were "a few Restless, uneasy Men not having the good of either of the States at Heart, but their own private Interest and Emoliment." Ethan labeled the Dartmouth group "a Petulent, Pette-fogging, Scribbling sort of Gentry, that will keep any government in hot water," and after a trip to Philadelphia, reported that Congress would annihilate the republic of Vermont if it kept the sixteen towns. Accordingly, a year later in 1779, the towns were disowned by Vermont.

All this time the Allens were consolidating their properties. If they could retain title to the vast acreage of the Onion River Land Company, the value of their holdings was bound to increase two- and threefold with the inevitable rush of settlers at the end of the war. Providing, that is, that they could nullify claims of the neighboring states. The return of the sixteen towns, however, seemed to place Vermont's chances for statehood in the deadliest peril. New Hampshire about-faced and claimed all of Vermont. New York again took to the warpath, and pressed her claims in Congress. Even Massachusetts put in a bid for a large chunk of Green Mountain land. North of Ticonderoga the British were still in control, for no other reason than that the United States did not occupy or garrison the land. Since Onion River could not be persuaded to change its course, its fate was dangerously uncertain.

For the moment, however, the neighboring states presented the worst threat. If they all fought over who would get Vermont, maybe none would get it. This, some said, was Ira's new strategy; he now seemed to be working for a sort of balance of power among the claiming states. He lobbied in Congress. He wrote pamphlets.

He went to the legislatures of states such as Pennsylvania, Delaware, New Jersey, and Virginia, which had no territory to gain or ax to grind in the Vermont matter, gaining friends who could be counted on for help. Not underestimating the power of women, he even made friends with wives of those representatives who were lukewarm toward Vermont.

Meanwhile Ethan, never in better form, was everywhere present, guillotining New Yorkers and their agents with his razor tongue. Since Vermont had decided to seize the lands of New York partisans, Ethan felt it his duty to make sure that it was done right. On one occasion, when a superior court was trying a group of Yorkers caught in defiance of a state-wide draft for the army, the lawyer for the New York party had just bolstered his case with a reference from Blackstone. Ethan, who had been sitting in the back of the room, clumped forward in full regimentals, which included a cocked hat filigreed with gold lace and a tremendous sword at his side.

"I would have the young man know," he thundered, "that with my logic and reasoning from the eternal fitness of things, I can upset his Blackstones, his whetstones, his gravestones, and his brimstones." The judge recovered sufficiently to say that the court would hear the colonel as a private citizen but not as a soldier armed with a sword. Unbuckling his belt, Ethan boomed:

> For forms of government let fools contest;
> Whate'er is best administered is best!

And then:

Fifty miles I have come through the woods with my brave men to support the civil with the military arm; to quell any disturbances should they arise; and to aid the sheriff and the Court in prosecuting these Yorkers, the enemies of our noble State. I see, however, that some of them by the quirks of this artful lawyer Bradley, are escaping from the punishment they so richly deserve, and I find also that this little Noah Smith

is far from understanding his business, since at one moment he moves for
a prosecution, and the next wishes to withdraw it. Let me warn your
honor to be on your guard lest these delinquents should slip through your
fingers, thus escape the rewards so justly due their crimes.

"Ethan," reports Hiland Hall, "with great dignity replaced
his hat, and having buckled on his sword, left the courtroom with
the air of one who seems to feel the weight of kingdoms on his
shoulders."

10

"HIS EX'CY IS AT A LOSS"

$\mathcal{T}$HE dispirited and tattered armies of the newly declared United States allowed American generals no promise of victory. Neither, in 1778, did the commander in chief of his Majesty's forces in America, Sir Henry Clinton, nourish the illusion of easy triumph. Endless black forests and obdurate lakes and rivers diffused his armies. Since the colonies rebuffed any terms except complete independence, England could win only when she had decimated George Washington's armies and forced the last state militia to hoist a white flag.

In the final months of 1778 it occurred to Sir Henry that he might try to detach the colonies one by one. And he believed he knew where to start—Vermont. This slice of mountain terrain, bordering on the lake that was the gate to the country, had served as a buffer between the Iroquois and the Algonquins, the French and the English. Now, as a strategic wedge, might it not crack the solidarity of the United States? Clinton wrote of his plan to Lord George Germain, secretary of state for the colonies, who promptly replied:

> The separation of the inhabitants of the country they style *Verdomont* . . . from the provinces . . . is a circumstance of which I should hope much advantage might be made by discreet management. I see no objection to your giving them reason to expect that His Majesty will erect their country into a separate Province . . .

Germain's happiest contribution was that Britain should allow all the present owners of Vermont land to keep it. He doubtless knew how appealing such a provision would be to Vermont leaders who, in trying to protect the Onion River Land Company, had tackled all comers for six years. "Your situation may enable you to have more ready access to [the Vermonters]," Germain wrote General Frederick Haldimand, commander of British forces in Canada, "and it is the King's pleasure that you should endeavor to open a negotiation with them upon the same ground . . ." Haldimand was advised to have his agents get in touch with those of Sir Henry in New York, and to contact the Vermont leaders.

During the summer of 1779 Clinton, from New York, tried twice to communicate with the Allens. The first time he sent a mutual friend, who fell sick on the way and had in turn to dispatch another messenger. This agent is said to have returned with a report from Ethan Allen that if the British commander would guarantee separate status for Vermont, Ethan would join Clinton with four thousand men. Clinton doubted the authenticity of this. He suspected that the Allens had no such intention at that time. In the second message, however, he suggested that Ethan either go to Canada and join Haldimand or unite with the British forces in New York. In the latter event Clinton would join him up the Hudson. This message, too, apparently failed to reach Allen, and for the moment the center of intrigue shifted to Canada.

General Frederick Haldimand, a Swiss soldier of fortune, had performed competently in the armies of the king of Sardinia, Prince William of Orange, Frederick the Great of Prussia, and, under the banner of George II, in the French and Indian Wars in America. He had served as military governor of West Florida, and as commander in chief at New York when General Gage was in England. This man was admirably equipped to deal with the Allens, for he had watched another small country, Holland, rise as a direct result of the personal fortunes of the Prince of Orange.

But Haldimand wrote Lord Germain that he could not entertain much hope regarding Vermont. "They are a profligate Banditti, and are now become desperate." He nevertheless started sending agents southward to spread the news among Vermonters that Britain would treat them with generous terms. At the same time he watched Vermont's unsuccessful battle with Congress for entry into the Union, and the advances of the "claiming states," New York, New Hampshire, and Massachusetts. During the latter part of 1779 and the first months of 1780, as he set the stage for formal conferences with the Allens, Haldimand moved carefully.

From the south, meanwhile, Clinton sent another letter to Vermont through his agent, Colonel Beverly Robinson, a New York loyalist.

I can make no proposals to you until I know your sentiments, Robinson wrote Ethan. But I think upon your taking an active part and embodying the inhabitants of Vermont in favor of the crown . . . that you may obtain a separate government under King and constitution of England, and the men formed into regiments under such officers as you shall recommend.

Ethan looked the letter over, sent back word that he would consider the matter, and at once held a policy meeting of the triumvirate. It seemed to Allen, Allen, and Chittenden that the fact that Vermont prisoners were held in Canada was of utmost concern, and that they ought to have a meeting with Haldimand to see if an exchange could be effected. In October, 1780, One-Eyed Tom wrote Haldimand and suggested that the exchange take place on a British warship on Lake Champlain. With the knowledge that they had a British ace up their sleeves, the triumvirate began to write defiant letters to Congress saying that unless something was done to make Vermont a state its people could not be blamed for turning toward Great Britain.

Haldimand was pleased. In suggesting an exchange of prisoners the Vermonters had devised a most ingenious subterfuge. The Canadian commander had been ready to send an expedition up Lake Champlain to divert the New York and Vermont militias from Clinton's operations in the south but, having received Chittenden's letter, decided to attack only the New York forces. In October, 1780, he dispatched Major Carleton up the lake with a large force. Two New York strongholds, Fort Anne and Fort

George, at once fell to the British. But except for a raid up Onion River conducted by a British lieutenant commanding a substantial number of Indians, Vermont did not suffer.

On October 26, 1780, Captain Justus Sherwood, a former Green Mountain Boy who, having turned Tory, had become Haldimand's agent, left Carleton's camp, crossed the lake, and advanced into Vermont accompanied by a drum, fife, and two privates under a British flag. At a meeting of ten field officers, on October 29, Ethan pointed out that the British agent desired to arrange the prisoner cartel, and that since his business was discretionary, the Vermont leader should first meet him alone. To this the officers agreed.

Sherwood first stated that if the important business he was about to discuss did not prove interesting, he must in advance request that Ethan would not take advantage of him. Ethan said he would not, provided "it was no dam'd Arnold plan to sell his country and his own honor, by betraying the trust reposed in him." Sherwood said his business was honorable but that, since opinions might differ, he must insist upon a solemn pledge that Allen would not expose him. After deliberating a few moments, Ethan agreed. Sherwood then said that General Haldimand had followed closely Vermont's battle for recognition as a state, and that it was quite obvious Congress only awaited for the right moment to step in and crush the Vermonters. He then related Haldimand's detailed offer to make a crown colony of Vermont with special privileges which included making Ethan a high officer of the line. Ethan replied that the promotion "had not the weight of a straw with him" but that, since the proposals affected the whole people of Vermont whose liberty and property had been in danger for years, he would seriously consider the matter.

At this point the two joined the other officers and arranged a truce with the British to last until the prisoner exchange had been carried out. Later, Allen and Sherwood again talked alone. Ethan said that the Vermont leaders intended shortly to put more pressure on Congress for admitting Vermont as a state, but that he didn't have much hope of success. If Congress continued obstinate and sent a force against him, Ethan declared he would march on Albany with his own troops. If obliged to retreat from there he would make a stand at Ticonderoga—and call for help from Canada. He hoped Haldimand could supply plenty of troops and that British naval forces were strong enough to prevent a French invasion up the St. Lawrence. Ethan warned Sherwood, however, that all this depended upon Britain's guaranteeing the Vermont land titles of the present owners. He also made it clear that Vermont would have to be a great deal more independent than other colonies. Finally, it would take some time to prepare Vermonters for such a change, and General Haldimand of course must realize that if Congress made Vermont a state the negotiations were all off.

The meeting ended pregnant with possibilities for both the British and the Vermonters. Sherwood's message regarding the truce was sent to the legislature, which at once disbanded the Vermont militia and appointed Ira Allen as one of two commissioners to treat formally with the British for exchanging prisoners. In November, 1780, Ira started north to Canada with Captain Sherwood and Jonas Fay, a Bennington confidant of the inner circle since before the war. But winter suddenly congealed the north country. Ira had to turn over Ethan's pamphlets and papers to Sherwood, with strict instructions to conceal them on the shore each night, lest they be captured by raiders from New York.

Sherwood reached Haldimand's Quebec headquarters late in November after a trip filled with hazards to his person and Ethan's papers. Haldimand was satisfied with the progress made. His own troops were widely scattered, however. Should negotiations with Vermont prove satisfactory, he was not too sure that he cared to have Ethan with four thousand men in Canada—since the Vermonter had once tried to storm Montreal and might again try to deliver Canada to the United States. But Haldimand could not help but think that the Vermonters were really interested in the British offer.

2

When Ira got on his horse to go to Canada to see the British in 1781, Ethan tried to dismount him. "My brother Ethan," reported Ira, "was greatly exercised in his feelings about my going into the enemies' country—he came out and tried to pull me off my horse, declaring I should not go, for, if I did, I would be, in one week, on my way to England in irons to be hanged, or to die by inches in a prison ship."

All this Ira knew. But Vermont by May, 1781, was in a desperate way—which is to say that the Onion River Land Company was in a desperate way. Congress had invited New York, New Hampshire, and Massachusetts to a conference to decide how the Vermont carcass should be picked. Philadelphia chose to ignore the 14-karat services of the Green Mountain Boys, Vermont strategy at the Battle of Bennington, and the rest. The United States simply did not want Vermont except, apparently, as part of New York, New Hampshire, or Massachusetts. The triumvirate reminded Congress that it was hard to find a motive to continue to fight Great Britain "and maintain an important frontier for the benefit of the United States for no other reward than the ungrateful one of being enslaved by them."

The truce between Vermont and Britain for exchanging prisoners bore to George Washington "a very suspicious face." Since the previous fall it had been falsely reported that Ethan had gone over to the British with a large force and truly rumored that a movement had been afoot in the Vermont legislature to impeach him. Although this failed to pass, Ethan indignantly submitted his resignation to the Assembly as brigadier general of the militia— which they accepted, thanking him for his services. Yet the same Assembly had appointed Ira Allen as a single commissioner to meet with the British to make further arrangements for the prisoner cartel.

Arriving at Isle aux Noix on May 7, 1781, Ira steeled himself for a word campaign of double-entendre with the British, which would have taxed the talents of Talleyrand. With open-faced sincerity in a 17-day series of conferences with the British emissaries, Sherwood and Dundas, he railed, as Ethan had, against the injustices committed by New York against Vermont. He said Vermont so hated New York that it would rather be a part of any other government on earth, and gave the British agents every reason to believe that Vermont was ready for an agreement. Sherwood and Dundas turned to each other and laughed, while Ira, according to his own report, "perceiving I had made just the impression I intended . . . laughed out of the other side of my mouth." The British officers said that Vermont should declare for England without delay. Ira replied that this would be a delicate job. It would take time. The people were afraid of an invasion from Canada, and nothing could be done to bring them on Britain's side unless the armistice was continued.

Disappointed at the prospect of further delay, Sherwood and Dundas decided that "Mr. Allen is sent here to spin out the time that they may see how Congress and the three states who lay claim to Vermont will act on account of their having sent a flag here." At the same time Sherwood remarked in his journal that "Allen and his family have large fortunes which they do not intend to lose, if there is a possibility of saving them. At all risks he is determined that Congress shall not have the parcelling of his lands to their avaricious minions."

To Haldimand, the military advantage of a chance of getting the new republic as a colony was still mouth-watering. Allen had declared that Haldimand would hear from Vermont by mid-summer, and that its representatives would have the power to determine whether Vermont was to become a province. Haldimand therefore extended the armistice, and Ira went back home with the

knowledge that ten thousand of his Majesty's troops poised in
Canada would not resume hostilities until after the Vermont legislature met, and maybe not at all.

In June Ira reported on his trip to the Assembly in Bennington. The actual business of his mission had been a secret to all except Allen, Allen, and Chittenden and their inner circle of confi-
dants. The ostensible business had been to make arrangements
with the British for the exchange of prisoners, and these arrangements actually had been made. Now he addressed the Assembly,
filled with spies from neighboring states as well as British agents.
According to Charles Miner Thompson's *Independent Vermont*
"he had to satisfy not only the men who wanted to be sure that he
was not betraying Vermont, but also men who wanted to be sure
that he was." The speech was a compound of all things to all men.

The British found the Vermonters' subsequent letter-writing
an extraordinary mixture "of perhaps Truth, Falsehood, Candour
and Deceit . . . it is perfectly Honest or perfectly Jesuitical, and
his Ex'cy is at a loss what to make of it." His Excellency (General
Haldimand) decided to go along for a while in the hope that Allen
was on the level. Ira meanwhile journeyed to Philadelphia to circu-
late information that the time was running out for Congress to declare Vermont a state. On July 31 that body was shocked by the
contents of a letter taken from a captured British ship. The letter,
written by the British secretary, Germain, stated that the return of
the people of Vermont to Great Britain was an event of utmost importance, for it would present a stumbling block if George Washington and the French were trying to hatch a revolution in Canada.
Members of Congress immediately offered resolutions to prepare
for Vermont's admission into the Union.

Meanwhile, aboard a British warship on Lake Champlain,
the Vermont leaders continued to meet with Sherwood and Dundas under the pretense of completing arrangements for the exchange of prisoners. In this way the Allens wore out the summer
of 1781. There was no end to letters, conferences, proposals, and

counter-proposals. By locust time, Haldimand had reached the end of his rope. He issued an ultimatum that he would either get a definite commitment from Vermont or send an army up Lake Champlain. Ira once more pacified the general by suggesting that the British commander draft a proclamation offering independence to Vermont. The proclamation would arrive by messenger under a British flag when the Vermont Assembly was in session. The seal of the document would be broken by the speaker before all the legislators, so there would be no suspicion that the Vermont leaders had had anything to do with it. Although Haldimand realized that this would provide the Allens with more publicity which would show the American Congress the seriousness of Vermont negotiations with Britain, and force the issue of statehood, the British general at once went to work to prepare the proclamation.

In the interim, however, rumors reached the north country that the French Admiral de Grasse had arrived in America with twenty-eight ships of the line and had dealt the British a stinging naval blow. It was even reported that Lord Cornwallis was a prisoner. Ira at once advised Haldimand that this was certainly not the time to try to influence the people toward Great Britain, and that in his opinion delivery of the proclamation should be postponed. "Should the General's patience hold out," he wrote, "and the frontiers not be invaded to rouse that spirit which there has been so much pains taken to allay, these matters may yet crown our most sanguine expectations . . ."

On October 19, 1781, Lord Cornwallis went down in defeat at Yorktown and there was no longer any reason for Haldimand to send an army up the lake. Turning toward Philadelphia, Allen, Allen, and Chittenden hastened to point out to Congress that their truce with the British had caused ten thousand of his Majesty's troops to stay in Canada all summer instead of meeting with Cornwallis, an obvious service to the United States. "Thus ended," wrote Ira, "the campaign of 1781, with the accidental loss of only one man on the frontier of Vermont . . . exposed to an army of ten thousand men."

"Vermont being thus driven to desperation by the injustice of those who should have been her friends was obliged to adopt policy in the room for power," One-Eyed Tom wrote General Washington.

"As you unbosomed yourself to me," replied Washington, "I thought I had the greater right of speaking my sentiments openly and candidly to you . . . if they should produce effects which I sincerely wish, that of an honorable and amicable adjustment of a matter which, if carried to hostile lengths, may destroy the future of my country, I shall have attained my end, while the enemy will be defeated in theirs . . . " Regarding the vacillating eastern townships, Washington wrote: "I would ask you candidly whether . . . your claim on New Hampshire was not . . . a political manoeuvre. . . . if so, you have nothing to do but with-draw your jurisdiction to its own limits, and obtain an acknowledg-ment of independence . . . of New York, New Hampshire, and Massachusetts."

On February 22, 1782, the Vermont legislature, with Washington's letter in hand, gave back the sixteen towns it had re-cently reannexed from New Hampshire. It also returned to New York some more towns to the west that it had annexed on the basis that offense had been the best defense. Even so, statehood did not come. The southern states were afraid that Vermont's entry into the Union would give the North too much influence, for it would destroy the balance of power. Also, they did not want to encourage their own western settlers to break away, as Vermonters had done, and demand independence. Congress therefore ignored Washing-ton's promise to the Vermonters.

But the Green Mountain triumvirate was too wise in politics not to have withheld a trump card. Allen, Allen, and Chittenden had been careful not to break off negotiations with Canada com-pletely. "I shall do everything in my power to render this State a

British province," Ethan promised. The British eagerly co-oper-
ated by again promising Ethan the rank of brigadier of the line,
and the others of the triumvirate, field ratings, and it was all very
tempting, so tempting, Congress suspected, that something ought
to be done about recognizing Vermont as a state.

Not until nine years later would Vermont be admitted as the
fourteenth state of the Union, but the half nelson of the claiming
states was forever broken. For $30,000 New York at length
agreed to give up all land claims in Vermont, while New Hampshire and Massachusetts just gave up. Now at last the Allens
could go in victory to their Onion River lands, the lands Ira had
never for a moment forgotten "that my soul delights in."

> May Allen live to use the quill,
>   While York in envy reigns,
> With ready mind and active will
>   T'expose their wicked plans.
> May all contagion flee away,
>   And at a distance stand;
> No hypochondrics plague his mind,
>   No palsy shake his hand,
> Till nature's great diurnal wheel
>   Some future day rolls on
> When all the Yorkers courage fail,
>   And all their hopes are gone.
> Then may our ALLEN have repose,
>   Before his days shall cease,
> And sing and see his labours close
>   And leave Vermont in peace.
>   —*T. Rowley*

11

"NOTHING BUT HURRY-CANES"

$\mathcal{I}$T IS doubtful if any person ever caused Ethan and Ira Allen more embarrassment than their brother Levi, black sheep of the family. He did not lack the qualities that made his brothers conspicuous. He was involved frequently in large, even dramatic, operations during which he showed enterprise and courage. He was concerned with politics and had a strong sense of property. As in Ethan and Ira, there was a certain uncultivated aura of poetry about him. The fact that Levi became later in life a brooding alcoholic dogged by misfortune everywhere he went was the result of his betting on the wrong horse in the Revolution. He was a Tory.

His career started auspiciously enough. He had been in the general merchandise business in Salisbury, Connecticut, with his brother Heman. He pioneered in the tanning industry and for three years, beginning in 1770, scouted west through hostile Indian country as far as Detroit, risking his life on every trip to hunt skins. He became adjutant of the Green Mountain Boys during the days of Yankee-Yorker skirmishes, but when war was declared against England, he declared for the British. Levi was caught supplying provisions to British ships on Long Island and was thrown into jail in New London, Connecticut.

When Ira put through his act confiscating Tory property to pay for mobilizing the state militia, he and Ethan confiscated Levi's Vermont property without so much as an official bat of an eye. *"Damn* his lukewarm soul!" Ethan complained. No sooner was Levi at liberty, after serving a six months' sentence in New

London, than he challenged Ethan to a duel. Ethan ignored the challenge. Levi wrote that he had no doubt that his brother would have fought him had not Ethan's friends argued that he had gone mad as a result of long confinement in jail.

Levi left Connecticut for South Carolina, where he served with the British through the rest of the war. During this time he engaged in extensive land speculations in Florida but lost all his property there when eastern Florida was ceded to Spain in the

peace of 1783. "The land business hath occupied the attention of our Family for many years past in which I have had no small share, particularly the foreign department. I was very successful till the unhappy dispute commenced between Great Britain and her then Colonies in which I suffered much and my Brother Ira made a fortune." He rather shamefacedly returned to Vermont and started land operations in lower Canada. Following the war, Ira had begun extensive rafting of timber for masts on the Onion and Levi, in business down Lake Champlain at St. Johns, Quebec, was forwarding them to the British. He made frequent trips to Onion River to discuss lumber operations and journeyed to England to obtain a contract for masts for the Royal Navy. In a London coffeehouse he was insulted by a Major Jessup, whom he immediately challenged to a duel. The major backed down and Levi issued a public statement to the effect that he was a coward. Levi conducted himself badly in London, ran into debt, and used pseudonyms to avoid imprisonment. He alternately signed his name as D. Alonzo, Christiana Vala De Arabi Constantine Americanus Calvo Almando De Alonzo, or, "when pressed for time, simply Bumber D." In the face of poverty he philosophized that "Gout . . . only attacks the rich, so I am in a good way to avoid Death and bodily inabilities." Returning to Canada he resolved, however, that "nothing but Hurry-Canes, Earthquakes, or a more awful lingering death, can prevent my success . . . "

From St. Johns he seems to have traded extensively with Ira at Onion River Falls not only in lumber but in general merchandise. Gradually, however, he became preoccupied with Canadian land speculations—and with drink. Nancy, his wife, apparently could not join him in Canada and he therefore sought consolation through the mails. His letters show a consuming restlessness—though he had already been a farmer, ironworker, Indian trader, merchant, land jobber, politician, and preacher in "Phisick." Nancy wrote that she was sorry to hear "that Bacchus and yourself are still on so friendly terms—your intimacy has been of so long standing and no probability of the friendship being desolved, that Venus is jealous of a preference in Bachusses favour."

Levi obtained employment as a British agent at £100 a year to try to influence the republic of Vermont to become a British colony, but the republic became the fourteenth state and Levi lost his job. He was thrown into jail by the British in Canada for irregularities in his land operations. He was, in fact, doomed to die forgotten in a Burlington jail on Onion River at the turn of the nineteenth century.

I was totally rong in political matters and my brothers right. I have done them no damage but on the contrary my blackness thro's a greater light on their brilliance, but it is too late as well as too mean now to turn about and from their brilliance to attempt to draw a ray to obscure my own darkness.

12

ONE-EYED TOM

*O*NE-Eyed Tom Chittenden, Vermont's first governor, was a rough man, rawboned and homely. He had innate humility and natural wisdom that came from a life lived near the soil. And he was shrewd. Ethan Allen said he was the only man he had ever known who was sure to be right even in the most complex cases, without being able to tell the reason why. Chittenden could sum up a situation in a few clear words. He could detect a four-flusher at fifty paces. His was perhaps one of the original Vermont senses of humor. His aggregate traits molded a sort of political Gibraltar of dimensions exceeded by none in the state of Vermont, and perhaps matched—though in an entirely different way—only by the Allens. He served for eleven years as the only governor of the republic of Vermont, and almost continuously, until his death, as governor of the state of Vermont.

Dubartis Willard, who sometimes made his way to the General Assembly on foot and sometimes on horseback, one evening stopped at One-Eyed Tom's to spend the night.

"Well, Barty," the governor said, "Where are you going?"

"To the Assembly, your Honor."

"What! You going to the Assembly!"

"Yes, your Honor. I am representative from the town of Essex."

"Well, well," Chittenden said. "In new countries, when they can't get iron wedges, they have to use wooden ones."

"Yes, yes," Barty agreed, "and when they can't get good

78

ironbound beetles to drive them with, they have to use basswood mauls." Such was the relationship between the governor and his constituents.

Tom Chittenden, who had been born in Connecticut, sailed at the age of eighteen to the West Indies, where, with his shipmates, the French captured and imprisoned him. At some point he lost the sight of one eye. He finally returned to the colonies, married, and settled in Salisbury, Connecticut, where he served as a member of the provincial legislature, as colonel of the militia, and justice of the peace. There he knew the Allens, who, having formed the Onion River Land Company and knowing a good man when they saw one, either gave or, for a nominal sum, sold him a rich tract of land at Williston just above their own at Winooski Falls. Chittenden moved to the Onion in 1774, left during the Revolution, and returned immediately after. During the formative days of the republic and state he was a strong and vital link in the Allen, Allen, and Chittenden triumvirate. Ira thought up most of the schemes, Chittenden passed on, negotiated, and popularized them, and Ethan enforced them.

"A low poor house," a 1789 visitor called Tom Chittenden's farm, "a plain family . . . hard fare, a very great farm—1,000 acres, a hundred acres of wheat on the Onion River, two hundred acres of extraordinary intervale land. A shrewd, cunning man, skilled in human nature and in agriculture—understands extremely well the mysteries of Vermont . . ." Visitor Nathan Perkins arrived somewhat later. "I perform this day . . . ye office of physician and nurse to Mrs. Chittenden, who is very sick with a disorder called St. Anthony's fire . . . They seem to love me as a brother & ye governor as a son. I struck them upon ye right key. His Excellency picked me out to understand human nature at first sight . . ."

Hard work and frugal living transformed his Onion River acres into a garden of husky crops. Before many years he built a brick house with a ballroom on the top floor, one of his few ventures beyond the plow and the desk. Yet One-Eyed Tom stuck to his double service coat—blue on one side for civil affairs and red on the other for military occasions. His frugalness began and ended with his personal life. There had been the time the British were on their way up the lake and Vermont faced the problem of raising money for troops. "Gentlemen," Tom Chittenden had said to the Council of Safety, "this thing must be done. . . . I have ten head of cattle, my wife has a necklace, a family heirloom. We'll start with those." Ira Allen's suggestion of confiscating and selling Tory estates made this severe measure unnecessary.

Recently there had been the year when the cold above the valley had frosted the crops and the long white winter reduced the mountain farmers to near-starvation. The rich lands on the Onion had, however, filled Tom's barns with corn. This message came to the mountains: "I have plenty and to spare. Come and get it." They came down the frozen hill roads with their homemade sleds, carrying scanty possessions which they offered Chittenden in exchange for his corn.

"I have no corn to sell to hungry men," he told them. "Help yourselves. Leave me only enough for seed."

In spite of the governor's tooth-and-nail opposition, a man named Stannard was one year installed as justice of the peace in Chittenden's own county. The governor had offended a close friend by opposing Stannard, the friend's brother-in-law.

"Well, you have appointed him a justice of the peace, after all," he said to his friend one day.

"Yes, and I think we have done right."

"Well, well," said Vermont's competent fence mender, "I don't know but you have. I really believe he will make a better justice of the peace than I think he will."

A persistent legend about Chittenden concerns a man who, evidently anxious to make a good impression on his Excellency, one day galloped to the Chittenden house and dismounted. With a certain amount of ceremony he called to a man working in the front yard and bade him hold his horse, which the man did without hesitation. Entering the house, the visitor asked if he might talk to the governor.

"I think so," was the reply. "He is in the front yard holding your horse."

13

DARKNESS AT NOON

$\mathcal{I}$N August, 1784, Ethan wrote Ira on the Onion to "git the Bords Sawed" for a house two stories high, 34 feet long and 24 feet wide, that he would be up with his dashing new wife in the spring to supervise the building. His desire to get his house built in a hurry was as impetuous as his plans for augmenting his family. In the fall a son arrived whom he named Hannibal Montressor Allen. About this time some people in Connecticut wanted him to lead a rebellion of some Connecticut settlers who said their land was part of Connecticut, against some Pennsylvanians who said it was part of Pennsylvania. Ethan, who for some time had been looking around for a good rebellion, was glad to go, but nothing much came of this one.

It was time, he decided, to put the epaulets and sword away, and so he took Frances and Hannibal Montressor to Onion River, where he built a fine farm on high land near the upper Falls with a sweeping view of his hard-won Green Mountains. Though his first wife, who died a year previously, had never been able to curb his various excesses, it seemed as if his new spouse, Fanny, had at least partly tamed him. Spirits were something Ethan had always been familiar with, even downright fond of. After they moved to their new farm Fanny decided to prove that he came home inebriated oftener than he would admit. She drove a nail in the wall of the bedroom. "There, Ethan," she said. "When your watch is hanging on that nail in the morning, I shall know that you came home sober." It looked so easy at that point that he at once agreed. Having made the bargain, he would not give up. Night after night he would stand before the nail making quick thrusts with his watch, only to find that the elusive peg had dodged him. After numerous tries he would usually succeed, then go to bed satisfied that everything would be all right with Fanny.

Onion River Falls had, since the Revolution, become the busiest place in Vermont. Below Ethan's new house, on a knoll overlooking the valley, Ira built a handsome dwelling for his own bride. Under the Falls Ira had started a shipyard where the river's first craft, the schooner *Liberty,* now took shape. To service the shipyard he built two forges and a furnace, where he started making hammers and anchors. Not many springs after his dam at the Falls was finished, a freshet came down the river and demolished it. The cost of building it had been considerable, and the number of available workers critically small. Ira was furious. He rebuilt it, this time to withstand great pressure. When it was completed, tradition says he stood on the bank and shook his fist at the river. "There, old Onion, I defy you to move that dam for forty years!" (At almost precisely the end of the allotted time, in 1830, the river was destined to do it.)

The dam on the upper Falls made available abundant water power for Ira's two sawmills and gristmill. Already the logs cut from the vast watershed of first-growth pine and oak were tumbling downstream to be made into masts for export, or floated in rafts to the river mouth, and down Lake Champlain through the Richelieu to the St. Lawrence. On the Millpond Ira placed a ferry. It was Heman Allen who had originally started the Onion River store, which Ira now continued, in order to supply his workers and the growing stream of settlers who arrived to lease his river lands. Sold outright to good prospective political friends of the future state were other choice tracts. Upstream at Williston, One-Eyed Tom Chittenden was busy building a saw- and gristmill. The sound of hammers, saws, and the rumble of millstones proved the intense energy of settlers along the lower Onion. By the late 1780's all the newly cut roads focused upon Ira's Onion River development. He was now one of the richest men in Vermont, a magnate of state-wide reputation.

With his 1,000-acre farm Ethan had become a country squire of a somewhat different character, more exclusively a farmer—not gentleman, but active. He gave up his share in some 400-acre lots around Ira's mills in exchange for an agreement that for seven years Ira furnish him goods, valued at £100 a year, from the Onion River store.

In 1786 Captain Daniel Shays, who was planning to capture the Springfield arsenal, dispatched two officers northward from Massachusetts to offer Ethan command of the insurgents. Indignantly he turned the project down. In 1787 after Shays's rebellion had disintegrated, Shays, Parsons and others fled to Otter Creek. Some of them were arrested stealing horses on the Onion. The commanding general of the militia of the republic of Vermont, far from seeking any more revolutions, was content to bask in the comfortable light of his military achievements, which had led the settlers so far along the road to statehood—now only four short years away—and had established the Allens as the unquestioned masters of the Onion.

Ethan, however, never lost any of his old fire. He took much not-so-secret pleasure in keeping alive the legendary Ethan of Ticonderoga. For many years he had ridden a large white horse and when fellow settlers saw a cloud of dust preceded by a galloping white charger, they always knew it was Ethan. One day in Colchester he came streaking up the road and drew up before a knot of people in front of a store.

"So, Ethan," one of the village wags called out, "you are the Rider on the pale horse!"

Wheeling around so as to bring his village cronies in the rear, and starting off again, the general hollered over his shoulder, "Yes, and *hell* follows after."

He believed in the transmigration of human souls into fish

and beasts, fowls and reptiles, and trusted he would live again as a large white horse.

One May Day, according to plausible tradition, Parson Amminidab Robinson appeared at Ethan's farm on a bony steed which seemed as undernourished as its rider. Ethan sent the horse to the barn for hay and oats, and led the parson into the house where Fanny could line him as she did all ministers, with spareribs, sausages, flapjacks, pumpkin pies, and cider. When they wanted to build a church, they came, strangely enough, to Ethan. Though he claimed he was an infidel, he supplied glass and nails, and usually sent men to help build the meetinghouse. On this particular day, toward evening, Ethan sat down with Robinson to talk over the parson's plans for a new church. After dinner Robinson was shown his chamber, "but in consequence of an unusually full stomach and fleeting fairy visions of the new meetinghouse, did not so quickly fall into the arms of Morpheus as usual."

Hearing somebody stirring about before dawn, Robinson got up and found Ethan watching for the sunrise over the Green Mountains. The parson, who was not able to understand why Ethan helped build all the churches but refused to join any, now asked for an explanation.

"God's rain," said Ethan, "descends upon all and his mercies are over all his works—no monopolies or special privileges."

The parson agreed Ethan was right in one sense. "It seems you believe in a God. Many of the Christian world have supposed you to be an atheist." In his singularly adept manner Ethan tied up Parson Amminidab in theological knots and wound up asking why there were wars if old Beelzebub was not still around. Furthermore, he had declared he had no patience with peace folks in war, and war folks in peace.

"I must say," said the parson, "this don't seem profitable conversation—let us leave temporal things and talk about a hereafter."

"Very well," the colonel-commandant agreed. "I am as willing to talk of things which either of us know nothing about." Robinson pressed Ethan for details of his concept of the hereafter.

"They no doubt keep a true account of our doings here, and if they find we are brave, generous, clever fellows," Ethan began, "they enter our name upon the muster roll of the grand army above."

Robinson found this brief and unsatisfactory. "Well, Parson," said Ethan, "I'll try to give you a sketch. In the first place there is the Rev. Mr. B, of the Congregational church, Elder C, of the Methodist church, and yourself and myself. They arrive at heaven's gate, nobody knows how, and rap. A voice from within cries, 'Who's there?' The two Christian ministers, after a little dispute who should have precedence, agree that the Congregationalist should go ahead, and he answers, 'The Rev. Mr. B, pastor of the Congregational church in—, awaits your pleasure.'

" 'Look and see if you can find his name', is heard.

" 'Yes, the charge against him for hypocrisy and selfishness is balanced by a long, painful fever, and repentance before he died. Let him enter.' "

Then, according to Ethan, the voice directs a search for the name of Elder C, of the Methodist church, and the voice says, "Yes, it is here. The long account against shameless improprieties while on the circuits is balanced by matrimony and sincere repentance soon after he was located. Let him also enter and direct both where to go."

"Now," said Ethan. "I'll suppose you march up next and rap."

" 'Who comes there?'

" 'Amminidab Robinson, pastor of the *Especial* Calvinist Baptist Church of Christ in —.'

" 'See if his name is there,' the voice says.

" 'Yes,' answers the second voice, 'it is written also that a meetinghouse was built about ten years ago by old Ethan Allen, the patriot, whom they improperly call infidel. He has left a numerous church and large estate.'

" 'Open the gate and let him enter.'

"You walk in," declared Ethan, "and there behold in glory the representative of the Majesty of Heaven, seated on a golden chair a little back of a table, upon which are large folio books with leaves of gold and silver; and in front of the table, the first bookkeeper, or recorder, of the deeds of those who come from one of his small planets, by us called Earth. You will next see the Deputy Grand Master rise and speak as follows: 'Ariel, take down that key and conduct Elder Amminidab Robinson to his people— they are enclosed in that northwest corner and locked up together; for they held *close communion* on earth, so they must in heaven. If they were honest there, they'll be happy here. After you let the parson in among those of his faith, lock the door and bring the key.'

"Thus you'll get among your Calvinist Baptist brethren, Parson, and be likely to remain in *close communion* through all eternity, for all I can see."

The parson was not very happy about the way he had been pigeonholed by Ethan, and asked the colonel just how *he* expected to fare, not being a minister or even a member of a church.

"When my body and soul dissolve their temporal copartner-ship," Ethan went on, "my soul will start up on its own hook, to ascend home from whence it came. My soul will carry no church certificate or commissions, any more than I had when I took Ti. Perhaps I may have the company of one of the brave fellows who went there with me. Not a minister or a deacon will accompany me; they will strive to accompany my wife. When I and my old comrade arrive at the gate, I shall rap stoutly, for I believe my right to enter is as good as the best of you.

"A voice from within will be heard saying, 'Who's there?' Perhaps my fellow soldier, wishing to add, the 'colonel,' may quickly reply: 'Colonel Ethan Allen, of Colchester, Vermont.'

"I shall then say to him, 'Away with your nonsense,' and scream out as I did to de la Place, 'No! It is old Ethan Allen that took Ti and Crown Point; and the armed vessel upon the lake, without any orders but *yours*, in one day!'

"A voice will be heard from within saying, 'Ah, yes, you need not look in the books, for the brave Allen has credit upon every page of them; open the gate to him and all his comrades, for he never would be seen in bad company.' So in we go, and the Deputy Grand Master, with a countenance beaming with love and goodwill, rises and says: 'Colonel Allen, in the name of the Majesty of Heaven, I bid you and your friend there welcome to paradise. In imitation of Him, you have contributed as far as you could to the happiness of all his creatures, and as you identified yourself with no one sect on earth, so you have *no bounds* set for you in heaven. Go where you will, except should you wish to see your old friend, Amminidab Robinson, call upon Ariel, who will at any time take the key, and let you in among the Calvinists, and out when you are pleased to go, and lock the door after you!' "

Parson Amminidab Robinson got help for his new church but could not recruit Ethan as a member.

Ethan had a daughter by his first wife who has been described as a lovely young girl and as pious as her mother. She became desperately ill, and when she realized she was about to die, tradition says she called Ethan to her bedside and told him she was about to cross the dark river.

"Shall I trust to your opinions or to the teachings of Mother?" she asked, her blue eyes the only remaining color in her face.

There was a pause and then Ethan said, "Trust to your mother." Perhaps for the only time in his life he covered his face with his hands and cried.

On a cold winter's day in 1789 Ethan took his mulatto man, a horse and sleigh, descended the river on the ice, and went up the lake to the island to get a load of hay at Ebenezer Allen's. He remained there all night convivially renewing old friendships. The following morning he and his man started back with their load of hay. About noon, as the sleigh entered the mouth of the Onion toward the broad acres of his farm, he said suddenly, "It seems as if the trees are very thick here."

These were the last words Ethan Allen spoke.

2

"Arrived at Onion River Falls & passed by Ethan Allen's grave," wrote Nathan Perkins. "An awful Infidel & one of ye wickedest men yt ever walked this guilty globe. I stopped & looked at his grave with a pious horror." Ezra Stiles, president of Yale, wrote in his diary under the date of February 13, 1789: "Died in Vermont the profane and impious Ethan Allen . . . 'and in Hell he lift up his eyes . . .' " The appraisal of Nathan Perkins and Ezra Stiles was not shared by others. Ethan's funeral was an event of great solemnity. It seemed to the people of the valley that a force as strong in a way as the river itself had gone from among them.

When he had been seized with a stroke as the sleigh slipped homeward over the ice at the mouth of the Onion, Ethan struggled so fitfully that his mulatto man, Newport, had to hold onto him to keep him from rolling off. Then the leader of the Green Mountain Boys was still, but he was living. Reaching the farm, the hired man carried him over his shoulder into the house. At first supposing him to be drunk Fanny was not overly alarmed but the next morning when Dr. Stevens came from Pottier's Point to bleed him, the blood would not run. Ethan Allen was dead. Hundreds of people came from neighboring communities to pay their last respects at Ira's river home where Ethan was laid out. There they partook of a keg of spirits, which Ethan had expressly set aside for the occasion according to the custom of the day.

The funeral procession of military companies, paced by muffled drums, halted every minute to the salute of a cannon. One such halt, perhaps most appropriate of all, was made over the ice behind the dam, for Ethan was crossing his beloved river for the last time. Over a fresh fall of snow the cortege wound along the riverbank toward the lake to the west, and the steel of two drawn swords, crossed over the casket, flashed like white fire. At the grave six platoons discharged their muskets and the casket was lowered. There could have been no final resting place more suitable to Ethan than this, for Green Mount Cemetery is high on a hill overlooking the Onion as it meanders across the intervale to Lake Champlain. To the east the proud high peaks of Mansfield and Camel's Hump touch the sky.

14

TO A MAN OF SPIRIT

*T*HE higher the pine stretches upward the more vulnerable it becomes to strong winds from the north. In the valley of the Onion the tallest and straightest trees first felt the ax's sting, for they were needed as masts and brought greater reward to woodsmen. A human parallel is found in the career of Ira Allen. Ira was a man whose aspirations knew no limit. He already owned entire townships on the river and all the houses in them. He owned dams and mills and farms and even a college which he had endowed in 1791, and placed in Burlington on the high pine table which overlooked blue Champlain and the Adirondacks. Kindled by Ira's imagination, an associate declared, "Burlington will rise and Washington will fall." The town would be "a great commercial center, its streets crowded with merchants, its warehouses filled with goods drawn from the four corners of the earth and its harbor providing anchorage and wharfage for large sea-going vessels."

More completely than ever Ira Allen was directing the destinies of his community and his state. But the richest man in Vermont might become richer; more power might come to the most powerful. The eyes of his imagination saw a deep shipway from Lake Champlain through the Richelieu to the St. Lawrence. They saw, too, some say, a Canada liberated from the British—a Canada whose destiny might be welded to that of the United States. Geography tempted such an alliance. The Winooski and the lake emptied north and bore the only carriers of trade—ships.

By 1793 Ira's wealth had burst the confines of manageability—he lacked working capital. Since he would not diminish his holdings by selling part of them to raise cash to pay taxes, he was borrowing from Peter to pay Paul, and running a dead heat with the sheriff. Failure to pay even a small sum when it was due sent a debtor to jail, a law he must have occasionally regretted. A large-scale operation such as buying western lands from the Indians was what he wanted, something with a 200 or 300 per cent return on the investment. He toyed with the Indian land-buying scheme and formed a company with his cousin, but this wasn't the answer, for to deal profitably with lands you had to be on the premises—and besides, Onion River had considerably slaked his land thirst.

It was in 1795 that he determined on an expedition to Europe to buy muskets for the Vermont militia of which he had been lately appointed major general by One-Eyed Tom Chittenden. There were few good muskets in the New World, almost none in Vermont, but east of the Atlantic in the land of eternal warfare there were plenty. He would purchase the muskets with his own money and resell to Vermont at a profit, a legitimate operation, but, with Napoleon at large in Europe, enterprise and courage were necessary.

Arriving in England he found the British hostile to the idea of selling arms to an American who lived near the Canadian border. It seemed likely he could buy muskets in France, for muskets he must have if the Onion River Land Company was to be maintained in the flush of health, or even saved from dismemberment, and so he sailed for France.

In Paris Ira bought a silk coat and waistcoat and went to dine at Luxembourg with Carnot, president of the Directory. It was here under glittering crystal with far vistas of statuary set in the precise greens of the palace gardens that Carnot on behalf of the Directory agreed to sell Ira 20,000 muskets and 24 field pieces for $50,000— $10,000 down and the rest on time over a period of seven years, with interest at 5 per cent. Carnot agreed to deliver the muskets at Ostend and it would be only necessary for Ira to find a boat in which to ship them home. Finding none in France, he hurried back to England to search there. By September, 1796 he had chartered the ship *Olive Branch,* which was scheduled to go from England to Spain, then to Ostend to load the muskets. Unknown to Allen and in violation of wartime edicts, however, she sailed to Dunkirk, France, discharging her cargo there, and proceeded to Ostend. Ira planned to return to France only to check on the delivery of the arms by the French at Ostend and then to sail from Amsterdam on the first boat to America. He wanted to be in Vermont at legislature time to ensure passage of a bill for purchase of his muskets by the state. Furthermore, his eight-month absence was not good for his Onion River holdings— continued delay would place them in jeopardy. Reaching Ostend, he found that the arms had been delivered, that the *Olive Branch* had arrived and was ready to load. The day after the loading began the French government—as a security measure to protect impending operations of its fleet—decreed that all ships were prohibited from clearing French harbors for thirty days. This was the most disappointing luck, but Ira at once started for Paris to obtain his ship's release. Some of the officials who had made the original arms agreement were no longer in office, so it took more time and the utmost ingenuity to secure permission to sail.

Some of the English sailors on the *Olive Branch,* having meanwhile observed the cargo of muskets and believing the Admiralty would tip its coffers for such information, stole a boat and rowed quietly across the Channel by night. As a result of their information two English frigates cruised outside Ostend harbor to ensure that the *Olive Branch* did not sail.

Every costly day that she lay in port under charter to Ira Allen his investment was being vaporized. He determined that she must sail, and at once. The 90-foot ship weighed anchor in early November, slipping out of port unobserved. As she passed along the Channel she sailed near twelve English warships—but they did not know her, for Ira, before embarking, had procured paint and brushes and insisted that the captain streak her sides with new and brilliant colors. She reached the broad Atlantic safely and as she turned west, with the wind filling her sails, the fresh salt spray was good to feel and the song of the rigging good to hear. Ira would soon be back on the banks of the Onion River with the precious cargo that would secure the future of the Land Company.

But eight days out, on Sunday, November 20, 1796, in latitude 47 degrees north and 10 degrees west at two o'clock in the afternoon, his Britannic Majesty's 74-gun ship *Audacious*, after three years in foreign waters, hove into view from the west and signaled the *Olive Branch* to take in her canvas. Boarded by an officer from the *Audacious*, the *Olive Branch* stood by, while her captain and Ira boarded the man-of-war at the summons of its master. In the cabin of Captain Gould the officers "in a rude confused manner asked questions respecting the ship and cargo, from every side of the table." Ira's papers were in order and complete to a copy of the Jay Treaty guaranteeing freedom to ships of neutral countries, and their cargoes. Gould determined to take her back to England as a prize, and to retain all the papers, asking Ira if he wished to put his seal on a large envelope in which they were placed.

"I will not permit you," said Ira, "to impose on my senses to believe that putting my seal on papers that will be broken open in my absence, can be any security to me." He informed Gould that his action was a disgrace to the United States flag. Gould admitted he could not properly seize the muskets, but the log of the *Olive Branch* showed she had recently carried contraband from London to Dunkirk—and she was a legitimate prize. Turning back her prow, the *Olive Branch* reached the cold gray shores of England in mid-December, almost a year from the day Ira had sailed from Boston. The vessel was placed under guard in the harbor of Portsmouth while her captain and Ira underwent Admiralty examinations. The squire of Onion River then left immediately for London, where he contacted an old acquaintance of the Yankee-Yorker days, Rufus King, now United States minister to England.

The battle of the muskets, which was to involve four nations and lead from the polished salons of men in high places to the dungeons of France, began quite literally as Ira Allen versus England. Aged and fusty Sir James Marriott, who dispensed justice in his Majesty's Court of the Admiralty, had no intention of releasing the illegally seized muskets. To do so would commit his government to paying Allen the costs of the seizure. The court instead chose to prove that the muskets had been destined for delivery in Canada, where it claimed Allen was hatching a revolution against British authority. However great a diplomat, Ira couldn't have forged a sovereign state or created his Onion River land empire without gathering enemies on the way. It was these men whom the court selected for evidence proving that the guns were intended for a Canadian revolution.

Prescott, the general who had thrown Ethan in chains when he tried to take Montreal, promising he would grace a halter at Tyburn, wrote the Duke of Portland:

Our friends in Vermont are more inclined to favour the projected attack on Canada than we supposed. Ira Allen has contracted at Paris for a quantity of arms, ostensibly for the Vermont Militia. This, however, is not probable, because as I am informed, the Militia in Vermont are by Law bound to furnish their own arms . . . I certainly believe the arms he mentions are destined either for the People of Vermont or for the Canadians . . . (Continuing his attack, Prescott later wrote the Duke of Portland that the Governor of Vermont) is a man of the meanest education and was lately Keeper of a Country tavern. I mention these particulars to show the utter improbability of Mr. Allen's being empowered to make a purchase of the arms . . .

Isaac Tichenor who, with Allen abroad, was rising fast in the Vermont legislature, had been a long-standing enemy. Pro-British Tichenor wrote pro-British Timothy Pickering, secretary of state in the cabinet of Federalist John Adams, that the legislature of Vermont had not authorized the purchase of the muskets.

On the other hand, United States Minister Rufus King, one of Ira's numerous powerful friends, exerted every influence to ensure that justice be done. He consulted with Lord Grenville, later to become prime minister of England, and helped Ira engage Slade and Nicholl, two of the best British lawyers, for his trial before the Admiralty Court in May, 1797. King advised Ira to return to the United States to look after his lands but he refused to go. From the Onion, One-Eyed Tom Chittenden wrote Matthew Lyon, Vermont's congressman in Washington, to request the British minister at the capital to assure his government that the muskets were purchased at the governor's request. With such irrefutable official evidence in hand, the British minister did so at once. Both the secretary of state and President John Adams now requested that the property be returned to Allen.

On May 19, 1797, the Court of the Admiralty heard the case. The *Olive Branch* was released but the muskets were not. The court adjourned until June 13, on which day parchment-skinned Judge Marriott observed:

> . . . What, the state of Vermont want twenty thousand stand of arms? No such thing, four or five hundred would be enough for them; why they are a young sucking state, the people were a banditti, transported for crimes from France and England; not well settled in government . . . The claimant was like Romulus and Remus who sucked the wolf, full of fight and revolution . . . his name (Ira) denotes rage, revenge and madness.

On the Onion Jerusha Allen gathered every available affidavit showing that the muskets were intended for the militia— newspaper clippings, sworn testimony of state officers and signed statements of Governor Chittenden. She sent copies of these to England on four or five different ships to ensure their arrival. When Judge Marriott received them on July 5 he announced to the court:

> As to Governor Chittenden, I know nothing of him, he may be in league with France for anything I know, and Mr. Allen, not but Mr.

Chittenden encourages him clearly, gives him his largest credentials for the French Government, so that I suppose Governor Chittenden has some conversation with the French Government . . . well, he goes after this canal at Lake Champlain, perhaps for better reasons of his own . . .

Ira was becoming unnerved. He was receiving letters from his wife and associates that the Onion River Land Company was crumbling. He must return, yet he could not since the muskets represented an immense sum. He offered to sell the guns to the British government, but wishing to condemn, not purchase them, it refused the offer. The strategy of the Admiralty Court was to drag out the case until Allen had become so impoverished he could no longer fight. On December 12, 1798, two interminable years after the *Olive Branch* had been seized, Marriott condemned Ira's muskets.

Delivering his opinion the judge said to Nicholl: "I have nothing further to say to you; you have led this gentleman round about; I think if I had been his counsel I would have managed his business better."

"This I know," Marriott said before rendering his verdict:

I know a man that comes from America, and who describes himself with an estate the map of which would cover this table, and yet I do not believe that he has a single acre there; I do not believe that he has a shilling of property . . . Now there is a singular circumstance as to the seal of Vermont; it strikes my idea, and shews the character of the people of Vermont; there is in that seal annexed to one of the affidavits, there are the other colonies represented by a number of small trees, and there is the colony of Vermont like a great tree in the middle, and Mr. Allen I suppose, is to be the Caesar, the Bonaparte of America, but that I do not know; and I will do nothing in this case but stick close to the point before me.

Just before Marriott condemned the cargo, Lord Duncan entered the courtroom ostensibly to pay his respects, but it was later learned that he slipped before the judge the letter Burgoyne had written to Lord Germain in 1777: "The district of the New Hampshire Grants, a wilderness little known in the last war, abounds with the most hardy, active and rebellious race of men on the continent, who hang like a gathering storm, ready to burst on my left."

Allen immediately had the judge's decision and commentary published verbatim in London. Soon thereafter Marriott lost his judgeship and was replaced by the king's advocate, while Ira's brilliant and industrious attorney, Dr. Nicholl, became king's advocate. "In justice to the government of Great Britain," Ira subsequently recorded, "and in apology for the aged judge Marriott, it is proper to observe that several years before . . . Mr. Pitt tried to get the judge to retire and offered him an Irish peerage with a pension equal to his salary—the Judge was then very aged and declined the offer."

One faint flutter of hope remained—the Lords Commissioners of Appeals in Prize Cases, which would convene in December, 1798. His lawyers told him there was no chance whatever, but they had not yet come to know the fierce stubborn flame of resolution that burned inside Ira Allen. He put on his major general's uniform and circulated in the anterooms of the Court of Appeals, mingling with the lords and plying "finnesse" as of old. In this way the affair of the muskets became inextricably associated in the minds of the commissioners with Allen's pleasant nature so that he was able to obtain a delay further to prepare his case for an appeal in their court.

His enemies were meanwhile redoubling their efforts. A group of London merchants had purchased the claim on his muskets from the Admiralty captors, who in turn had determined on a course of having him declared bankrupt and thrown into debtor's prison. They knew his finances were strained to the breaking point and that he was forced to sell some of his Onion River lands to pay the staggering costs of his case. They knew that his best friend, Chittenden, the governor, had died the previous summer, that his old enemy, Isaac Tichenor had replaced Chittenden, and that the legislature of Vermont had levied a tax of a cent an acre on all the land in the state. The British Foreign

Office, in league with the captors, knew in fact more of Ira's affairs than he himself. They gained their best information from one of their own operatives, William Tatham, whom Ira had innocently selected as his London agent for the sale of Onion River lands. The British government was intent upon destroying the man who had played a dominant role in wrecking one of its campaigns of the Revolutionary War. It knew that ten thousand of his Majesty's troops had been held in Canada awaiting the moment when Vermont would become a crown colony—a moment that never arrived.

Ira secured the services of Thomas Erskine, one of England's renowned barristers, for his hearing before the Court of Appeals in Prize Cases on March 30, 1798.

My Lords [Erskine said in a tense courtroom] I am to address you on the part of General Allen, and I by no means intend to address myself to your lordships' humanity or to your lordships' commiseration; but I mean to address myself to your lordships' justice, and so according to the rules which have been immemorially established for the examination of facts . . . I would charge your lordships against confounding, in the smallest degree, suspicion and proof.

Erskine exhibited the original certificate given Ira by Chittenden for purchase of the arms, outlined his career and the offices he had held in Vermont—surveyor general, treasurer, *emissaire extraordinaire,* major general of the militia—in sum, father of the state of Vermont; and he told the entire transaction of the muskets from the day Ira left Boston in 1795.

". . . My Lords, in this case I am in a most singular predicament as I am counsel for a man whose character was never wrecked from the first period of his life, whose conduct was never disputed, who was leagued with no enemy, and without any possible interest which the fertile and able mind of the King's Advocate can find out . . ." Erskine castigated Marriott as a blight on the tradition of English justice before the law. His words left such a lasting impression on the tribunal that, though the King's Advocate followed with his prosecution—the decision of the

Admiralty Court was reversed, the muskets were ordered turned
over to Allen while he gathered more evidence in France relative
to the sums paid the French government for their purchase.

It was now May, 1798, over two and a half years since he
had last been at Onion River. From letters he knew that his land-
holdings there, pilfered by local real estate sharpers and laden
with taxes and mortgages, were in a state of accelerated disinte-
gration—yet he left Dover for France full of expectation that he
would soon procure the required evidence and be back in America
with his muskets before the end of the year. Reaching Grave-
lines, France, on May 20, however, he was seized by the French,
put in a house and guarded by a sentry. What he did not yet sus-
pect was that the English Admiralty captors, who had much at
stake in preventing him from ever reaching Paris, were bribing
the French to control his every action.

In July, 1798, two months after he had arrived in Grave-
lines, an American disembarked who seemed to be having an
equal amount of trouble leaving for Paris. A common language
was basis enough for friendship. Lodging in the same house, they
freely discussed their problems until one day the American suggested an easy way for Ira to leave Paris without a passport. Becoming suspicious, Ira found out that the American was an agent
of the Admiralty captors and had been spreading a rumor among
the people that Allen's anxiety was driving him crazy.

The captors next sent two women, English-speaking and
beautiful, who seemed to take to General Allen immediately,
and it was doubtless most tempting to the general to reciprocate,
but this ruse of the captors seemed obvious. He would not talk,
walk, or dine with them. On another occasion, when making purchases in a neighboring town, he decided to pass the night there
instead of returning in the dark. As rumors spread about Grave-
lines that he had escaped, a local posse mounted the stairs of his
flat and were preparing to open his trunk when they looked out
the window and saw Ira strolling unconcernedly homeward

through the courtyard. The posse retired in haste and confusion. At last there arrived a special passport, for which he had written to his friends Talleyrand and Tom Paine, and he set out at once. His stage overturned en route but he was able to get out and extricate the others through a broken window. A new carriage and fresh pair of horses were procured and the journey resumed.

Two French Ladies were in the Coach one by the side of me, the other on the seat facing me when the latter discovered a Flea on the former who with Difficulty caught it which made amusement for all the Company when she in order to get shed of the flea and some satire attempted to throw the flea out of the coach window hinting that it got off me ('by accident' I understood her) when the flea with Great Dexterity gained the Lap of his old Friend . . . I interfered in the Dispute, seized the Flea and Threw him out of the window declaring him to be no American, but a Native of France which added to the Mirth of the Moment.

In Paris he found that Carnot had left the government in great haste and was now in Switzerland living on the down payment of Ira's muskets—for there was no record that the French government had received it. The intrigue of those next August days of 1798 involved the highest officers of France. Meanwhile Talleyrand attempted to procure for Ira all the papers relating to the muskets. A galaxy of forged documents and the intrigues of the captors, who were still trying to prove the guns were for Canada, further complicated the picture.

The minister of police, an unscrupulous and decadent man named Barras, who had provided Napoleon with Josephine—a cast-off mistress of his own—was trying to use the affair of the muskets to discredit Talleyrand, who had been a close associate of Carnot. Through no fault of his own, Ira's business had thus almost hopelessly involved him. He did, however, gather papers necessary to satisfy the English courts that he had paid money for the muskets and was preparing to leave Paris when, early on the morning of September 1, twelve officers with fixed bayonets entered his room and arrested him. He was thrown into Temple Prison with the worst criminals of France. He wrote Paine, Talleyrand, the French Directory, the president of the legislature, his lawyers, his wife—and had to bribe the jailer to be sure each letter was mailed. He became hungry, then sick, but he was not yet destitute of hope. Two months later, surrounded by filth and disease, he was still there—and still fighting.

It is unpleasant [he wrote the Directory of France] for any man to be necessitated to give details of the history of his life in justification of his conduct. But when life liberty and property, the three governing principles of human nature are exposed, self preservation . . . attachment to a rising family and the means of supporting them are considerations that will apologize for exertions . . . Have been detained in France more than five months without being able to learn the cause, confined in a prison in bad health, banished from society, necessitated to be my own physician . . .

And on November 28:

I see nothing but that I must remain in prison till the Christian resurection when it is said that all truth shall be brought to light. But I am for more decided measures . . . I have too often risked my life for the liberties of my native country to be detained in a land of liberty by misrepresentation, mistake or otherwise . . . This place swarms with spies . . . Some may receive money from more than one of the Beligerent powers . . .

The painful hours in Temple Prison finally ended in December 10, 1798, when he was released only to be followed by two fellow inmates of the prison—agents of the English captors. They trailed him for a week, at the end of which he spoke to them. Suspecting that their identity was realized, they disappeared. On December 30 he was again seized suddenly and thrown into Sainte-Pélagie, a prison even worse than Temple. Here for two weeks he slept on the floor in the wet cold of an unheated room with one filthy blanket as a cover. He pawned his watch to obtain enough food to keep alive and bribe money to continue his letters to French officials. He sent one to the foreign minister detailing the advantages to France of constructing the Suez Canal, outlining a plan to keep it from filling with sand. He felt it would be a great and rewarding project for the nation that built it. This was seventy years before France undertook the project.

On January 22, 1799, since he no longer had enough money to bribe the jailers, he proposed that he be released in Paris for one day in order to obtain a map of Onion River from his papers at the Ministry of Police. He wished to obtain a loan or to sell some lands outright to relieve the brutality of prison life. "I do not value the loss of property so much as the loss of my liberty and to be beat by such an infernal combination extending from England to America." Again on February 20 in another letter to the president of the Directory: "I once more take my pen to acquaint you of my situation. I have long since requested to know . . . the cause of my detention, to see my accusors face to face, if any there were . . . that I might have an opportunity to speak in my own defense. Nine months are elapsed since my detention." He described how his Onion River interests were disintegrating, and of the plans he had for his new university on the pine plains near the river mouth . . . "I had concerted measures to establish a most extensive plan of education, not to be under the superstition of the clergy, and in place of paying too much attention to the Hebrew, Greek, etc. to institute the French and other languages of the present day and such other studies as might be most useful and applicable to the genius and views of the students . . ."

He asked that his room be changed to separate him from the common criminals with whom he was placed. Immediately a rumor gained credence that he wished to be alone in order to kill himself. He refuted this by writing: "I take the earliest opportunity to assure you that I am a man of too much firmness of mind ever to change my political principles or to commit suicide. If I die in this place it will be by sickness or starvation for I assure you I shall never join the crowd to run for a ladle full of soup. Death before dishonor . . ."

For months the prison officials would not allow a doctor to treat Ira and they even appropriated the medicine sent him. His friends were at last able to secure permission for a doctor to visit him—in the company of the jailer. He was so weak he could barely walk. His condition alarmed the doctor, who was not permitted to call the next day. Some pills were sent to him and Ira carefully noted their size and color before the prison physician borrowed them for "examination." When the box was given back he saw that the pills were not those he had first received. He nevertheless pretended to take them and the next morning feigned death by lying very still. One of the spies of the English captors, who had posed as a prisoner, entered his cell five different times, examining him closely. After the examining prisoner had performed his "autopsy" and departed, the corpse arose, dressed and ate breakfast. When at one o'clock in the afternoon the prisoner-agent again appeared, he was quite startled to find Allen alive. Inquiring into the state of his health, he asked if he had taken any of the pills sent him and Ira reported: "I know too much to take such damned things." The man went away. A fortnight or so later the turnkey added two prisoners to the four who inhabited Ira's cell. They looked to him like hired assassins and he did not sleep that night. Pretending to be sick, he frequently arose, offering them no chance to slice his throat. The next morning they disappeared but somewhat later two other dangerous-looking men appeared who seemed bent on the same purpose. Ira's razor was always within his reach and he was up and down all night. Though England and France were at war, it was obvious that the English captors hoped to liquidate the man who had managed to keep the muskets and who might now obtain proof that would gain him heavy costs. It was quite evident that Police Minister Barras was being handsomely bribed to keep him in jail and to kill him if possible.

He was now extremely ill, suffering night sweats and intermittent pain from his feet, which were numb much of the time. On the unhappy occasion of his forty-eighth birthday—twenty-six years after the late summer day he and Remember first set foot on the bright lowlands of the Onion—he wrote: "In ancient times when the Jews were waiting the coming of a Messiah, Jesus Christ came from Nazareth and ministered unto them. The Jews murmured, saying one to another *can anything good come out of Nazareth?* They derided and persecuted him. In modern times men coming from *England* into France are in like manner persecuted."

From London his lawyers were writing:

My Dear General—Your absence for almost a year and your silence for five months have been very distressing to your friends here and detrimental to your interest respecting your arms which have arrived safe at New York but not disposed of when the last news about them left that country . . . Your longer silence will cast down the spirit of all your friends and I fear prevent your lawyers giving further attendance on your concerns in Court . . .

On July 9, 1799, realizing that there was another plot afoot to kill him and suspecting the prisoner in number 9, Ira wrote "To the gentleman of No. 9, same lane—I will have nothing more to do with you or No. 11, and I think that the French government has been lenient in sentencing you to only five years imprisonment."

Thoughts of death began to occupy his mind. He wrote the minister of justice that, being one of the oldest Republicans, made the idea of dying unnoticed in a solitary prison more painful to a man of spirit than death itself. He sent a final letter to the French government in which he pointed out he had written a friend, the chief justice of the United States Supreme Court, who was coming to France on a commission that year and who knew the particulars of his case. The prospect of altercation with the chief justice made an impression on the old Directory. Talleyrand had for months been working faithfully in Ira's behalf but he had not been successful even in getting a release for his fiancée from India, who had also been thrown into jail; for he was on the outs with the current Directory, particularly the corrupt Barras, who held absolute power in the Police Ministry. Only when that Directory was deposed and the friends of Allen were once more in power was he released on September 12, 1799.

The new minister of exterior relations said there had never been any good reason for Ira's imprisonment and that he had often told his predecessors of the unjust treatment he had received. As for Talleyrand—it had been to him Ira had planned to pay the balance of the musket money in order to take back a clean bill of sale as proof to the British. But on the proposed day of the payment to Talleyrand, Ira had been arrested by Barras.

Now in October, 1799, with Napoleon back in Paris and the old Directory abolished, the shoe was on the other foot. Talleyrand was minister of foreign affairs and Ira's good friend General Clarke was commander of Bonaparte's forces in Paris. To complete a little pressing personal business, Talleyrand prepared a written form of resignation to be signed by Barras—and delivered it himself. He found the minister of police in his bath at the opulent country estate that bribe money had been maintaining. "A guilty conscience," reported Ira, "made him like wax in the hands of Talleyrand." Revenge was succulent for France's greatest diplomat, who now forced Barras to sign the resignation he had brought.

Ira went to the Boston Hotel, where he remained five months to convalesce. He bought velvet knee breeches, silk stockings and waistcoats, and once again found himself dining in the gold-encrusted halls of Paris. He worked unceasingly to obtain the necessary proofs and send them on to England—for five seemingly eternal years had passed since he left America. On November 23, 1800, the wind filled the sails of a ship leaving Bordeaux for America, her bowsprit pointing west.

The squire of Onion River was coming home.

15

APPARENTLY WITHOUT PAIN

*W*HEN news arrived that the ship *Neptune* had docked in Philadelphia with General Ira Allen aboard, eyebrows lifted along Onion River. In the households of those who had been stealing his lands there was consternation. The guilty parties hastily met and determined to escort the general home with a cavalry company and fete him with a public dinner. Asked if he deemed this a fitting tribute, a Burlington judge said he thought General Allen would consider it a greater compliment for them to give up the lands they had stolen.

Ira came home to find the 28-year-old Onion River Land Company a derelict ship on an empty shore, the superstructure and fittings gone, the ribs bleached like old bones. Local real estate operators had taken practically everything that the state had not seized and sold for unpaid taxes. Unraveling the tangle of outright thievery required energy, time, and money, and the general now had none of these. He petitioned the legislature to grant him two years free from suits and imprisonment to straighten out the snarl. His ancient enemy Governor Isaac Tichenor, who had succeeded in thwarting Vermont's purchase of his muskets, now exerted every effort to prevent his gaining this period of immunity. But the representatives moved that the general be heard. When he appeared, his eloquence elicited the respect of younger representatives who did not know him, and regained the respect of the older ones who did. They voted him a year's immunity from imprisonment.

His health, broken down by French prisons, was, however,

so mean that he could no longer carry on with his old vigor. Without capital to hire lawyers he could not regain title to his Onion River lands. Tichenor could have solved his entire problem by purchasing the muskets the militia so badly needed, but the governor chose to quash every possibility of that. And since the state would not purchase the muskets, all the old British suspicions that they were for Canada arose anew, eliminating any hope of gaining the heavy costs he had suffered fighting through the English Admiralty Courts. Even while Tichenor was crucifying Allen by throwing every obstacle in his path the hypocrite was saying:

> . . . It may not be unprofitable to look back to the infant state of our republic, from thence trace the measures persued by our venerable fathers to whose wisdom and firmness we are indebted for the rank and privileges of an independent state. It is a tribute justly due to their virtues . . . Their appointments to offices were on men whose disinterested zeal for the public good was manifested more by their acts than by their profession. They subdued the wilderness, they sowed the seeds of science and the arts, and the elder states saw . . . united citizens demanding . . . an honorable station among her sister states . . .

Since the chief justice of the Vermont Supreme Court was a Tichenor appointee, Allen found little more justice before the law than he had in England. His enemies were bringing him to complete ruin. He was gradually losing everything he had—even a voice in the affairs of the University of Vermont that he himself had endowed.

The firm of Bird, Savage and Bird, his bankers in England, failed. Then the incredibly short year of his immunity from suits and imprisonment was over. He tried for an extension of time but, failing to get it, was soon buried under an avalanche of suits. He shortly found himself looking through the bars of a prison, this time in Burlington, the town he, Ethan, and Remember had created on the pine plains above the lake. Availing themselves of the debtors' law, the jackals who were his creditors found it a simple matter to have him thrown into Chittenden County jail. During the months the Father of Vermont was suffering the acute indignity of being a prisoner in his own community he must have thought of the remark attributed to Talleyrand, that there are services so great that they can be repaid only by ingratitude.

Late on a March Saturday night three years after his return from Europe he obtained bail by sacrificing for merely $20,000 most of his remaining lands in Burlington, Colchester, Sheldon, Essex, and Georgia. Knowing that his poor health would not permit him to fight any more suits, he turned over his papers and the rest of his property to his nephew, Heman, and provided for his wife and children to the extent of his resources. The next day, Sunday, was his last on Onion River. He passed it quietly with his family and toward evening stepped into a small sailboat and started up Lake Champlain. He had every intention of returning as soon as his health improved, but he was seeing the lands his soul delighted in for the last time. From the broad lake, the bustling young port of Burlington, and to the north the sails of river sloops at Colchester Point, were a panorama before him. He may instead have seen a river meadow where the blue joint grass was thick. Cousin Remember behind the bar where he kept "Sperets for Sale" in the log fort, the river boiling through Bolton Gorge, smoke curling up from a Yorker encampment below Lightning Ridge. "Skin for skin, yea all that a man hath, will he give for his life," he thought. His Onion River lands were indistinguishable in the distance.

The boat sailed through icy water, landing at the head of Lake Champlain. Lake George was next, then a long ride to Philadelphia, where he found a small flat in view of Independence Hall. When his health permitted he worked with government officials in an attempt to gain an award of costs from the British in the musket affair. At the request of Jefferson, James Madison wrote James Monroe in England that delay in Allen's case amounted almost to "a refusal of justice," but the British had never entertained any intention of doing more on Ira's behalf than releasing the arms.

Since his enemies had gained control of the University of Vermont, Ira with a heavy heart decided to send his sons to Middlebury College. "Herewith I commit to your care my two sons, Ira and Zimri," he wrote to its president,

whom I intend shall receive an education at Middlebury College and while I return my acknowledgements for your Kindness in consenting to take them into your family I hope that you will not consider them as mere boarders, but as under your immediate care and protection subject to your commands, and particularly that they be enjoined to pay strict attention to their studies, that they be refrained from keeping bad company, from being out late nights and such other vices as boys of their ages are liable to fall into, that they attend public worship and all other regulations thought best . . . Ira is attentive to his books. Zimri's disposition I esteem to be equally good, and who is a boy of genious, but from some cause or other, has not that relish for study that the other has. I have hopes however that he will improve . . .

He must have had hope of regaining title to some of his Onion River lands and of returning home, for he sent numerous circulars to state, federal, and Canadian officials favoring his canal project from Lake Champlain to the St. Lawrence. He still hoped Vermont would buy the muskets but on one occasion when the purchase was suggested in the legislature, a Tichenor henchman arose and proposed a bill "authorizing Ira Allen Esq. to apply to the President of the United States to hire gunboat No. 1 of the American Navy for the purpose of importing arms for the use of the Militia . . . which resolution being read, Resolve that the same do not pass."

The attorney general of the United States, having reviewed the entire case of the muskets, delivered in May, 1808, the opinion that General Allen's "situation is peculiarly hard and distressing . . . he is entitled to redress. The special interference of the Government of the United States will not only be proper, but is an act of real justice due an injured individual." Jefferson urged immediate action but the bitter events leading up to the War of 1812 ended all hope that the British would settle with Allen.

ALLEN'S ROCK

In 1811, ill and without his family, acutely homesick, he read this ad in a newspaper: "For Sale—A valuable farm in Colchester, on the bank of Onion River at the Lower Falls adjoining Burlington about 1 mile and a half from County Court House and one mile from the College. On the premises there is a handsome convenient dwelling house, barns . . . a good garden well stored with fruit, and two bearing apple orchards. The situation of the house is healthy and aggreeable, affording delightful views . . ."

Philadelphia, 22d January, 1814

Heman Allen, Esq.
Dear Sir:

It is with much pain I have to inform you of the death of General Ira Allen. You know that his health for a long time past was declining. During last week he was extremely debilitated and on Saturday evening, died without a groan and apparently without pain . . . I am, Sir, very respectfully yours.

John P. Ripley

The legislature, still controlled by Federalists, met in October, 1814. No mention was made of the death of the Father of Vermont.

16

MORNING ON A WARPATH

$\mathcal{I}$N the last quarter of the 1700's a sprinkling of hardy souls plodded miles into the woods and there settled, with only the strength of their arms and backs between existence and extinction. They could not bring their animals because there was nothing in the woods for them to eat. Since they could not bring their animals they could not bring all their tools. Since they could not bring all their tools, their accomplishments were limited to what could be done with the axes and augers carried on their backs.

Thus the first homes on the Onion were just log shelters with blankets hung up for doors. Cracks between the logs were plugged with mud. Roofs were of bark. Floors, if any, were of hewn logs. Fireplaces were of stone. Flues consisted of holes in the roof. Furniture is a term too dignified for what passed for it. After the shelter came the work of hacking out a clearing where some corn, beans, pumpkins, turnips, and potatoes could be planted. When there was enough room for wheat and barley, animals could be brought to share some of the work. But until sheep could be brought no wool could be spun, and until cows came no tallow for candles could be made. Even fire was scarce—there are many stories of walking miles to get it. Though the woods supplied game, and the Onion, fish, there were winter months when the woods were snowbound and the Onion was frozen. And there were even the occasional summer months when for one reason or another crops didn't grow. Then food was simply fish, nuts, roots and herbs—sometimes not all of these.

. . . Got lost twice in ye woods already—heard ye terrible howling
of ye wolves . . . Woods make people love one another & kind & obliging and good natured. They set much more by one another than in ye old
settlements . . . Several women I saw had lived four or five days without any food, and had eight or ten Children starving around them—crying for bread & ye poor women had wept till they looked like Ghosts.
Many families have lived for weeks on what ye people call Leeks—a sort
of wild onion—it poisons all ye milk & Butter of ye new settlements . . .

The sound of hungry children crying at night was not any
pleasanter to pioneers than it is today. The nearest neighbor was
often seven miles away. A Mrs. Lawrence lived in the vicinity
of the Onion for ten months without seeing another woman. The
only way she and her widely scattered neighbors knew ten months
had passed was by the noon-marks notched in their doorsills.
When sickness struck, there were only herbs and old wives' rem-
edies, and when babies came—they just came. Some areas were
lucky enough to have a midwife. Mrs. Whitmore, a celebrated
pioneer, delivered two thousand babies. Despite danger from
wolves and catamounts she was known to travel six miles through
the woods at night on snowshoes. Mrs. Whitmore lived to be
eighty-seven.

It took three to four years to make a farm under such circumstances. By that time the farmer might have collected a cow,
a horse or ox, pigs, and some hens. He might have accumulated
buckets enough to tap his sugar maples, or enough children to
gather honey from the trees in the woods, or wild strawberries,
blueberries, and cranberries. He might have been able to import
some glass to substitute for the oil paper in his windows. His wife
might have acquired a spinning wheel and some pewter dishes.
Instead of buckskins, their sons might now wear homespun, their
daughters, homemade flannel dresses and pantalets. There might
even be shoes enough so that moccasins could be laid aside for
Sunday meeting. There might even be time of an evening to make
candy of sweet-flag root or to crack butternuts before the fire.

But all the progress made by the pioneers who first came to
live on the Onion was swept away by the Revolutionary War.

Roderick Messenger, one pioneer farmer, buried his hardier possessions, loaded his family into a canoe, and paddled downstream. Landing at Hubbel's Falls, he went down over the rapids as far as Colchester, where he unloaded the canoe and let it plunge over the Falls. At the mouth of the river they waited for a lake sloop to take them south. When one appeared, Grandmother Messenger directed young Phebe and Rachel to climb a tree and wave their aprons, with the thought that the boat would not mistake people waving aprons for Indians.

Among those who decided to stay was a Joseph Brown from Great Barrington, Massachusetts. Having located in Jericho, six miles from the nearest Indian trail, he considered himself secure. In the spring of 1777 he decided, however, to use some of Messenger's land near the Indian trail in the vicinity of the blockhouse where Matthew Lyon's men had gone over the hill. One day while he and his two sons were building a fence around the corn, Indians came whooping from adjoining woods and took them prisoners. They were taken to Isle aux Noix, where they met Burgoyne, who let them go after making them acknowledge the supremacy of the crown. After a variety of vicissitudes they returned to their farm.

On October 15, 1780, three hundred Indians, led by a British lieutenant from Canada, quietly made their way up the old Onion highway. They seized and made prisoner a hunter named Gibson, who shortly before had been sick and had convalesced under the care of the Browns. Gibson now told his captors that if they would let him go he would take them to a white family. He led a detachment of Indians to the Brown farm, which they sacked with their usual fury. An Indian, who bore down on Mrs. Brown with a knife, was diverted by the gold beads around her neck, and failed to take her scalp. Other redskins cut open the beds and filled the rooms with a snowstorm of feathers. They took everything they found, set fire to the house, and made prisoners of the entire family. They let the Browns' betrayer, Gibson, go as they had promised but before he had gone two miles they again took him prisoner. "We said we let you go," the Indians told him, "and we let you go, and now we take you again." Gibson was herded to camp, where he was placed with the Browns. There his conscience, if he possessed one, had an opportunity to work on him. The Indians butchered one of the Brown dogs to eat. When they approached the other dog to do the same he leaped at the throat of one Indian bringing him crashing to the ground. Before the others could kill him, the dog was off into the woods to join white men miles away.

The main body of Indians went upriver and before dawn attacked the small frontier settlements of Randolph, Tunbridge, and Royalton east of the Onion. There was wholesale sacking, scalping, and burning. One villager, Hannah Handy, ran from the scene as fast as she could with her two children, but the Indians caught up and took the elder, a son. Mrs. Handy asked what they were going to do with him. They said they would make him a soldier. They left her then, and there was no course for her but to continue in the direction in which she had started, with the little girl hanging onto her dress. When she saw a large group of Indians on the opposite bank of the White River, she thought there might be a chance of getting back her son. As she started to cross the river, an old Indian, supposing she was giving herself up as a prisoner, offered to carry her and the little girl across on his back. Her daughter screamed that she didn't "want to ride the old Indian," but the Indian insisted. From the opposite bank Mrs. Handy hastened to find the British leader, Richard Houghton, who told her that such boys as her son would not be hurt but would be trained as soldiers. She told Houghton that mere boys could not stand up under the trek to Canada and that when they could not continue, the tomahawk and scalping knife would be the only relief. She furthermore told him that, were he a parent, he might know what it was like to have his first-born taken away. Houghton said he could do nothing—that the Indians were an ungovernable race and would never give up anything they'd decided to take.

"The curse will fall upon you for whatever crime they may commit," she warned. "All the innocent blood they spill will cry for vengeance on your head." At this, Houghton broke down. He said she would have the boy back as soon as his captors appeared. When they returned him, she started away with mixed gratitude and fear, but was overtaken by Houghton, who advised her to remain at his camp until the scouting parties had returned or they might again take her child away. While she waited, other Indians brought into camp several of her neighbors' children who, when they saw her, clustered about her, and held onto her dress. She again approached Houghton on their behalf and made such a warm appeal that he released these children too. Before she started back an Indian came and took her son by the hand. As she would not let go of the other hand, the Indian began to wave his sword over her head, which brought the other Indians to the scene. Since the lives of the other children were in danger, she let the Indian again take her son, but once more approached Houghton, who, after much altercation with the redskin, again obtained his release. She now led eight children away, all holding onto her and each other.

As for the Browns, whom the detached force had imprisoned on the Onion at Jericho—they were delivered to the British at $8 a head. Three years and six months later Brown once more returned to Jericho in absolute poverty, owing so much back taxes on his lands that he lost most of them. Nothing, however, had happened to Joseph Brown's calloused hands or strong back—he died leaving his children well off.

17

LATE ICE AND FIRST GROWTH MEN

$\mathcal{Y}$OUNG Stevens lost his girl to another man. He had a good carpenter's business in Corinth but he gave it up and bought traps and a gun and went into the woods in the fall of the year. He made his camp about a quarter mile up from the mouth of the eastern tributary of the Onion. Nothing was heard of him until, the following spring, two hunters found his body. A fallen tree lay along the edge of the stream, making an eddy and a likely fishing spot. On the bank just inside the tree was Stevens, one hand resting on a fishing pole, its half-rotted line lying over the log and in the water. Not far from the body stood a hunter's camp with traps, a gun, a hatchet, and a blanket spread over the boughs. Skins were hanging on a tree outside the rude cabin. Over the charred bed of an old fire hung a camp kettle with water and herbs for sickness in it. The hunters buried Stevens nearby but that was not all that was heard of him, for the Onion's tributary near which he died is called Stevens' Branch.

There are six other main tributaries feeding the Onion out of the Green Mountains. Among these is the Dog River, which comes down out of Roxbury and Northfield and enters the Onion near Montpelier, the capital of the state. The reason it is called Dog River is that a pioneer hunter's dog got caught in a beaver trap and drowned in the river trying to free himself. Then there is Kingsbury's Branch, which drains the country up around Calais and Woodbury. A pioneer named Kingsbury fished in it a great deal of the time and always referred to it as *his* branch. His neighbors agreed.

Up in Cabot there are two large ponds called Joe's Pond and Molly's Pond. The latter, draining south, is a source of the Onion. Joe's pond drains north, although the ponds are very close. The Joe for whom one pond takes its name was a St. Francis Indian who came to live peaceably in Vermont with the first English settlers in the valley of the Onion. Molly was his wife. Though Joe did not like war and declared he "never pointed the gun," he hated the British for slaughtering his St. Francis tribe. Once he visited George Washington, who shook hands with him and invited him and Molly, his squaw, to dine. Later, some of Joe's St. Francis kinfolk came to Vermont and tried to get him to go back to Canada with them, but Joe so hated the British that he would not set foot on Canadian soil. One time Joe is said to have trailed a moose for two days. When the moose crossed the line into Canada Joe said, "Good-bye, Mr. Moose." The St. Francis Indians subsequently kidnaped Molly, taking her into Canada thinking Joe would follow, but he would not go even then, and Molly later returned to Vermont.

By a former marriage, Molly had two sons called Toomalek and Muxawuxal. It is written that Muxawuxal died young without bringing sorrow to the heart of Molly, but Toomalek brought bitter sorrow. He was somewhat disfigured, heavy-set like an ape, and with stiff black hair down to within an inch of his small eyes, had an ugly face. He fell in love with a young squaw, Lewa, but because he was ugly she did not love him. Instead, she married another Indian, Mitchell. Consumed with jealousy, Toomalek waited until Lewa and Mitchell were in their wigwam. Sneaking up, he raised his gun and fired on Mitchell. The bullet entered Lewa's breast and she died that night. The Indians tried Toomalek for murder but decided that "as he did not kill Mitchell, and did not intend to kill Lewa, he was no murderer." Toomalek, however, still hated Mitchell, who had married a second squaw whose beauty was as great as Lewa's. One day he took a bottle of rum and with a white man went to Mitchell's tent. Being careful to drink little himself, he saw to it that Mitchell drank a great deal. When Mitchell became drunk, he began to heap abuse on Toomalek for murdering Lewa and when he made a threatening gesture, his heart received the blade of Toomalek's knife. The ugly redskin was again tried for murder, yet he was again acquitted because Mitchell had made the first move.

Later, Toomalek and Pial, the son of John, chief of the tribe, were with several others on a drunken lark. In Haverhill they met a young squaw from Newbury who made some remarks about Pial's love affairs. Pial, who was a good-natured Indian, in return made some remarks about the young squaw which angered her. She took Toomalek aside and whispered in his ear. A few minutes later he slipped a knife into Pial's throat—and he too died. Their other companions seized him for murder and took him before Pial's father, Captain John, who was deeply grieved to think he had twice spared Toomalek from death. The unanimous sentence was that he should now die, but the Indians first asked the white minister at Newbury if their sentence was in accordance with the word of God. He said he believed that it was. The next morning Captain John raised his gun and pulled the trigger. The gun did not go off. Toomalek mocked the snap of the firing pin, "Click, click." John stepped closer, fired again, and ugly Tooma-lek was no more. Molly and Joe, who were present, each took an arm of the dead Indian and sorrowfully dragged him away to bury him. The reason for her grief could be clear only to Molly. She alone had understood Toomalek.

2

Colonel Jacob Davis never suspected that one day the gold dome of the capital of the state of Vermont would rise among the trees near which he chose to make a clearing on May 3, 1787. He arrived with his cousin, a hired man, tools, and a horse. His family followed later. Reaching the Onion, his son took a line and hook he'd brought from Massachusetts, some raw pork, and a half-bushel basket, went to the banks of the Little North Branch, baited his hook and threw it in. He expected fish but not the chaos of the next few minutes. The water seemed to boil with trout. They came from every direction and it was only a question of which trout would get hooked first. In half an hour his bushel basket bulged with half-pounders upward to two-pounders—the small ones he'd thrown back.

In a few years, Colonel Davis was able to build a fine house which helped to fend away the roughness of the frontier on every side. There were constant reminders of that. The first ball of the first Thanksgiving observed by Montpelier was held at Colonel Davis's house. From miles around they came—it was the region's first real social event. The dance was not over until just before daylight, when Theophilus Brooks and Isaac Putnam escorted the fair Hobart sisters home. At the Middlesex landing they all got into a log canoe and started for the other shore. The Onion, swollen by rain, flowed high and fast. At the deepest point the canoe turned over. Putnam, the only one who could swim, managed to right it and get the two girls and Theophilus back into it. The canoe became water-logged, however, and shortly overturned a second time. Putnam was exhausted. He spent his remaining energy swimming to the bank with his partner. Her pretty sister was lost and they didn't find Theophilus until the ice broke up the following spring.

3

Twelve miles downriver from Colonel Davis's was the tiny settlement of Waterbury. The experience of its first settler, James Marsh, was the greatest hard-luck story in colonizing the Onion. After becoming well settled in New Hampshire Marsh found his claim there was covered by a prior title, and giving up his farm with no compensation for all his improvements, he trekked into the Onion wilderness, cleared some land in Waterbury, and raised a crop of corn. Heartened by this, he brought three of his children to his farm in the spring of 1783, but upon his return he found the corn gone. The children, Elias, Rene, and James thus had nothing to eat except what Marsh had brought on his back. Supplying them with a week's provisions, he went back to get the rest of his family. By the end of the week he had not returned and the provisions were gone; so the children decided to go to the Falls to catch some trout. On their way they met a bear, which, tackled by their dog, finally made off into the woods. They next had to cross the Onion tributary, the Waterbury River, with only a tree stretched across as a bridge. Elias carried James over on his back, but Rene, deciding to cross by herself, became dizzy about midstream and fell in. She went down twice before she could be rescued by Elias, who had hard work to resuscitate her. The two brothers returned to the bank from which they had come, supporting Rene as best they could, built a fire of driftwood, gave her the rest of the food and without anything to eat themselves turned in for the night. The next morning, after Elias carried both James and Rene over the stream, they tramped fifteen miles down the valley to the house of a neighbor in Jericho. The neighbor kept them for a week.

Meanwhile their father had returned to Waterbury with the rest of his family, this time with a horse. On each side of the horse dangled a kettle and on his back rested a feather mattress. On top of the mattress was Mrs. Marsh with one child in arms and one strapped to her back. Her husband and three other children were on foot, carrying whatever else they could. When he found the three children gone Marsh went into the surrounding woods on a search, calling out desperately. During his absence, James returned from Jericho and then had to hunt for his father to tell him he, Elias, and Rene were all right.

With his provisions again nearly gone, Marsh set out downstream for Onion River Falls, where he went to work as a laborer on a dam being built there. Marsh was promised that he would be furnished with provisions for his family until they were grown—and a boatload of food and supplies from Skenesboro was expected within a week. When three weeks later the provisions had not arrived, Marsh announced he would have to leave to look after his family. Having installed him as foreman of the dam builders, they refused to let him go, and told him that if he left he would not be paid for the work he had done. Marsh left anyway and, upon reaching Waterbury, found that his family had subsisted for two weeks on wild onions and cow's milk. Though he was hungry, he would not eat the wild-onion goulash that his wife served up. Instead he started for New Hampshire, where he got a bushel of corn which he carried to his family on his back. This kept them going for a time, and their growing corn looked good. In the fall, however, the river overflowed and washed it all away, so starvation and Marsh continued to run a tight race. The only way he kept ahead was by swapping moose meat for corn. In the second winter he went to Williston to cast some spoons in Mr. Brownson's spoon molds. Crossing the river on his way back, Marsh fell through the ice to his death and his new spoons settled to the bottom of the Onion. It was not until the following Sunday that they found his body. On the day before the funeral there was a heavy snowstorm and it must have seemed to his family, who had to snowshoe fifteen miles to the ceremony, that even the elements had conspired against James Marsh.

4

Upriver from Waterbury and Montpelier stood some houses which a few years later, in 1793, would become the town of Wildersburg. The settlers thought the name uncouth, and in a meeting resolved to change it. A number of names, including Paris, were suggested but none seemed to ring the bell. Two vociferous voters were present whose suggestions outwore all others. Captain Joseph Thomson from Holden, Massachusetts, thought the name should be Holden. Jonathan Sherman from Barre, Massachusetts, thought it should be Barre. Between the partisans of Holden and Barre agreement seemed impossible.

Finally Thomson and Sherman decided to fight. The meeting
moved to Calvin Smith's new shed where a pole was erected
across which Thomson and Sherman would box. From the point
when one knocked the other down, no holds would be barred.
Thomson shortly landed a blow that brought Sherman to the
floor. Following it up, he jumped astride Sherman and began to
pelt him with quick jabs to the face and head. Though Thomson
was on top, Sherman was able to dodge the main force of these
blows so that Thomson's knuckles were shaved by the floor's
rough hemlock planks. Sherman delivered some fast jabs to
Thomson's solar plexus. The fight suddenly went out of the
latter. His blows became tremulous and he was heard to groan.
Sherman, disengaging himself, jumped up and proclaimed breath-
lessly, "There, the name is Barre, by God!" And Barre—the
name of the world's largest granite center—it has been ever since.

5

By 1791 when Vermont was invited into the new Union as
the fourteenth state, the Onion was no longer a wilderness, though
some travelers failed to appreciate the refinements two dozen years
had wrought. His Royal Highness, Prince Edward Augustus, son
of George III, destined to be father of Queen Victoria, found
little similarity to life along the gentle Thames.

Arriving from Montreal at the Champlain port of Burlington in 1791 en route to Boston, he took over the largest house in
town—none too large since he was accompanied by a squad of
tasters, lest he be poisoned by Yankee barbarians. This posse and
his elaborate ostentation in a land of dawn-to-dark labor, did little
to endear the royal family to the people of the Onion. He was a
chip, they decided, "off the old basswood block."

Reaching Montpelier he put up at Colonel Davis's house
where his tasters continued to sample each morsel of food placed
before him. The Colonel at length found it impossible to restrain
himself from indicating that settlers did not crawl about at night

with knives between their teeth, nor was raw meat eaten unless necessary for survival. Savage chants did not emanate from meetinghouse windows on Sundays. Indeed, one was quite apt to hear a chorus of voices raised in Christian song.

Thus reassured, the prince somewhat reluctantly decided to send the tasters and bodyguards back to Montreal, and with courage born from continuing fair digestion, he set out for Williamstown. Somewhere along the road he stopped for a few moments at a shoemaker's house where, having lost many of his inhibitions, he grabbed and kissed the shoemaker's wife. Startled because she recoiled, Prince Edward announced, "Oh, never mind! You can now tell your people you have had the honor of being kissed by a British prince."

"Oh, never mind, sir," said the woman's husband, delivering a kick to the prince's posterior which sent him staggering over the threshold, "you can now go home and tell your people you have had the honor of being kicked out of doors by an American cobbler."

Williamstown did little more for the prince's ego. He chose to stay at the home of Judge Elijah Paine, who was noted for his fiery sense of justice. Once, according to local legend, the judge and a neighbor were drawing two sleighloads of wheat along a road whose borders were piled with snow five feet high. At one of the narrowest parts they were stalemated by meeting a team drawing a sleigh with salt. Since there was no passing or backing up, it was necessary to unload the sleighs and tip them on their sides. After this was done, the judge and his neighbor assisted the salt-sleigh driver in reloading—expecting him to return the favor. As soon as the salt was loaded, however, the driver jumped to his seat and with a crack of his whip was off down the road. For a moment Judge Paine watched the retreating sleigh with eyes that flashed fire, then throwing off his coat, sprinted down the road faster than his neighbor had ever seen anyone run before. Overtaking the team he was on top of the stranger with one leap, catapulting him into the snow. He then hustled him back, and pointing to the bags of wheat in the snow with the polite dignity of his office, counseled, "There, friend, if you will take hold of those bags and load up both of our sleighs, we will be much obliged to you—very much obliged to you, sir"—the frightened man complied to the last bag.

The same sense of justice now attended the stopover of Prince Edward at Judge Paine's, though this time the judge's good wife expressed it.

"I suppose, madam," said the prince at the dinner table, "you here never read anything but your Bible and Psalm Book."

"Oh, yes we do," said Mrs. Paine promptly. "We are all quite familiar with the writings of Peter Pindar." This was enough to color the face of one even so callous as Edward. He had not supposed that Peter Pindar's scorching and hilarious travesties on his father, George III, had reached the valley of the Onion.

18

TAKING THE SNAKE

The men who laid this smuggling plot
Was Sheffield, Mudgett, Dean and Mott,
And many more who were not clever
Spread out their sails on Onion River.

*C*HE river meanders through country lying only sixty miles
from the Canadian border, while its outlet, Lake Champlain, no
respecter of man-made boundaries, spreads unconcernedly over
the line. In the early 1800's there was an ugly tar-smeared cutter
called the *Black Snake,* a reconverted ferry, with six oars on each
side and a sail. On December 22, 1807, Congress passed an Embargo Act which prevented boats owned in the United States from
trading with Great Britain or her colonies. The citizens of the
Champlain valley, whose trade with Canada had been their life-
blood, regarded this law as a grave injustice and many of the
people of the Onion chose to disregard it.

Soon after the embargo had been adopted the *Black Snake*
began a wild nocturnal career. The most celebrated of many smuggling vessels, the *Snake* did not smuggle diamonds or Scotch, furs
or watches into the U.S.—as have many later vessels—it smuggled
potash out. Ever since woodsmen had first started cutting timber
on the Onion, rafting it to Canada had been a profitable business.
Potash, vital in the manufacture of glass and soap, had been loaded
into barrels and had been secretly sailed over the border in sloops.
The first patent ever issued by the United States government,
signed by George Washington, president, and Thomas Jefferson,
secretary of state, had been granted on July 31, 1790, to Samuel
Hopkins of Burlington for a pot and pearl ash process, and so the

community had something worth while to smuggle. For months after the embargo was law the *Snake* successfully carried one hundred barrels of potash per trip, selling it in Canada for $6 a barrel. Well hidden by bushes from the eyes of enforcement officers, she would load at night on the Onion below the Falls, sail to the mouth of the river and down Lake Champlain. Then in order to avoid the *Fly,* a twelve-oared cutter, manned by revenue officers at Windmill Point on the border, she would detour into St. Albans Bay and creep through marshes, creeks, and short lengths of man-made canal into Missisquoi Bay where she was in Canada.

> Then Farrington sailed down the lake,
> And thus he to the rebels spake,
> "Orders I have to take the *Snake*
> And all the smugglers on the lake."

On August 1,1808, a Lieutenant Farrington, with Sergeant David Johnson and twelve infantry privates manning the *Fly,* received orders to seize the smugglers and bring them to book, whatever the cost. On that day the *Snake,* after delivering a load, had been hugging the North Hero shore and at night sailed through the darkness to the mouth of the Onion. She was equipped with her usual defenses—spiked poles to keep off revenue boats, big clubs, a basket of stones, a gun for each member of the crew, and a blunderbuss with a barrel eight feet two inches long and a bore of one and one-fourth inches. On the following night the crew was engaged in hunting up extra ammnuition because they had heard that the *Fly* was after the *Snake* in earnest this time.

Having been told that the *Snake* was somewhere on the Onion, Farrington landed the *Fly* on Wednesday morning, August 3, near the mouth at Colchester Point, and there breakfasted with his men. Then he sent Sergeant Johnson out to gain what information he could from settlers on the point. Johnson shortly met a man who thought he was a smuggler and asked if he was after "a load." Johnson replied he did not know whether he could get a load because he understood there were already some boats upriver. The settler said there were two and that one was the *Snake.*

There would be no difficulty in getting a load, he said, unless, as he had heard, a revenue boat was on its way upstream. Johnson reported to Farrington and the *Fly* shoved off, carefully making its way along the bank under an arch of willows which dipped into the warm August water. Half a mile upstream a boy in a canoe appeared around the bend, saw the *Fly* and quickly turned about, paddling away in great haste. From the shore an Indian shouted: "Canoe come down, see you, turn back." The men of the *Fly* bent to their oars, gaining on the canoe, but the boy, whom they suspected of being a spy, made for the north bank, took his gun and powder horn and disappeared through the trees.

Farther up, a man named Day approached the bank and called out: "What, are you going up the river after the *Black Snake?*"

"We are," said Johnson.

"You won't find her," said Day, "but if you go up the river you will find something more terrible than the *Black Snake,* for there are thirty men armed."

"Boys, row on," ordered Johnson.

At a point some distance above, Day again appeared, this time in a bateau tied at a place called Joy's Landing. "Are you going to take this boat?" he demanded.

"If it's a smuggling boat, I will," Farrington said. "I have orders to take all suspected boats, and if this is one, I will take it.— Where is the *Black Snake?*"

"She went out of the river last night. You didn't see her?" asked Day. "I warrant you went within eight rods of her."

"I don't believe she's gone," Farrington said, "because you are one of the crew and you would have gone with her."

"That's not true, but if I did own the property," said Day, "I would fight until every man was killed before I gave up." At this he departed. The *Fly* landed while Johnson went down the bank a piece to a place where the rushes had parted to admit a vessel, but it turned out to be the track of a stone boat, not the *Black Snake.*

When he returned to the *Fly*, the lieutenant was talking to another man who had come down the bank to say that the *Snake* was up-river fifty or sixty rods. The *Fly* once more shoved off. After a few minutes' row it turned another bend, and there was the *Black Snake*.

> Then Mudgett gave the threatening word
> To all the men that was on board,
> "The first that steps into the *Snake*,
> A lifeless corpse of him I'll make."

Standing near one end of the *Snake*, which was made fast to the beach, was smuggler Mudgett who warned Farrington not to land.

"It's a free country," Farrington snapped. "We have a right to land anywhere we please." The *Fly* was brought alongside the *Snake*.

"Don't lay hands on the boat," Mudgett hollered. "I swear by God I will blow the first man's brains out who lays hands on her!"

"I have orders to take her," Farrington said. "She is forfeited and I shall take her." Johnson and part of the crew of the *Fly* boarded the somber smuggling vessel, while Mudgett ducked behind some small trees to talk with a fellow smuggler, Mott, who had the gun with the eight-foot barrel resting over the crotch of a tree and trained on the *Snake*. Farrington ordered his men to search for the *Snake's* oars but they could not be found. Four oars were then borrowed from the *Fly*, and the sails were brought aboard from the beach.

"Come on, boys," Mudgett cried to his men in the trees, "parade yourselves. You are all cowards—they are going to carry the boat off." At this Mott and two other men emerged from the rushes carrying guns. "Come on, boys, you are cowards," Mudgett repeated, and two more men came out of the woods. On board the *Snake* and *Fly* the revenue men were preparing to shove off. As both boats left the bank one of the smugglers called out: "Lieutenant, prepare to meet your God—your blood shall be spilt before you get out of the river."

"That man with the red facings is a good mark to shoot at, and I will have his heart's blood," announced another.

"I'm a good mark if you want to fire," the lieutenant answered as the boats got underway.

> It was Sheffield, with his Indian skill,
> The crimson blood of Drake did spill—
> Ormsby and Marsh then prostrate fell
> Before these wicked imps of hell.

There was a shot, then a series of shots. Drake, one of the men in the *Fly*, who had been preparing to take over the rudder from Farrington, sank down amidships. His hat fell overboard and the colors just behind him came down.

"They've killed Drake!" shouted the lieutenant. Farrington, whose men were now lying down in the bottom of the *Fly*, was trying to row first on one side, then the other. Johnson took up his gun.

"Don't fire back," the lieutenant cautioned Johnson. "Row for the bank." Returning to the shore a little farther downstream the revenue men clambered up the bank in the face of a second charge, this time from the eight-foot blunderbuss. Private Asa Marsh and Captain Jonathan Ormsby, a farmer whom the shooting had drawn to the scene, fell grievously wounded. The firing then stopped, but in the next few minutes before a doctor could be brought, Marsh and Ormsby were dead. With Farrington wounded, the revenue men, headed by Sergeant Johnson, recruited settlers to form a posse, and made a spirited raid on the smugglers. They were able to round them up and march them off to jail. During the climax that followed, flaming handbills appeared, claiming that Isaac Tichenor's Federalists were trying to shield the outlaws.

> It is done! The cup of guilt is full! Treason, rebellion and murder stalk abroad at noon-day! Our land has been stained with the blood of our citizens acting in defence of the . . . laws of our country. By whom? A foreign foe? No . . . by the bloody hands of domestic traitors! . . . Certain federal characters who even lay claim to the name of high respect-

ability . . . throw the whole weight of guilt on the part of the government. Says one, "The men were sent here . . . to steal an empty boat, and died like fools" . . . Says another, "I should care but little if I did not fear it would influence the ensuing election." Says another, on hearing of the melancholy event, "I am glad of it, if they are republicans who are killed."—Such was the current expression which poured from the mouths of federalism . . . within the boundaries of that town which boasts itself of being the stronghold of federalism, and some of whose principal merchants furnished the insurgents with powder and ball . . .

Despite the influence of the Federalists, Cyrus Dean, the smuggler who fired the blunderbuss, was convicted of murder, and Samuel Mott of manslaughter. On November 11, 1808, Dean was taken to the courthouse, where he heard his own funeral sermon. Then a crowd of ten thousand persons from all over northern Vermont marched behind the prisoner to the scaffolding which had been erected at the top of Ira Allen's pine plains in the town of Burlington. There they witnessed the first hanging in the state of Vermont.

Mott escaped the gallows by a technicality and was sentenced to one hour at the pillory in the village square, to receive fifty lashes on his bare back, and to serve twenty years in the state prison.

> These men were tried all for the same crime,
> Why not alike their sentence find;
> Dean was sentenced to the halter,
> The rest convicted of manslaughter.

19

VICTORY IS A DUTY

"*You* are to understand," wrote Secretary of the Navy Jones, "that upon no account are you to suffer the enemy to gain the ascendancy on Lake Champlain." These were simple, positive instructions. One might presuppose that 27-year-old Lieutenant Macdonough—the only commissioned officer stationed by the navy on Lake Champlain—had merely to cruise forth and with well-placed cannonading, scuttle his Majesty's sloops. There was one difficulty—there was no American fleet. On Champlain it seemed to be a tradition for the American commander to build his fleet as well as deploy it in battle, so, borrowing a leaf from Benedict Arnold's scrapbook, Macdonough went about the lake collecting old ferryboats and whatever else could float a couple of cannon.

"My poor forlorn-looking squadron," Macdonough called it as he put it in winter storage at Shelburne harbor in the fall of 1812. He then went off to Connecticut to get married and returned with his pretty bride to spend the winter in Burlington.

Military companies were being recruited from along the Onion, and the town of Burlington, which was spreading among the trees of Ira Allen's pine plains, became the headquarters for the Northern Department of the United States Army. They made a battery on a high bluff overlooking the lake and brought sods from fields two miles away to build the parapet. Four thousand men soon bivouacked around the battery, the number of desertions daily reflecting the poor morale of an area which was finding it difficult to understand why the war was being fought.

133

Brother Nathan's nation mad—
　I think as how he's right, sirs,
Mama's sick, and sister's sad
　And I's right hot to fight, sirs—
For I've no 'lasses for to eat
　Along with pumpkin pie, sirs,
Now, Tom, take off the embargo soon
　And Nate and I will thank ye.

Since the end of the Revolution trade with Canada, which meant Britain, had been brisk. The Non-Intercourse Act had run athwart a strong Yankee instinct—trading. To many Vermonters James Madison's promise to declare war, if re-elected, was little justification for a fresh flow of blood. So New England and New York had refused to let their militia serve outside their own boundaries; Yankees were driving cattle through the woods and back roads into Canada, and receiving British manufactures in return.

There is a deep notch at the foot of Mount Mansfield through which the herds were driven on their way to the border, the same route over which the finished goods found their way back to Boston. They say that is how *Smuggler's Notch* received its name.

From the tiny settlement started by Colonel Davis, Montpelier had in 1807 mushroomed into the capital of the state. The countryside abounded with old veterans of '76, most of them flaming Democrats. One venerable character, Joseph Goodenow, who had been one of the original settlers of Berlin but was now living two or three miles above Montpelier, regularly hobbled on two canes into town to learn the latest machinations of the Federalists —Tories, he called them. At Montpelier he usually lost his temper and at dusk could be seen returning home at a much greater clip aided by only one cane. On a particular occasion, after a heated argument with some villagers, he was seen returning home at great speed, aided by no canes at all.

The friction between the Federalist and Democratic parties in a war meeting at the capital in the winter of 1812 generated white-hot sparks of political acrimony. The roads were choked with men on foot, horseback, in cutters and double sleighs. Th

issue in the tightly packed hall of representatives was clear—war
or no war. The Democrats wanted a resolution to encourage Congress to declare it. Federalists used every means to defeat them.
The war party outnumbered the Federalists in the meeting room,
though the latter, under the leadership of Isaac Tichenor, had been
in control of the state government for a number of years. After a
great deal of stamping and shouting, the meeting was brought to
order and the Reverend Chester Wright, resident minister of
Montpelier, was invited to offer the prayer. Wright was not in the
hall, and it was announced that owing to conscientious scruples
about war he would not pray at the meeting.

There was a rumble of indignant muttering until someone
suddenly shouted, "Uncle ZIBA!" Others took up the cry and a
Democratic committeeman mounted the platform and asked
tensely: "Is the Reverend Ziba Woodworth present in this audience? If so, he is respectfully invited to come forward onto the
platform and open this meeting with prayer." The Reverend Uncle
Ziba, a Christian—and a Democrat—stumped forward, hitching
along his game leg, stiffened by wounds received at the siege of
Fort Griswold. Mounting the platform he seized a chair, dropping
down on one knee, and, with a jerk and resounding thump, threw
out the game leg behind him. In an emotional voice he gave the
Democrats what they wanted, a properly slanted prayer blessing
"our rulers for farseeing wisdom and notable patriotism in so
fearlessly taking their stand in resisting the aggressions of British
tyranny," and castigating "the enemies of war and the enemies of
our blessed country—God's pity on their blindness for their trea-
sonable dereliction of duty."

The prayer was received with enthusiasm by the Democratic
majority, which now proceded to recommend a string of resolutions calling for war against Britain. A Federalist arose and was
launching a vitriolic attack upon President James Madison for his
warmongering when Matthew Wallace of Berlin, an intelligent
Irish immigrant, got up and interrupted the speaker in a ringing

voice: "Can't stand that! Can't stand that, Mr. Chairman! Anything in reason, but by Heavens, sir," he shouted, shaking his fist, "I shan't sit here to listen to outright treason." The Federalist was permitted to proceed but had to temper his remarks, which were barely audible for the hissing and booing of the Democrats.

But the day was still young. In the morning the Democrats had been in the majority, but toward noon a band of Federalists marched into the hall, almost outnumbering the war party, and the Democratic chairman, Ezra Butler, could not bring his pro-war measures to a vote. A scene of great confusion followed. "In his slow deep-toned and peculiarly emphatic manner, Butler announced, 'Silence in the house—I say SILENCE!' " The Federalists, now clearly in a majority, forced Butler off the platform and elected their own chairman. But by afternoon a great number of out-of-town Democrats started forcing their way into the hall. Shouting down the opposition, they carried the meeting with "hurrahs for Madison and war that made the State House shake and tremble from mudsill to reach pole."

Whether the majority of the people wanted it or not, war and all that went with it was again transforming life on the Onion. In the Burlington battery several hundred were dying weekly of smallpox, and there was an attendant increase in desertions. Before Colonel Clark on a white horse, deserter John Cummings of the 4th U.S. Infantry, blindfolded and kneeling on his coffin, slumped forward at the sharp volley of the firing squad.

By the summer of 1813 Lieutenant Macdonough had been able to build at the Vergennes shipyard on Otter Creek a small but respectable squadron, one proud vessel having been converted from a steamboat. Mounted with eleven guns each, his sloops bore such names as *Growler* and *Eagle,* rechristened from *Hunter* and *Bulldog.* At 2:30 in the afternoon of August 2 some British ships appeared outside the Burlington harbor on a mission to determine the size of Macdonough's squadron. They lobbed a few shells toward the parapet in the battery. Captain Chapell of the artillery, who had loaded a 12-pounder on each of two scows, fired from the wharves, while three of Macdonough's growing squadron succeeded in driving the British off to the south.

It was not until the second week in September, 1814, when the booming of cannon from across the lake at Plattsburg rumbled up the valley of the Winooski, that war was really brought home. Heard even as far back into the mountains as Stowe, it was evident that whether there was any good reason or not, the war should be fought and the enemy repulsed. The spirit of '76 surged in the hearts of old soldiers who had not yet joined up. Without guns, ammunition, rations, or adequate clothing, fifty men tramped down through the valley in a night rain reaching Waterbury at dawn. There, a similar group (certainly not a company) was forming. From Waterbury the enlarged contingent trooped twenty-eight miles along the Onion to the lake, swelling in numbers as it went. At Burlington rations of wheat, beef, and pork were procured along with a large kettle for boiling the meat. The famished volunteers had it only half cooked when the roll of a drum signaled the order to march to the wharf to prepare for crossing the lake. Stuffing their meat in bags which they slung over their shoulders and spearing the loaves of bread with sticks, they started for the docks, the grease from the meat trickling down their backs. After drawing muskets they were taken across the lake in small groups, for all vessels of any size had been commandeered by Macdonough.

On September 11, 1814, the British Navy, supported by troops marching south from Canada, met Macdonough in the bay at Plattsburg, where they proceeded to fight the bitterest naval engagement in any American waters up to the time of the Civil War.

"The havoc on both sides is dreadful," reported Midshipman Lee of the British ship *Confiance*.

I don't think there are more than five of our men out of 300, but what are killed or wounded. Never was a shower of hail so thick as the shot whistling about our ears. Were you to see my jacket, waistcoat and trowsers you would be astonished how I escaped as I did, for they are literally torn all to rags with shot and splinters; the upper part of my hat was also shot away. There is one of our marines who was in the Trafalgar action with Lord Nelson, who says it was a mere flea-bite in comparison with this.

Macdonough was knocked down twice, once by the spanker boom, which fell on his back, and the second time by the severed head of a gunner, which drove against him while he was sighting a gun, and threw him into the scuppers.

The contingent of old veterans and farmers from the Green Mountains and Onion valley arrived before, during, and after the battle. It was chiefly Macdonough's day, for by sundown he had smashed his Majesty's fleet. But by land the king's troops had been stopped also—by the same rough assortment of men who once before in their lifetime had turned the invader away from their green valleys.

> Old seventy-six has sallied forth,
>   On their crutches they do lean;
> With their rifles leveled upon us,
>   And with their specks they take good aim.
> There's no retreat to them, my boys,
>   They'd rather die than run.

20

PRAY FOR YOURSELVES

ON certain old maps the Onion appears as French River. The first English settlers knew it as the Onion but after the early 1800's the Indian name for the vegetable which grew in wild profusion on its banks—Winooski—gradually reappeared. Perhaps the freshet of new settlers finding homes in the towns along the banks thought Winooski more dignified, though from the vantage point of years and considering records of goings-on in the early nineteenth century, it would seem that the people were little qualified as judges of dignity.

Chester Wright, the "moral Hercules" of Montpelier—the man who refused to pray at the capital's war meeting, claimed that in 1809 the inhabitants, without religion, "became generally dissipated and a deplorable state of morals was the result. The Sabbath, instead of being observed as a day of holy rest was improved as a season of relaxation from ordinary business, only for the purpose of amusement, convivial entertainments, public houses or shops, sleigh riding, trading or gambling; and the language of profanity was the common dialect." The frequent appearance of the words "tavern" and "dissipation" in the writings of historians and reformers suggest that the wild West had nothing on early Vermont. Self-righteous Puritans had never extended their domain to the rough, wooded north-country. Refugees from that stern oligarchy had swarmed north out of Massachusetts and Connecticut into Vermont and fashioned a relaxed moral and religious pattern to their liking.

Ethan Allen, a godless creature according to missionaries,

had written a ponderous tome called *Reason the Only Oracle of Man,* which became a bible for the freethinkers along the Winooski, and Tom Paine's *The Age of Reason* was "greedily received" up and down the valley. The majority of settlers were rebels of one kind or other and they were rebelling in this case against the power of orthodox religious doctrines. "The harvest is great and the workers few . . . There is more business than ten missionaries can do this side of the mountains," cried one religious magazine. Little wonder that a galaxy of preachers, their eyes lit with the fire of a crusade, prepared to invade the Winooski religious frontier.

Certainly the most electric of these was "Crazy" Dow, a native Methodist who drew the north woods of New England as his first circuit. With an untamed beard, a sharp nose, wide-set eyes, and hair straggling to his shoulders he was quite in character. A shapeless oilcloth cloak with a hole cut in it for his head served to protect Dow and most of his horse as he charged from meeting to meeting and gave him the appearance of a Messiah. His first appearance in the Winooski valley was in an old barn on Methodist Hill in the high township of Mansfield. He arrived early dressed in tow pants and shoes without stockings, and lay down on a long bench. As the people gathered they made several efforts to arouse him with the news that there was to be a meeting and that the minister was due to arrive. The moment the service was scheduled Dow jumped up, clambered to the makeshift pulpit, and delivered a sermon that transfixed the assemblage.

"Is there anyone in the room who wants to be prayed for?" he asked in conclusion. "If so, pray for yourselves." He seized his hat and departed.

At the end of his first sermon in Montpelier he announced in a voice ringing with destiny: "One year from this day I will again preach here." One year from that day to the very hour he reappeared to the astonishment of the community and began the service with "Crazy Dow is with you once again." During the

three hours he preached he so completely held the congregation
that those with tobacco forgot to chew and there was real regret
that they would not again hear him until a year from that day.

His fame spread through the valley. Eager crowds in Cabot,
Calais, in Barre and Plainfield awaited his annual message. Sorely
distressing his fellow preachers he frequently arrived while they
were holding their services. If they denied him use of a building,

he would mount a woodpile outside the church and begin his sermon. One by one members of the congregation would abandon
the church until only the ministers and deacons were left, and
Dow would have a great multitude before him.

Often he would stop and preach to a small group in the
remote countryside. Once while riding through some woods he
encountered two woodcutters who had just felled a tree. Dis-
mounting, he climbed the stump and announced: "Crazy Dow
will preach from this stump six months from today at 2 o'clock

P.M." Six months later a huge crowd assembled around the stump. Dow was in the vicinity but had not yet appeared, for he had met a poor man who complained that someone had stolen his ax.

"If you will come to the meeting," Dow advised him, "I will find your ax." Before mounting the stump at the meeting place he picked up a stone and put it in his pocket. After the sermon he said: "There is a man here who has had his ax stolen and the thief is here in this audience and I am going to throw this stone right to his head." He quickly drew back his arm. As he did so a man in the audience ducked.

"You have got this man's ax," boomed Dow. And the man had it.

On another occasion he suddenly stopped in the middle of a sermon and announced: "There is a man present who has been considered a very respectable person, but he is guilty of hugging and kissing another man's wife. Both parties are present. The man has a white feather on his head and the woman blushes deeply." A man in the audience grasped his head. Pointing an accusing finger Dow declared, "Thou art the man." He then pointed at a woman who was blushing deeply. "Thou art the woman." Whether psychic or gained from local gossip and carefully pre-arranged, such devices were good stage business and helped his reputation spread with his broadening circuit from the Winooski valley and the rest of Vermont and New Hampshire south even into Mississippi.

Some roughnecks with knives were butchering his hand-some beaver hat which he had left some distance from the stand one day. "The laws of society condemn you," Dow proclaimed, turning to them. "The laws of your country condemn you; more-over, the laws of God condemn you. The word condemned means damned. First, you are villains. Second, you are condemned villains, that is, you are damned villains. Third, God condemns you by His law, that is, He damns you. Hence you are God damn villains."

Said to have had a photographic memory, Dow exhibited a profound knowledge of the Bible, of history, politics, and literature. He was obsessed with Methodism, and his mission was to lead a holy life on earth that he might be happier in the hereafter. Had he not been a realist and the possessor of an acute sense of humor in dealing with the foibles of humankind, he never could have gained such popularity among the rough north-woods people who so often strayed from the paths of righteousness.

A driving Vermont snowstorm one night forced him to take refuge in a small log house. After much knocking on the door he was admitted by a woman who at first said she would not accommodate a stranger. After throwing himself down on a cot he found that there was a reason she hadn't wanted to admit him— but not because she was afraid of strangers. Through the flimsy, crack-ridden partition separating her bedroom from his, he heard her conversing with a man who Dow decided was a paramour. In the middle of the night the front door burst open and her husband, a perennial drunk, came staggering in halloing and stumbling about. In the bedroom his wife hastily secreted her friend in a cask of tow, then rushed out to quiet her husband by telling him that Lorenzo Dow was in the other room. Hearing this the husband announced in a loud voice that he had heard Dow could raise the devil, and he then weaved toward the door to Dow's room and shouted for him to come out and do it. Pretending to have just awakened, Dow emerged yawning and rubbing his eyes. The husband demanded that Dow raise the devil, and said he wouldn't take no for an answer.

"If you insist," said Dow, "I will do it, but when he comes he will be in a flame of fire, and you must set the doors wide open so he will have plenty of room." The front door was opened, and Dow, proceeding to the bedroom with a candle, lit the tow in the cask. In a moment it was a sheet of flame. The man inside catapulted out, streaked through the front door and up the road, bits of burning tow falling into the snow in his path. The husband was so filled with terror that he was at once a sober man. He retired for the night in proper humility, a stanch convert to the far-flung flock of Lorenzo Dow.

In his third year in the valley of the Winooski the eccentric spellbinder arrived in Montpelier with his new wife, Peggy. They both were clothed in ankle-length cloaks of homespun, wooden shoes, and broad-brimmed hats. Each carried a walking stick. Dow ascended the platform, sat down, studied the audience for a few moments, then rose to his feet. At a signal Peggy, who was in the audience, also stood up gravely.

"This woman," declared Lorenzo, "is Peggy Dow. I have brought her with me that she may teach the women subservience to their husbands." He then addressed Peggy. "Stand still!" Peggy did not move. "Be seated!" Peggy sat down. Dow then commenced his sermon and Peggy later led the singing.

His fame spread to Europe. He crossed the ocean fourteen times but one of his favorite stamping grounds was his first—the valley of the Winooski. For fifteen years Peggy was his constant companion but she finally contracted consumption from the strenuous life of the circuits. When she was dying Lorenzo took her in his arms and prayed: "Lord, thou gavest her to me! I have held her only as a lent favor for fifteen years and now I resign her back to thee until we meet again beyond the swelling flood!" Peggy said, "Amen," and died shortly. On her tombstone these words were carved:

PEGGY DOW

Shared the Vicissitudes of Lorenzo

Fifteen Years

And died January 6th, 1820

Aged 39

Lorenzo married again but it had been with Peggy and her

singing that he had reached the height of his popularity in the Winooski valley. The curious couple have not been forgotten. Today there are certain people in Montpelier who can show you valued, well-worn tomes inscribed, "Peggy Dow's Hymn Book."

21

TOM DAVENPORT'S MACHINE

$\mathcal{N}$APOLEON Bonaparte offered a reward of one million francs in 1810 to any man in the world who could invent a machine for spinning flax, to be driven by water power. An imaginative Vermont cabinetmaker, Elisha Town, informed an enterprising neighbor, Sylvanus Baker, who was installing a cotton mill on the Winooski, that he didn't see why a machine to spin flax couldn't be built, and would Baker back him while he did some experimenting. Baker thought the money would be well spent.

With visions of the million francs stimulating his mind, Elisha went to work and tinkered for eighteen months with one rough model after another, gradually removing all defects. He at length completed a handsome model which he exhibited in Boston before taking it overseas to be judged by Napoleon's commissioner for the million francs prize. Town's machine was a specimen of Yankee ingenuity, and with the turn of a crank spun flax competently. It should have won the prize. Town should have lived in opulence the rest of his life. Napoleon was currently trying to annex Russia, however, and Town's hopes and energies along with Napoleon's, came to naught. Napoleon soon went into exile, Town went back to cabinetmaking, and Baker returned to his Winooski River cotton mill.

While Town was working on his flax spinner, there was in Williamstown, at the source of Stevens' Branch, a poor farmer named Davenport who was about to die of spotted fever in the epidemic of 1812 and leave his family poorer. But poverty and distinction are not uncommon bedfellows. Tom Davenport, only ten when his father died, hired out as apprentice to the Williamstown blacksmith, and labored indifferently for nine years. "He works too much with his head to make a good blacksmith," complained his masters. While he was working and the clang of the anvil rang across the green hills at the top of the Winooski valley, he would stop the bellows and pick up a book, or sing or play his fife, as he pondered over what he had read. For one thing, there was electricity—the perplexing force described by Faraday and Henry.

In 1823, at the age of twenty-one, Davenport left Williamstown for Brandon, where he married Emily Goss, a beautiful and spirited girl. He started a blacksmith shop there, yet from the routine of the forge he still took refuge in the riddle of electricity. By 1832 Davenport was consumed with the idea that he might help put the elusive force to work. He crossed the lake to Port Henry with $18 in his pocket to buy iron, but instead purchased an electromagnet at the Crown Point ironworks. On the night he returned, he sat down and started to unwind the magnet, which was in the shape of a horseshoe, while Emily, who shared his excitement as he dismantled it, wrote down a description of the magnet and the way the wire was wound. During the days that followed he made a horseshoe of soft iron much larger than the model. Then came the tedious business of applying the windings. There was the problem of insulating the wire but Emily got out her wedding dress and tore it into silk strips which served well, and when the large magnet was finished and connected to galvanic batteries in glass jars, it lifted impressively heavy objects. Money and time for experimentation had exhausted their savings and Davenport had to make a side show of the magnet to pay living expenses. He meanwhile considered ways and means of making a wheel revolve by magnetism. He felt certain that this force would someday power railroad cars and ships, yet he said little about it because his instability and crazy ideas were amusing the solid people of the community.

He spent hundreds of hours trying to make the magnets revolve a wheel which had irons attached to it but he found it would turn only until the irons were opposite the magnets and that it was apparently impossible to break the current fast enough to prevent the wheel from stopping. "There's no power," he said to Emily, "this side of Almighty God quick enough to do that."

"I wonder if quicksilver isn't a conductor," volunteered Emily, and they tried it. At three o'clock one July morning in 1834 the ponderous machine with quicksilver circuit breakers was ready. When the wires from the glass jars were attached the wheel started to turn. As they stood by in excitement, it made a complete circuit and gathered speed. What is considered the first electric motor in the world was running. When the news spread, scientists such as Henry and Morse hailed Davenport as a genius. Some declare, and with sufficient reason, that Morse during a visit obtained the idea of the telegraph from the backwoods blacksmith, who had constructed several different types of telegraph sets at an early date. The models exist today.

Davenport made improvement after improvement on model after model of his motor. He went on to construct a miniature electric train and a rotary printing press run by electricity, on which he printed the first journal about electricity. A patent for his motor was finally granted in 1837. It recognized that "the discovery here claimed . . . consists in applying magnetic and electromagnetic power, as a moving principle for machinery in the manner above, or in any other substantially the same in principle." If the patent existed today, it would cover every electric motor in the world, for the principle of its operation has not changed since that July morning in 1834.

The world was not interested in Davenport's machine except as a curiosity. No way of generating quantities of electric power was known and Davenport did not discover that by driving his motor in reverse with an external power, such as a steam engine or water wheel, it would make electricity. He worked for nineteen years to prove the value of electric power but a world moved by steam did not care to listen. Since he would not give up his endeavor and return to his trade as a blacksmith, he and Emily lived in poverty and had to move to a backwoods farm. There he died in obscurity in 1851, having realized nothing from a discovery worth billions today.

But on Otter Creek, where he developed his invention, and in the valley of the Winooski, where as a blacksmith's apprentice he dreamed his dreams, there is no forgetting, for his motor, working today at countless tasks about the valley, speaks for Tom Davenport. There is a marker in Williamstown which says: "Near this tablet stood the blacksmith shop . . . He had a VISION of the great future of electricity . . ."

22

THE CABOT ENIGMA

$\mathcal{T}$HE Winooski is a trout brook where it rises in the township of Cabot, yet the largest river in the world must begin with such a ribbon of water. On September 1, 1804, the sixth child of a carpenter named Colburn was born in Cabot, an inconspicuous event, except that Zerah had six toes on each foot as did his father and one brother. But on an August day five years later, when the child was playing in the chips below his father's workbench, occurred the first unearthly episode of a story which was to confound the world of mathematics.

The 5-year-old said suddenly: "5 times 7 are 35, 6 times 8 are 48." The father stopped work at his joiner's bench. "7 times 9 are 63, 10 times 12 are 120." Colburn turned unbelievingly and looked down at the child, who in a casual manner continued his multiplications. At first it struck him that Zerah was repeating what he had heard older children say, but he soon dismissed this possibility. He got down on the floor and asked Zerah how much was 13 times 97. "1,261," said Zerah with no hesitation. Colburn could not have been more shocked if someone had risen out of the earth and stood erect before him. He examined Zerah further and the child responded unerringly. Colburn brought him at once before the neighbors, who were no less astounded when Zerah agreeably supplied products of any numbers they asked.

In a matter of weeks his fame had spread throughout Vermont. Zerah was examined by members of the bar in Danville, by judges of the court, and in October, 1820, by the legislature. He was taken to Hanover, New Hampshire, and questioned by Dart-

150

mouth mathematics professors, and by the president of the college, Dr. John Wheelock, who at once made an offer to educate him. Large numbers of people came to witness the phenomenon, and one man, an uncompromising Deist, was, when he heard the child's mathematical recitations, at once converted to Christianity. During his sixth year Zerah was taken to Boston, where he supplied his interrogators with the products of two- and three-place figures, square roots and cube roots of large numbers—and even the factors of numbers, for which, mathematicians agreed, no formula existed. The boy was unable to read, to trace a number on paper, or tell how he made his computations. His father took him to England, Ireland, and Scotland, where he was visited by prominent educators and royalty including the Dukes of Gloucester, Cumberland, and St. Albans. Princess Charlotte, daughter of the king of Belgium, asked him to give the square of 4,001. He replied at once that it was 16,008,001. The Duke of Cambridge asked the number of seconds in the time elapsed since the commencement of the Christian Era—1,813 years, 7 months and 27 days. "57,234,384,000," Zerah said.

The duke then requested him to raise 8 to the sixteenth power which he did at once, naming the figure 281,474,976,710,656. Another interrogator asked him for the factors that produced the number 247,483, which he revealed to be 941 and 263—the only two factors that will produce it. He was asked to name the multiplicands of the figure 36,083, and after pausing a moment, announced that there were none, which is true. French mathematicians had declared that 4,294,967,297 is a prime number, but Leonhard Euler, after much computation, discovered that 641 times 6,700,417 would produce it. Zerah supplied these factors in a matter of seconds.

On one occasion he was asked the square of 999,999. He could not answer this, but proceeded to multiply 37,037 by itself and that product twice by 27 to give the figure 999,998,000,001. He announced he would multiply this figure by 49, and obtaining the answer—48,999,902,000,049—multiplied this figure in turn by 49 which gave 2,400,995,198,002,401. He then proposed to multiply this immense number by 25, which gave 60,024,879,950,060,025.

Zerah had no interest in figures and his mind, unless directed to a particular problem, did not dwell on mathematics. This was an enigma to the high priest of the mathematical world. who determined that, however young he was, there must be some method behind his computations. He was sharply questioned as to how he arrived at his answers. Zerah replied: "God put it into my head, and I cannot put it in yours."

His father exhibited him for three and a half years before he began to receive even the rudiments of formal schooling, although offers to educate him had been made in nearly every country he visited. Before such mathematicians as Laplace, he was examined by members of the French Institute, who placed the meeting on record in their journal for August 4, 1814. Washington Irving, in Paris at that time, became interested in Zerah's education and appealed to the French government to place him in one of its schools. Napoleon, who had returned from Elba, granted the request and on May 30, 1815, he entered Lycée Napoleon.

The strange fate that befell Zerah was that the more he learned, the less he knew. His powers of calculation began to fail at the Lyceum and by the time he was twelve years old, when he entered Westminster School in England, it had become much harder for him to provide instant answers when asked to multiply three- and four-place figures. By 1821 he was teaching at a school in Highgate, England, and by 1825—his father having died—he returned to Cabot, Vermont. Though his mother neither recognized him nor cared about him, he started a school in Cabot, which he taught for two months, then went down the Winooski valley to Burlington, where he held classes in French. He married and raised a family and for some years taught at Norwich University, but the remarkable powers of computation had long since left his mind. He succumbed to tuberculosis at the age of thirty-four.

23

JUDGMENT DAY

*T*HE Winooski gradually became—in the eyes of the clergy —a respectable river. During the 1830's yearly converts to Baptists and Congregationalists numbered in the thousands.

"Will you not say that you love God?" pleaded the Reverend Jedediah Burchard at a Montpelier revival meeting. "Only say that you love God." Some announced that they did, and the Reverend Mr. Burchard's assistant wrote down their names in a book. Many of the congregation were not yet converted. "Do you not love God? Will you not say that you love God?" persisted Burchard. He took out his watch. "There now, I give you a quarter of an hour. If not brought in fifteen minutes to love God, there will be no hope for you—you will be lost—you will be damned." Still no response. "Ten minutes have elapsed, five minutes only left for salvation. If you do not love God in five minutes, you are lost forever." Terrified lest they miss the last train to heaven, scores capitulated.

Vice, claimed an observer, had finally been "put to blush." Infidelity had received a "fatal shock." Respectability had come the hard way after months and years of earnest endeavor on the part of resident and itinerant preachers. The greatest battle had been against rum and whisky, detours indeed from the paths of respectability. As late as the first of the 1800's preachers had added fire to their sermons by imbibing in church. In the days before statehood the two thousand inhabitants of one Vermont town drank during a year $9,000 worth of liquor, more than the entire expense of running the town. The landscape was dotted with distilleries. To close the distilleries, to disgrace the bars and road-houses, and cork the thousands of jugs tipped daily by soldiers and traders, plowmen and trappers, was a task of ample dimensions—like attempting to persuade the river to flow east instead of west.

By 1825 religious and temperance leaders had been at work fifteen years trying to dry up the people of the valley and had made no progress whatsoever. The pronouncement of a man named William Miller that Christ would again appear on earth in 1843 almost decapitated the ogre of drink with a single stroke—for the Second Advent was at once used as a threat against intemperance. Orthodox churches, which so short a time before had a minimum of influence in a Deist-minded valley, now gained absolute control over the lives of parishioners.

Pathetic Emily S——, of the Essex Baptist Church, who apparently lost her virtue on the banks of the river, had to reckon with the disdain of the Baptist Church fathers.

Dear Brethern—As it respects the stories in circulation about me at Onion River as it relates to my virtue, they are entirely without foundation and were in my opinion malitious and wilfully reported to injure my Christian caricter and the Baptist cause generly, but in many respects I acknowledge I departed from the true caricter of a humble Folower of Christ and am sorry that I have injured the feelings of my Brethren and felt it a privalege to ask them forgivness and hope I shall receive the same . . .

                                                                    Emily S.

The disposition of Emily is not known, but sinners whose guilt was beyond question were expelled from the church (and thus the community) in a most humiliating ritual which took place before the entire congregation. The transgressors stood, eyes lowered in shame, while they were read out of the fellowship—they were "churched."

By 1832 Miller's premonition that Judgment Day was only eleven years off had begun to take hold. Hastening to purge any taint of sin from their personal lives, the people turned their backs on alcohol and the two hundred clubs of the Vermont Temperance Society brought distillers to their knees. The keg of rum in the field at harvesting time began to disappear; heavy planks were hoisted with sober industry at community house-raisings; the loving cup was not passed at marriages, and funeral companies marched in unalleviated gloom.

The Winooski would presumably cease to flow on March 21, 1844, slightly later than the first pronouncement. Inhabitants of the valley who had led a good life, according to Millerites, could expect to ascend to heaven on that day. Accordingly, as the year and day approached, scores of Vermonters, lately converted from orthodox faiths to Millerism, settled their affairs on earth— closed out their businesses and sold their farms. On the appointed day some had climbed to the roofs—some had trekked to mountaintops with wings strapped on so that their ascension would be easier.

> You will see the world a-burnin' . . .
> In the old church yard.
> And the band of music . . .
> How they'll sound it through the air!
> You'll see Gabriel with his trumpet . . .
> You will see the Lord a 'comin' . . .
> You will see the graves all openin' . . .
> You will see the dead arisin' . . .
> You will hear a mighty wailin'
> And a gnashin' of the teeth . . .
> And the band of music . . .
> How they'll sound it through the air!

But the sun rose in the east as usual on March 21, and by sunset the river was in its same old channel, carrying the spring snows from the mountains to the lake.

24

THE IRON LIGAMENT

Singing through the forests,
Rattling over bridges,
Shooting under arches,
Rambling over bridges,
Whizzing through the mountains,
Buzzing o'er the vale,
Bless me! This is pleasant,
Riding on the rail.

—John G. Saxe

*T*HE success of the Champlain Canal to the Hudson led Winooski River lumber barons to earnest consideration of a Winooski Canal, which would extend from Lake Champlain east to the Connecticut River and open the West to the Boston market. Conferences were held and plans drawn up for the "Onion River Navigation and Tow Path Company"—a 100-mile waterway through the Green Mountains following the channel of the Winooski for half the distance. But in the early 1840's the project was suddenly abandoned—the iron horse was coming to the valley.

Chief instigator of the first Vermont railroad was a polished promoter named Charles Paine—Governor Charles Paine. A skeleton in the Vermont closet seldom rattled by historians, Paine was not exactly a crook, but he was not exactly honest either. He was the son of Elijah Paine of Williamstown, the fearless judge who had helped give Prince Edward an uneasy time on his way through the valley in 1791. A Whig who on his way up had collected a lot of votes on the Anti-Masonic ticket, Paine had not only reached the top rung in the Vermont political ladder by 1841, but on the side was managing extensive business activities in his home town of Northfield on the Winooski's Dog River tributary. He bred high-grade cattle, ran a woolen mill inherited from his father, and owned the Northfield Hotel. At the first railroad convention held in Montpelier in January, 1844, a committee was appointed to make a survey from Lake Champlain to the Connecticut River. The best route without question was the main channel of the Winooski. Paine knew it and the engineers knew it. Everybody knew it. The river had carved a highway through the Green Mountains and, since there was not a single steep grade, the railroad could do no better than follow the river mile for mile.

Governor Paine, however, schemed to have the cars pass through his home town of Northfield, which lies in the mountains fifteen miles from the valley. He could sell his real estate to the railroad at inflated prices and perhaps have the shops and headquarters of the road established there. He went to work at once to influence the committee. Since he was governor of the state, the committee had little choice. They recommended that the railroad meander north from the Winooski and take advantage of the "easier" terrain offered by the Northfield route. It was claimed that this route would cost $423,000 less and present fewer engineering problems. Actually there would have been nearly six miles less track to build along the river and the road would have served an area with double the population. Paine got his wish, however, and today Central Vermont trains from Montreal to Boston leave the Winooski channel about a mile west of Montpelier, proceed through a narrow gulch, and climb a series of steep grades to Northfield. Owing to Paine's machinations, the capital of the state is not served by the Central Vermont except by a spur, and countless travelers have for years wearily faced the announcement: "Chaaange cars for Montpelier and Barre!"

On January 28, 1846, at two o'clock in the afternoon, ground was broken on Paine's farm in Northfield—a spot which would soon become the railroad station. Three thousand people assembled. Bells rang and two 6-pounders shot off one hundred rounds of ammunition. A public dinner was served at Paine's hotel and the recent governor was toasted as "the man to whom the people of Vermont are more indebted than to any other for the success of the Vermont Central Railroad." Paine, doubtless suffering twinges of conscience, responded by stating that, although a member of the committee to decide the route, he had never availed himself of the privilege of voting on this question.

As construction got under way and details of Paine's private blueprint were realized in brick and mortar, the public had a chance to gain a clearer perspective. The repair shops, served by water power supplied by Paine, were built in Northfield on land Paine sold to the railroad. The railroad station on Paine's farm was coming along nicely, and the decision to make Northfield a division point and overnight stopping place for trains as well as headquarters for the road, assured a year-around clientele for Paine's hotel. Some of the directors resigned and many people along the Winooski repudiated their subscriptions for stock. The Vermont Central was off to a typical railroad start.

One thing Paine did not have was a monopoly on Vermont railroads. In 1843, the year the Vermont Central started construction, work began on the Rutland and Burlington, which had the same object, to provide the region of western Vermont and northern New York, bordering on the Great Lakes, with a cross-country outlet to the East at Boston and connections north at Montreal. Coming up from a more southerly route the Rutland— like the Vermont Central—pointed at Burlington, the busy lumber mart on the Winooski. A hell-for-leather race to reach Burlington first created plenty of excitement in the valley.

The Vermont Central was having as hard a time negotiating the rocky narrows at Bolton by land as Ira Allen had by water on his exploratory expedition seventy-five years previously. For his agreement to purchase five thousand shares of Vermont Central stock, a man named Suel Belknap had been awarded the contract for building the road but at Bolton his resources were exhausted. The main reason was that the foundation of the Vermont Central had been built on financial quicksand. Paine was drawing three times the salary other railroad presidents were getting in the region; he was draining cash from his car-building shops in Northfield, awarding himself commissions, land damages, "incidental claims," and raiding the petty cash account. Like Paine, most of those in a position to "do" the railroad and unsuspecting stockholders were chiseling every available dollar from the abutments. In this way the money had run out at Bolton in the spring of 1847 and the road was now faced with an insurrection of Irish laborers. Two large settlements of Irish immigrants were encamped near the town, the upper colony called *Cork* and the lower, *Dublin*. As in the old country, there had been friction between the two camps. But when the railroad ceased paying their meager wages, Cork and Dublin presented a united front. Their inhabitants surrounded Jones's hotel in Bolton and demanded their pay, hurling angry epithets at the contractors inside.

"Highway robbery!" they yelled. "Miserable vagabonds cheatin' poor honest men out o' their pay!" The women "ran to and fro with their wide cap borders fluttering, arms gesticulating and tongues going like flutter wheels." Inside the hotel Belknap's subcontractor, a man named Barker, cowered in silent terror. Even when the militia arrived from Burlington and attempted to break up the siege by arresting some of the leaders, the crowd failed to disperse and Barker expected every moment to be dragged from the hotel and strung up to a tree on the riverbank. The riot was finally quelled by a Catholic priest. Troublemakers not previously apprehended by the militia took refuge in the Green Mountains, pressing in on both sides of the Narrows, and the rest withdrew in bitter resignation. The laborers were never paid. Work stopped until the spring of 1849, and by the time the Bolton section was finally completed seventeen Irishmen had lost their lives along the rocky right of way.

It looked as though the Rutland and Burlington was going

to win the race to the lake. Both roads were throwing up temporary bridge staging, and the track went down helter-skelter. On December 18, 1849, the first Rutland and Burlington train from Boston roared from the south over the approaches to the Winooski intervale, and wheezed into Burlington carrying a large group of chilled celebrities. An editorial writer condemned the "savage and headlong speed of the Rutland," declared that the engine had reached eighty miles an hour on a flat stretch just prior to its arrival, and said he "wouldn't be surprised to see the train in the streets of a neighboring town."

The Vermont Central, held up by bridge construction directly across the river at the town of Winooski, entered Burlington with a spur from the main line shortly after. The era of 6- and 8-horse teams which had carried passengers and produce along the river on the Montreal-Boston turnpike since settlement days was over. Now it was the iron horse.

> The shrill treble of the *Nantucket* and the *barytone* of the *Burlington* have been stretched far away into Colchester . . . stirring up grim visions of Catamounts and Tigers . . . We understand that when the deep diapason of the *Burlington* was first heard in Essex, a movement was immediately organized for the purpose of slaying the wild beast that was supposed to be prowling about . . . in the valley of the Winooski . . .

Paine had written Matthias Baldwin that he would pay $10,000 for a locomotive that could pull a train sixty miles an hour. The Baldwin Locomotive Works responded with a 25-ton engine which had an extra long boiler and a specially designed cylinder. A monument of steam-engine building, the finished product gleamed with polished brass and the green and gold colors of the Vermont Central. Its name, *Governor Paine,* was a foregone conclusion. The brass and the red wheels caught the morning sun as the *Paine* wound through the valley. There is a legend that, despite the weak bridges and unballasted track, an engineer once opened the *Paine's* throttle wide and roared a mile in forty-three seconds. The *Winooski* was another early engine, fancy and proud with her cabbage stock and shanty-cab.

The "iron ligament" had already begun to quicken the pulse of life along the river. "The fetters which have hitherto bound and confined us within the narrow limits of our mountains and our valleys have been broken," orated Judge Follett, president of the Rutland and Burlington at a Railroad Jubilee in 1850. "Great physical obstacles, mountain barriers which have hemmed us 'round since the world's creation have been removed . . . a great triumph of art over nature in her most stubborn form, has brought us into close proximity with our Sister States . . ."

Though the Vermont Central had become an operating reality, there stood not a single span among its hastily constructed river bridges that was weaker than the road's finances by 1854. Paine had hired a treasurer whose competence at stock watering put to shame the governor's balance-sheet sleight of hand. When this man had finished with the books Paine found him to be treasurer in a larger and more absolute sense—he was in almost complete personal possession of the treasury. The railroad was $295,000 in the hole. Paine had of course added handsomely to the deficit by drawing $43,619 for "incidental claims" in 1852. The next year the threadbare stockholders finally succeeded in forcing him out. The governor left the Winooski valley for Texas, where he promoted a transcontinental railroad. He died of dysentery before he got very far.

25

THE EMPIRE OF JUSTIN MORGAN

*N*O sun shines over the hills of Scotland brighter than the one that raises the mists in the valley of the Winooski. In the basin of the Congo few rains fall harder or faster. Nowhere in the East does the snow lie deeper on a February morning than on Camel's Hump, which lifts its head four thousand feet above the river. Though nature demands tribute from the men who live here—and the beasts—who can say that they are not the better for their struggle?

Over a century and a half ago a small bay horse with black legs, mane, and tail came to live in the Winooski valley. He was first brought to Randolph, Vermont, from West Springfield, Massachusetts, where they say he had been sired by an imported stallion out of a mare carrying Arabian blood. His owner, Justin Morgan, who put the colt to work on all kinds of jobs, soon realized that he owned a remarkable animal, but he sold him to a man who lived in Woodstock, who in turn sold him to Jonathan Shepard, a blacksmith in Montpelier. Full grown, the horse weighed 950 pounds and stood only 14 hands high but he could out run, out trot, or out draw any horse around—even after a day's work. He harrowed, he mowed, he raked, he pulled wagons and hauled wood. By instinct, it seemed, he was the gentlest riding horse ever to wear a saddle. Loaned by Shepard to the neighbors, he would ride the children along the river or up the steep hills of the valley.

Before many years stories of his strength and spirit had spread throughout the valley and east and west to New Hampshire and New York. "That Morgan horse," they called him after his

BLOOD OR ENVIRONMENT?

first owner. Justin Morgan had many masters and earned his living by hard work—the feats of strength and the racing were incidentals in his long career. He died as the result of an accident, when he was over thirty, in the winter of 1821, but to the last day of his life he was not an old horse. His step was firm, his neck arched, and his spirit showed in his quick eyes.

Of Justin's sons none was more nearly like him in action and style than Woodbury. "No horse ever had less fear. Martial music only roused him, the firing of guns in no way disturbed him, waving flags and gay uniforms seemed hardly able to attract from him a single glance, and he moved about as if he was himself the principal object of attention." Woodbury had the same lively eyes, broad chest, arching neck, legs wide apart, and smooth-rounded hindquarters. Justin's sons and grandsons, who founded celebrated families such as the Ethan Allen strain, won admiration everywhere. When "Green Mountain Morgan" rode through the streets of Saratoga an eminent horseman said: "The moment I saw him I was on my feet and with a great crowd was hurrying to get a closer view of that horse, and to find out where he came from and to what family he belonged . . . "

By 1860 the family Justin founded had grown immensely. His progeny were legion on the intervales and hillsides of the Winooski. Then one day a simple message arrived at Montpelier: "Washington is in grave danger. What may we expect of Vermont?—A. Lincoln." "Vermont," wired Governor Erastus Fairbanks, "will do its full duty."

The secretary of war wanted a regiment of Vermont cavalry and insisted that it be mounted on one thousand Morgan horses. Forty-two days later, in October, 1861, the thousand Morgans and their riders were down the valley at Burlington; and they were soon parading through the streets of New York. "The Regiment," remarked the New York *Herald,* "is a sturdy one . . . both as to men, horses and equipment"; and the *Times* said, "The regiment . . . is in all respects the finest one raised in any of the States." The 1st Vermont Cavalry rode through seventy-five battles and skirmishes. When the guns were at last silenced at Cedar Creek, General Custer reported: "The rapid pace at which my command had moved had necessarily extended my columns, and upon reaching the vicinity of the Creek I had but two regiments available—the First Vermont and the Fifth New York . . . Never since the beginning of the war has there been such a favorable opportunity for a comparatively small body of troops to acquire distinction as was here presented . . . " Gettysburg, Cold Harbor, Appomattox Court House. "I have never commanded troops in whom I had more confidence than I had in Vermont troops," said General Sheridan, "and I do not know but I can say that I never commanded troops in whom I had as much confidence . . . " The general had himself fought the war astride Rienzi, a jet-black Morgan with three white feet. "I rode him almost continuously in every campaign and battle in which I took part, without once finding him overcome by fatigue, though on many occasions his strength was severely tested by long marches and short rations."

Of the thousand spirited Morgans who went to battle eight hundred were killed. Of the remainder only a few returned to their green valleys in Vermont, but these carried on a race later fostered by the government at the Morgan horse farm near Middlebury.

Justin's characteristics are curiously strong in today's Morgans—the broad chests showing great lung power, necks thick and arching, short strong legs. These and their stout hearts are the purveyors of their strength but the source is more obscure. There are those who say blood will tell. Others declare it is environment—the rigorous climate, the rough pastures, the limestone bluegrass, the high hills and clear water.

26

WHEN THE MOON RISES

*S*OME treasure-laden Spaniards once trekked through the valley, they say, and had to bury their chest near the river in what is now the town of Essex. The last of the Spaniards, before he died in Ohio, told a friend and the friend came to Essex to dig up the chest. With a few trusted acquaintances, including a "juggling" doctor with a mystical stone in his hat and a forked stick, they set out one night "in silence and in fear," carrying shovels, pickaxes, iron bars, and lanterns which flickered dimly. Presently the forked stick poised on the forefingers of the doctor began to waver from its horizontal position and the mystic stone agreed with the stick that this was the right spot. They set to work with their implements and had soon dug a big hole, but finding nothing, started other holes around the first. At last their pickaxes thumped against a hard object. They dug around it in desperate haste. It was the chest. When they opened it their eyes feasted on such a glittering display of silver and yellow gold that their voices joined in a loud exclamation. But their shouts broke the charm and before their very eyes the chest disappeared forever in the solid earth below. Such were the stories told on winters' nights when the snow in the valley was "crotch-deep on a nine-foot Injun" and the moon came up orange and fat over Mansfield.

Just under the peak of Mansfield in the township of Stowe flows Gold Brook. In the old days an Indian lived along the stream. They claimed he traded gold nuggets for supplies at the camp store but when they trailed him to learn his secret he would lead them astray and disappear.

166

While Abial H. Slayton was fishing in Gold Brook opposite his farm in 1855, a bright particle which looked suspiciously like gold caught his attention. He took it home, examined it carefully, and determined that it was gold. Keeping his discovery to himself, he bought the farm through which Gold Brook flowed. He then hired several men, went to work in the spot where he had found the first nugget, and shortly washed out enough more to make himself a heavy watch chain, a bracelet, a cross, and several rings. Later he supplied gold out of his brook to plate the last spike for the Mount Mansfield Electric Railway. No one knows how much he mined over the years and none of the bright metal has since been washed from the stream, but when he was an old man Slayton told the newspapers that the gold in Gold Brook was no legend—but a fact.

Witches were not alien to Stowe, either. Nancy Sanborn, the wife of an early settler, was a full-fledged witch in the eyes of the townspeople because in her presence butter would not separate from cream. Her strange power prevented bullets from finding their marks. Apparently she was not a witch of the Salem variety; the people of Stowe did not molest Nancy Sanborn.

Near the village of Stowe is the precipitous V of Smuggler's Notch. There are legends about that, too. One concerns the 12-year-old son of the leader of a band of smugglers. The lad was knocked overboard during a skirmish with the revenue officers on Lake Champlain and was apparently drowned. Filled with remorse, the father withdrew with his wife and daughter to a log cabin in Smuggler's Notch, where for years he sealed himself from the unhappy world. During the fray on the lake it happened that the son had been hauled out of the water by a passing boat, and resuscitated. His rescuers were a family of rich people who took him west to live with them. He grew up to be a young man of wealth and high esteem but when he learned that his parents were living in a log cabin at the top of the Winooski valley he resolved to visit them.

One night a thunderstorm crashed over Smuggler's Notch

and the father went out into the rain to wail with the wind as was his custom. It seemed to him that he heard calls for help. Suddenly, during a blinding flash of lightning that momentarily turned night into day, he saw the form of the young stranger standing on the edge of the cliff above him. Seizing his lantern, the father made his way to the ledge and helped the exhausted young man to his cabin. There he recognized him as his son, and there was great thanksgiving in Smuggler's Notch.

Farther upriver, in the hills near Montpelier, stood an old log house, setting of one of the most bizarre legends of the valley of the Winooski. A frayed newspaper clipping from a scrapbook owned by Elbert Stevens of Bridgewater Corners divulged the fearful details, first set down by a Winooski valley traveler. His account of the cold storage bodies has been related recently by doctors before the American Medical Association.

It was lack of food that induced the people who lived in the wilds near Montpelier to undertake their gruesome experiment annually during the latter 1800's. As soon as the snow flew, six persons beyond the age of usefulness—four men and two women —were drugged into insensibility. Friends and kinfolk of the victims, on the occasion related by the traveler, then removed all the clothes except undergarments from the bodies on the dirt floor. They next carried the victims out into the frigid air of a January night and placed them on logs.

> The full moon shown on their upturned ghastly faces and horrible fascination kept me by the bodies as long as I could endure the severe cold. Soon I could stand the cold no longer and went inside, where I found the friends in cheerful conversation. In about an hour I went out and looked at the bodies—fast freezing.

The next day the bodies were as stiff as the logs they rested on. The traveler was horrified to see their frosty faces. After breakfast some of the men went off into the woods with a yoke of oxen. The rest nailed together a box ten feet long and five feet high. Straw two feet thick was put in the bottom of the completed box and three of the victims, with cloth over their faces, were placed in it.

Another layer of straw was added and three bodies were stacked on top of the first. After the box was sealed, the ox team drew it on a sled to the bottom of a cliff where other men had readied a bed of freshly cut hemlock boughs. The traveler learned that the snow would pile up twenty feet deep over the box, permanently sealing it until spring.

"If you want to see them come alive, you come here about the tenth of next May," advised one of the women whose husband was in the box.

The traveler often thought of the bodies during the winter but had no idea, as he plodded back over muddy mountain roads the following May, that there was a spark of life left in any of them. Except for occasional patches, the heavy snows had dissolved and rushed off to the Winooski far below. Here and there trillium and columbine challenged the drab brown mantle of the earth. Upon reaching the cabin, he found gathered there the same people who had deposited the body-box below the cliff in January. They said it was time to uncover it because they needed help for spring planting. When the traveler arrived at the ledge he noted that most of the snow had melted and the hemlock boughs above the crypt were visible. The men soon removed the brush and uncovered the box. The bodies, still as white and stiff as frozen cod, were lifted out and placed on snow. Nearby were large troughs made from logs. These were filled with hemlock boughs and warm water, which the boughs turned to a deep wine color. The victims were placed in the troughs with their heads raised slightly. Steaming water from kettles heated over a nearby fire was then added to the troughs and for approximately an hour the "corpses" were briskly massaged. The traveler, hardly believing what he saw, observed at the end of that time that the arms and facial muscles of the victims had begun to twitch. They soon started to gasp. Color was faintly returning to their faces. When spirits were allowed to trickle down their throats, they opened their eyes, began to talk, and at length sat up in their wooden bathtubs. They were then taken to the log cabin, where they ate heartily, as good as new apparently, and much refreshed from their four months' hibernation.

"Truly," wrote the traveler, "truth is stranger than fiction."

27

FREE LOVE IN NOVEMBER

$\mathcal{T}$HE river flows black through mountain gorges on cloudy days, while on summer afternoons in the open fields it is as blue as the sky. Passing through woodlands, it reflects the green of the willows lining its banks. But since white men came, it has flowed red only one summer, and then for merely a brief interval between the lake and Colchester.

By 1874 Orren Shipman of that town had hatched a utopia for "Celebates, Free Lovers and Believers in the sacredness of marriage." The colony was a "Community of Property by Investment of Capital and Labor" which emphasized "the Education of Head, Heart and Hands, Government by Enlightened Practical Goodness—and free criticism, hating no one—cultivating Love to God and Love to man, to Dwell with Freedom, Purity and Harmony, Passing on to the Highest Attainment to Know Self, Truth and Wisdom."

The Vermonter gained his ideas from the writings of a Midwesterner named John Willcox, to whom Shipman wrote suggesting a way in which these high principles could be put into practice. Shipman owned some heavily mortgaged lands on the river, and Valcour Island near the New York shore of the lake, which he offered for $31,000 as a properly isolated site for the Free Colony. The land was really worth twice that much, and the terms of payment would be easy. Willcox heartily accepted the proposal and came east to join Shipman and form "The Dawn Valcour Agricultural and Horticultural Association." A flurry of activity quickly established the colony on Valcour Island early in the fall of 1874.

On August 27 twelve of Willcox's followers left Chicago for the bright promised isle, where they could observe unmolested, their only governing law: "complete, universal free love." The twelve men and women were members of a Chicago group of "advanced" Spiritualists who "will be able," commented a Chicago newspaper almost wistfully, "to worship at the grand fountain of pleasure for this life . . . " When news of the Valcour Community spread, ten more recruits from the Midwest promptly joined the original twelve.

Orren Shipman, a rough man who had somehow acquired the title "professor," shuttled between the river and the island in a black boat rowed by his browbeaten, dried-up wife, Sarah, and the wife of his hired man, a rawboned woman who chewed tobacco. The guiding hand on the island was of course that of Willcox, but the counsel of a young and beautiful woman of twenty-seven from New York City, H. Augusta White, seemed to carry equal weight. A poet, author, and lecturer, she had arrived much earlier than the rest "in pure conjugal love" with a young man named Woodhouse. Augusta believed that every woman reaching the age of eighteen should be allowed to call herself "mistress" or "Mrs." and that children should not necessarily take the name of their parents. Woodhouse agreed. He pointed out that the children of the Oneida Colony were sickly and the reason was that the principle on which the New York community had been founded was not deep enough.

"Our children," he declared, "will be *love children*—cared for and educated collectively." A local newspaperman asked Woodhouse how a child of the colony would answer the question: "Who is your father?" Woodhouse replied that the child would wave his hand in a sweeping arc, indicating all the men on the 800-acre island, and say: "These are my fathers." When asked how he would feel if some other man in the colony chose Augusta for a companion, Woodhouse replied that he would not let his own selfish love outweigh the happiness of the two, and he would submit.

Willcox planned an elaborate building program for Valcour, to include several community buildings, a farm, and landscaped gardens. From the outset the Chicago press was suspicious of the "benefactions" of Professor Shipman, who made the sale of farm lands along the river, and the island itself, with the understanding that the property, with improvements, would revert to Shipman if anything happened to the colony. "If the community disband," commented the Chicago *Times,* "he (Shipman) is apt to receive it back when the current year's crops are eaten up, and there is a necessity for spring plowing." Shipman was able not only to participate in the happy communal life on the island, but at the same time watch his river and island lands appreciate.

In the Interval of the Peat Bed are nearly two miles of excellent ditching . . . We shall rejoice if any of our Brothers will help us to a Peat Machine . . . We have on the homestead an Osler Willow Plantation for willow ware manufacturers . . . We want a peeling machine. Who can send us one? . . . We want a small Propellor to run between our landings. Who can furnish us an Engine? . . . We invite you to *Invest* what you will. Lands—Goods—Merchandise or Funds. Will you send us a certain sum—say *Five* or *Ten* Dollars, or more, each month?

By the time the frosts came to Valcour in the fall of 1874, it was evident that community life was not quite living up to expectations. The splendid buildings envisioned by the architects of the society had not begun to materialize and the people on the island were shabby. By spring, 1875, "complete, universal free love" was nowhere less evident than on Valcour. Shipman had instructed Willcox to sell a stag grazing on the island, which Willcox did, but, instead of turning the proceeds over to Shipman, he used the money to settle a community debt with a local merchant. Shipman caused Willcox to be thrown into jail on March 4, 1875, but the trial that ensued in Winooski ended in favor of Willcox. Dissension rent the colony on the island. Three of the brothers departed and exposed the activities of the others. "When the history of this communal enterprise shall have been written," railed the community, "the names of these conspirators will rank with those of Benedict Arnold and Judas Iscariot." This was certainly neither "cultivating Love to man" nor dwelling with "Freedom, Purity and Harmony."

On October 5, 1875, the mortgage was foreclosed, and in November, Willcox and Augusta White, presumably followed by her friend Woodhouse and the other comrades, departed for New York City.

The winds blew cold over the peat beds and the willow plantation along the Winooski and withered the foliage of the island paradise.

28

THE FORTUNES OF MILLSTONE HILL

$\mathcal{T}$WO or three million centuries ago there was an explosion of molten, glasslike matter beneath the crust of the earth in an area that one day would become the heart of Vermont. The molten mass failed to reach the surface and become a volcano. It contented itself with bulging upward through layers of older rock where, through countless ages, it gradually lost its fire. As if resenting the intrusion, the heavy layers of rock above pressed upon it with enormous weight, but it was this weight that presently began to make of the invader a handsome rock of gray and white crystals.

Nature's most spectacular feat was yet to come. It pushed the older and newer rocks upward together, making high mountains of them. The overlying rock, now exposed to ages of frost, rain, and a series of glaciers, began to wear away until at length the granite underneath appeared at the surface.

When white settlers came to the Winooski Valley they discovered the outcropping of gray-white rock on top of a hill which descended sharply into the Stevens Branch tributary. In a few years they had begun to cart it away to make millstones. Other than diamond, sapphire, and ruby, it was the hardest rock in the world, a fact which must have been evident as they struggled to shape it with inadequate tools, and yet despite almost overwhelming difficulties the hill near Barre became the source of the millstones with which the rivers of New England and Canada ground their settlers' grain.

There was spasmodic activity on Millstone Hill during the

1790's and early 1800's but it was not until Vermont decided in 1832 to replace its wooden State House in Montpelier with a granite edifice that quarrying began in earnest. Twenty-three thousand cubic feet were needed for the Capitol. Since the granite weighed 167 pounds a cubic foot and had to be drawn fifteen miles to Montpelier, Joseph Glidden and his son Mark could not have expected to get rich when they agreed to deliver part of it on carts and sleighs at 8 cents a foot. They arose at four in the morning, harnessed their 4-horse team and yoke of oxen, drove to East Barre, climbed the hill a thousand feet over muddy or icy ruts, loaded up by means of skids and rockers, and descended the hill. In winter they dragged the granite to Montpelier over the river ice, unloaded it, and went home at ten o'clock at night. Eighteen hours of backbreaking work and a 25-mile trip for $4.

With winters when the thermometer dropped to 30 below, springs when the hill road was a slough of mud, and with granite a most uncompromising stone whatever the season, small wonder that a half century passed before the crystal wealth of Millstone Hill was again tapped. By 1880 news had reached the quarries of Aberdeen, Scotland, that some of the finest quality of granite in the New World was to be found near the town of Barre, Vermont. Fascinated by the prospect of life in America, granite cutters began to leave for the United States. News that a group was leaving would spread like a grass fire through the Aberdeen quarries. Struck suddenly with wanderlust, other workers hastened to join it. One man is said to have run home from the quarry, hurdled his wife who was scrubbing the stairs, and shouted over his shoulder: "Well, Mary, I'm off!" He bundled up his things and barely had time to say good-bye before joining the group at the station.

After a long sea voyage, usually by steerage, the Scots arrived in Barre and were there confronted with all the problems of a new industry. There was work on Millstone Hill but the boardinghouses and tenements were full. Because of unsanitary conditions epidemics of fever were breaking out. Wages were so low that only a bare subsistence was possible. The immigrants, however, were hardy young men from the farms and villages of Scotland, reared in a tradition of hard work and frugal living. They were, moreover, expert quarrymen with as much ambition as there was granite on Millstone Hill.

The age of steam had not yet come to the quarries—there were just horses, oxen, and men. Granite was drilled by hand. One man sat and turned the steel while two strikers alternated

blows with heavy sledges. There were derricks to swing blocks from the hole but the science of lifting by derrick was in its infancy. Teams of horses or oxen, treading a path around a winch, provided power.

There was always the transportation problem. Sometimes when mud in the road was three and four feet deep a load became mired, despite the best efforts of an 8-horse team. Then it was necessary to hitch three, four or five such teams together. Forty horses could start any ordinary mired wagon but a wagon freighted with granite blocks "six feet cube," shafts 30 feet long, or 40-ton mausoleum roof stones, needed every last foot-pound of energy from every horse. Ice on the river below and snow on the hill made the going easy for sleds in winter—too easy for those coming down. "Clog" chains were fastened to the runners at steep places but loads were so heavy and the pitch so great that the chains sometimes broke and over the bank went thirty tons of stone.

Among Scottish laborers there were those who, with previous savings or by virtue of pennypinching, were able to gain title to a bit of land on the hill and assume the role of employers. They would work in the pit all day as they always had, and do their office work at night. The office was frequently a walled-off end of the blacksmith shop or the dust loft at one end of a Barre finishing shed. They had to make every block of stone count, and every man-hour of work. A story is told of two men who, in finishing the top, or bed, of a block of stone, before turning it with the derrick, determined to "bull-set" off the excess themselves before the boss got back. They had the bad luck to fracture the stone, and ruin it. While they were measuring with their rules and squares to see if the block could be salvaged, the boss appeared. Realizing what had happened at a glance, he grabbed one of the workmen's squares and hurled it across the yard. The workmen protested. "Ye bugger," shouted the boss, "I should cast ye baith after't fer knockin' in sic a hole!"

The Scottish colony continued to grow through the 1880's and 1890's. First arrivals took pleasure in baiting greenhorns just off the boat. A newcomer was passed a bowl of gravy in a boardinghouse with the explanation that it was a special treat. He looked at it, took several potatoes, dropped them in, devoured the contents of the bowl and remarked: "That was fairly the best tatie soup I ever tasted!"

The average age of men in the colony was twenty-eight.

About half were married. The objective of the married ones was to save enough money to send to Scotland for their families. One wife, who had reached the valley of the Winooski at last, was afraid the train was going to carry her past Montpelier Junction, where she was supposed to get off. She spied a man with a coonskin hat. "Hey, you wi' the hairy bonnet," she hollered, "is this Montypeeler?"

The heart of such a woman in a strange land was in her throat. There never seemed to be enough housing on the hill and two or three families often had to crowd into space for one. Scottish women were accustomed to open coal-burning grates, and had to adapt their cooking to American ranges. Kerosene lamps were more difficult to manage than the gas jets of Aberdeen. The social pattern, too, was different from that of the homeland. But there was this about the Winooski valley: its scenery reminded one of Auld Scotia. On Sundays there was the freedom of fields and woods. In spring and summer the land was green and in the fall the air was as clear as ever it was in Scotland. There were nuts and berries to be gathered in the hills, and the river belonged to all of them.

The life of a quarry family was as hard as any in the valley, yet it was not without pleasure. There were picnics on Fast-Day and Thanksgiving Day eve, and every so often entertainment evenings in Barre. Following a concert, the hall would be cleared and refreshments served. Children played tag across the floor and square dancing lasted into the "wee sma' oors."

Hammer throwing, stone putting, jumping, and the sack race highlighted youth weeks. And during the rare free hours from the pits and sheds there was, for young men, the much-anticipated jaunt to Montpelier—to have their "likeness ta'en." "I wonder," wrote William Barclay, summoning up early days, "if the photographer's two pretty and vivacious daughters—who were invariably present to assist—were not the principal reason."

Single men lived in boardinghouses and tenements, in rooms

nine feet square. On long summer evenings there was "collar and
elbow wrestling" outdoors. A contestant, wearing a loose jacket,
grabbed his opponent's shoulder and elbow and struggled to throw
him off balance. In a tight spot a man could slip out of his jacket
without bearing the stigma of defeat, and try again. For those
who found it necessary to wash the granite dust from their
throats—and there were many—there was potent, poor liquor to
be had—cheap. Verbal brawls involved politics, history, current
events, or the merits of this quarry crew as compared with that.

Fevers and other severe illnesses which attended the crowding of tenements on Millstone Hill were, for the great number
of single men, particularly distressing. By forming clans they
coped with it after a fashion. It was the duty of two clansmen to
sit up all night with an ill member, but such a vigil did not excuse
them from work the next day. Through the many years before insurance it was the clan that took care of the destitute family of a
deceased member.

In 1889, when the Barre railroad—"The Sky Route"—was
built on Millstone Hill, the quarries entered a new era. From the
river bed, where the sheds were located, the track rose 1,740 feet
in three miles. Special engines with large boilers designed to make
the steepest broad gauge climb this side of the Rocky Mountains,
began to puff up the hill and return to deposit their heavy loads of
granite at the doors of the sheds. New methods of quarrying
transformed work in the pits as completely as the railroad had
changed transportation. Horse-powered sweeps for operating derricks gave way to steam-driven hoists and the chatter of steam-
powered piston drills echoed on the sides of the deepening quarry
holes. In 1894, seventy-two different quarries on the hill, employing two thousand men, produced $893,956 worth of monumen-
tal, building, and paving stone.

The two thousand men were not all Scottish. News that there
was work in Barre had reached other nationalities in granite and
marble quarries about the world, and during the late nineteenth

century and the first years of the twentieth immigrants from many lands began to arrive on the Winooski. There were the Italian carvers and sculptors whose trade was ancient in medieval times. Large numbers of French came from Canada. In rapid succession groups of Spanish, Pole, Finn, Scandinavian, Swiss, Austrian, Irish, and English stoneworkers appeared. Most of these had no desire to learn any trade other than stonecutting and settled peacefully, adding new patterns to the kaleidoscope of life on the hill. It is said, however, that the Poles, who arrived sometime after 1900, had ulterior motives. For months they would work their hearts out in the pits, and by patching their shoes and clothes, live on next to nothing until they had accumulated $400. When they had saved precisely that much, they would appear at the quarry office with the bills wound tightly in a ball and announce, "Me go to Canadian Northwest," and off they would go to buy their piece of land.

Conditions were not improving on the hill, where ugly tenements and shacks to house the influx of workers created "Stovepipe City." The black days of the Robber Barons had come to Barre. Many tenements were built by quarry owners, who made 25 to 30 per cent on the investment, while their tenants lived in squalor. Pneumatic drilling in the pits and machine polishing in the sheds raised clouds of granite dust which filled the lungs of workers, inevitably bringing dreaded silicosis in a few years and tuberculosis and death in a few more. A man starting to work in the quarries or sheds at the age of eighteen had a prospect of living to the age of forty-five or fifty, not longer. Thus Stovepipe City had inevitably to provide for widows and children.

By 1924 granite sheds, strung out along the Winooski between Montpelier and Barre, were producing $8,000,000 worth of granite yearly. Most of it was still coming from Millstone Hill. Pyramids of grout waste seventy feet high near the edge of the pits were testimony of forty years' intensive quarrying. Steam power, which had overtaken horse and ox power, was now giving way to electric power in the derrick engine rooms, though the industry was still young.

The seventy-two quarries which were operating in 1894 had shrunk by 1944 to five, yet since these five were larger than all seventy-two, more stone than ever was being quarried from Millstone Hill. The main pit of the Rock of Ages quarry, largest in the world, is a crater 350 feet deep. Men working on the bottom seem like small black dots to the observer at the top. Across the 40-acre opening stretches a network of cables attached like the ribs of an umbrella to masts of Oregon fir 115 feet high. All the anthill activity of the quarry focuses on the derricks. In the morning, when the shrill air whistle blows, men cluster on flying platforms on top of the pit, the 90-foot boom swings out over the hole and down 350 feet they go to their drills and channel bars. Shortly, the deafening clatter of pneumatic tools, powered by 7,000 cubic feet of compressed air a minute, announces the start of the day.

A single crew may work weeks to cut away one block of granite 30 feet square and 15 feet deep. This is done by drilling a series of vertical holes along a straight line, then cutting horizontally underneath with a channel bar. When this tedious operation is finished, the block is jarred loose with a small charge of dynamite. Once, a single block 200 feet long, 80 feet wide, and 24 feet deep was quarried. It weighed 32,500 tons—as much as a battleship—and when cut up required 1,728 freight cars to remove it. As soon as the most convenient size, 30 by 30, is freed, it is cut into 25-ton sections which are carried over to the derricks by means of "Blondin" cables—named after the man who walked above Niagara Falls on a tightrope in 1859. When the derrick is ready to hoist a 25-ton block, a whistle blows and all men on the quarry floor leave the area. By means of complicated hand signals between a man in the pit, another man on the rim of the quarry, and the derrick operator, who can see nothing of what is going on, a block starts up. When it reaches the surface the boom swings it over and deposits it on a waiting freight car as meticulously as a mother placing a baby in a crib. One day the haunting whistle of a squat mountain locomotive announces the block's departure for Barre. It winds down the hill to the river, where after a series of complicated machines in the sheds saw and shape it into a memorial, it is lettered by sand-blasting or carved by Italian stonecutters. One-third of the public and private monuments and mausoleums in the United States, it is estimated, came from Millstone Hill. There is no indication that they will not continue to come from there; the granite bed is thought to extend into the earth under the hill for two hundred miles. A shaft of Barre granite 51 feet high commemorates the Vermont birthplace of Joseph Smith, founder of the Mormon Church. F. W. Woolworth, Walter Chrysler and Carter Glass, John D. Rockefeller, Victor Herbert and John J. McGraw, Cyrus H. K. Curtis, J. W. Packard, Booth Tarkington, and Alfred E. Smith rest in mausoleums of granite that came from Millstone Hill. The Wisconsin and Pennsylvania capitols and the Chicago City Hall were hewn in the stone sheds along the Winooski. Had the Washington monument been built of Barre granite, it could have been half a mile high, since granite can withstand a pressure of twenty thousand pounds per square inch.

There is little on the hill, except the granite itself, that has not changed since the first settlers hunted millstones and Joseph Glidden drew his ponderous loads for the Vermont State House. Today there is talk of doing away with drills and employing new types of saws to cut the stone to size in the pits rather than later in the sheds.

Change comes more slowly to stonecutters. Italians in the sheds are not quite yet Vermonters—they are Vermont Italians. They still make their own "red ink" wine at home, eat their polenta and rabbit and ravioli. As their families did in the old country, they embark on mushroom hunts in the woods along the river on September Sundays. In back yards outside their neat houses in the north end of Barre you will see on bright fall days their mushrooms drying on window screens, for there is nothing like mushrooms to spice spaghetti sauce. Though conditions are infinitely better in the sheds, since suction devices were installed to clear the air of granite dust, there are still many Italians who have worked for years when the dust was thick. And so silico-tuberculosis, the grim unmentionable reaper of the stonecutter, is still with them.

It would not be surprising if these Italians were preoccupied with death: they spend their lives working on tombstones. Yet neither death nor sickness is ever discussed even if the emaciated head of the family, no longer able to work, sits quietly at home wracked by coughing and by pains in his chest. There is always a faint hope that the afflicted will get better, but if he does not he is prepared. In Hope Cemetery, on a high rise of ground above Stevens' Branch, he has set up an elaborate granite memorial which he has himself carved for his last resting place. It may have Corinthian columns or weeping figures. Sometimes it is the stump of a young tree with a granite scroll containing vital statistics hanging from a limb.

The carved letters and figures on memorials of granite workers tell their own story:

JAMES ADIE   JAMES S. GRIERSON
1864-1916   1878-1924

EUGENIO VILOLI   LUIGI CERUTI
1876-1924   1875-1926

29

AND THE WATERS PREVAILED

*H*AD it not been for the fat V that running water notched and then mortared with earth, there could have been no fields in the heart of the mountains. Without fields there could have been no farms, without water power no cities—and yet white men have rarely acknowledged their debt to the river. They have restricted its right of way, cut down the trees and choked the channel with sewage. Previous to the grotesque events of November 3 and 4, 1927, the Winooski had twice revolted. On July 27, 1830, responding to heavy rains which the dwindling forest mantle failed to absorb, the river rose quickly and swept away mills and bridges in scattered towns of the valley. Thirty-nine years later another freshet accomplished the same mischief.

In October, 1927, there was double the normal rainfall. Though the ground had become saturated by November 1, a tropical storm from the Gulf of Mexico was on that day carrying its heavy gray freight north to Vermont. Ordinarily it would have moved into the east to spend itself over the Atlantic but another storm was on its way from the Great Lakes area. Joining over New England, the storms locked themselves in a battle for celestial supremacy, with the Winooski valley under the heaviest engagements. The rain started on November 2. On the morning of November 3—though the weather bureau at Northfield predicted fair and colder—the sky, a dirty gray, was still overflowing like a gigantic bathtub. By noon the river was angry and black and there was no prospect of the rain stopping. By 4:00 P.M. water stood in the streets of the capital. By 5:15 all travel had stopped. When

the Waterbury fire siren began its unearthly wail, the people knew
the river was rising fast. As the water reached the post office,
telephone operators sent warnings over the wires and firemen
hunted for boats.

Since the rain was still falling in torrents, night came with
incredible swiftness. In a few hours the main streets of every
town on the river were impassable. Telephone circuits went dead;
lights began to go out. In Barre, Lieutenant Governor Hollister
Jackson stepped out of his car to his death in the swift black water
of a Potash Brook washout. In the Barre business section occasional lights glared on the water swirling into the entrances of
stores. The basement wall collapsed under one building and the
river rushed in over two young men carrying merchandise to the
first floor. The boat with which Helge Carlson had been trying to
save the Webster family overturned. Before he was sucked under,
a Webster child clung for a moment to Carlson's leg. The 25-
year-old Swedish granite cutter then swam to a pole sticking out
of the water. A raft or platform came out of the night, smashed
against the pole and broke his grip. He used the rest of his
strength climbing onto the raft. Hardly had he caught his breath
when the raft gained speed and went dizzily over Trow and Holden dam, hurling him once more into the flood. The Prospect
Street bridge was next. He grabbed it and held on a brief ten seconds before the current pulled him under. He was still swimming
when he passed beneath the railroad bridge downstream. Beyond
that he got hold of a compressor pipe that stuck out of the Hoyt
and Milne shed and was able to crawl to the roof.

In Montpelier a bridge went out taking the gas main with
it. Lights failed. People marooned on roofs, on freight cars, and
in the tops of trees could hope only that someone would hear their
cries and telephone for aid. At the telephone office by ten o'clock
no contact with the outside world was possible, and the local circuits had gone out one by one until the switchboard, illuminated
by two feeble candles, was dead. From then on rescue work was

without direction. A former mayor, trapped on the top shelf of his workshop, pressed his head against the ceiling in the narrow space of air above the water. He was rescued with a rope of twisted blankets. The janitor of the First National Bank managed for hours to keep his hold on the picture molding in the counting room, where he stood on a shaky iron grille above eight feet of water. A motorboat came down the street and took him aboard.

In the state mental hospital at Waterbury the lights were out. The staff and employees were trying to move the 872 patients to the third floor; the water was three feet deep on the second. Except for eight cans of milk there was no unspoiled food, although a stranded milk train, whose conductor, Frank Murphy, was perched in the water tower near the station, offered some degree of hope. There would certainly be no more milk from the 121 prize Holsteins trapped in the institution barns. The river at Waterbury was a lake 40 feet over its normal level because the water had created a sort of dam out of a stubborn old covered bridge calked with two houses, chunks of barns, player pianos, dead animals, furniture, and a pile of twisted lumber. The Winooski chose to cross the Waterbury graveyard and level 100 tombstones. The streets of the town were canals through which the few available rescue boats groped their way. Charles Parker, a furniture dealer, paddled to safety in two wooden caskets which he had strapped together. His wife held her baby with one arm and bailed with the other.

Harry Cutting had assembled his wife and three children on a raft. It became unmanageable and overturned in the current. They found Harry Cutting dazed in a tree, but they never found his wife or children.

The current at the Narrows in Bolton was frightful, although most of the houses were withstanding it. One that did not was that of Mrs. Hayes, who kept a boardinghouse. Sixteen bridge and highway workers staying there accompanied Mrs. Hayes, her daughter, and granddaughter over Bolton Falls to their deaths. At 2:30 A.M. a heavy bumping and scraping outside William Agan's house added to the agonizing noises of his animals trapped in the barn. Agan peered into the night. He saw a lantern in the second-story window of a house floating past.

"Where am I?" shouted John May as he held up his lantern.

"You're at Agan's." There was a pause.

"This is Jack May. We're gone! Good-bye." A few seconds later May, his wife, and four children were lost as his house disintegrated against the railroad bridge.

The flood made monsters of shadows in the streets and fields. Without light there was little hope of rescue for those who could not last until morning—and the lights in the valley had flickered out. Some of the Winooski's hydroelectric stations had been wrenched from their moorings and washed into the river. Others groaned under the weight of wreckage and silt. Yet there were certain sections of Barre and Montpelier where lights glared on the flood even at its crest. Outside the town of Marshfield, in the country where the river rises, stands a small power station with one generator. Above it a wall of water 5½ feet high and 40 feet wide was spilling over Molly's Pond Dam. Since the supporting earth was gone from underneath a 150-foot section of the penstock, which led from the reservoir to the plant under the hill, the huge tube dangled precariously in the air, supported at each end. The Winooski, here a small mountain stream, had swollen enormously and had thrown a bridge from upstream against the span leading to the plant, perched on land that had become an island. But operator Archie Bullard could take pride in the fact that his generator was still running. He had been on duty for three days and three nights. Men from town had climbed down over the hill to bring food. Under his guidance they had stacked sandbags and baled hay against the wall of the station in case the river came in. At midnight of November 3 six volunteers from town were bailing out the basement in an attempt to keep the water level below the storage batteries that powered the switches upstairs. Above them Bullard was busy at his control panel. The power system in the valley below was being ripped to pieces. He knew this because his switches, responding to one short circuit after another, kept tripping out. When they tripped he threw them back in, and if they tripped again, he waited five or ten minutes and threw them in again. Bullard was haggard for want of sleep but his generator was roaring at top capacity—5,000 kilowatts. By keeping his switches in, he knew his current was going out, but where it was going he couldn't know. All contact with the other plants in the system had long since been broken.

After 154 hours of continuous duty, another operator arrived to relieve Bullard at the switchboard. Then it was that he learned that his turbine had been the only one in the valley in operation, that his current had found its way to the operating rooms in hospitals at Barre and Montpelier.

By morning—Friday, November 5, most of the 8.63 inches of the 39-hour rain had fallen, but it was still raining. In Waterbury the water was 18 feet deep on the main street. Daylight, however, had relieved some of the tension and in the upper stories of houses people were thinking about getting something to eat. One hundred men from the high Mansfield township of Stowe had bridged the washouts on the road down to Waterbury with lumber which they had brought on trucks. Shortly after daylight they appeared with boats brought from Lake Mansfield and started rescue operations. On a dry rise of ground in the center of town the women in the kitchen of the Congregational Church were doing yeoman service, while the Stowe rescuers quickly gathered 150 destitute people and brought them back home to feed and shelter them.

Man and beast shared the tragedy. At Jonesville a man sat all night on the roof of a warehouse holding a kitten. On a high rise at the south end of an iron bridge in Richmond nineteen people composing four families were marooned with three horses, five pigs, and 250 chickens. At Winooski a large chestnut horse washed over two dams, swam out of the backwash to the bank below the cotton mills, and was there harnessed and put to work. Below this, on the lowlands, an old black horse and a young colt were swimming together. The old horse began to weaken and his head was seen to go under. The colt paused in uncertainty. As he did so the old horse thrust his head out of the water and set his teeth in the mane of his young companion who, with a burst of his remaining energy, set out for the shore. They reached it, too. It is related, but less authentically, that a farmer near the Heineberg covered bridge was attempting—with a rope hitched to his Model T Ford—to pull his prize bull out of the water and up the steep bank on the edge of the intervale. In excitement the bull instead pulled the Model T down the bank into the water. The bull drowned and the Model T was never the same.

As it reached the lower valley the crest of the flood passed over the dam at Essex at a height of 24 feet. It picked up the railroad bridge at the gorge like a piece of balsa wood and deposited it on an island hundreds of feet below. Twisting the trolley tracks like copper wire, it removed the iron highway bridge at Winooski Falls, which let go with a shriek and went over the dam. The flood then spilled out over the lowlands, turning its vast acreage into a bay of Lake Champlain.

When the rain finally stopped on Friday, the water started to subside and to reveal the wounds the river had inflicted during the twenty-four hours past. It had drowned 55 people. The 2,000,000,000 cubic feet of water it discharged washed out most of the 253 miles of track and 54 bridges lost by the Central Vermont Railroad. (On November 5 the C.V. promptly declared itself in receivership.) Since the river at the height of its flood had expanded its channel from 250 feet to a mile in some places, there was often no dry ground to which the animals—the dairy herds—could swim. Within a few miles of Waterbury there were thousands of dead cattle. At Montpelier, directly opposite the home office of the National Life Insurance Company, stood an immense elm which the state forester said was one of the last two trees of the original forest. It went down the river during the night of November 3, and, when the water subsided, all that was left was a gaping hole where its roots had spread. Another hole which the river had excavated in an hour that same night took two months and 3,000 loads of dirt to fill.

During the worst of the flood a Vermonter in rubber boots and a slicker was standing in the rain with a friend watching the remains of two bridges go floating down the Winooski.

"By George, Harry!" he said. "Taxes are goin' ter be steep!"

2

The valley tackled reconstruction in the manner of a barn-raising. The cavalry arrived from Fort Ethan Allen. Norwich cadets built a radio transmitter out of old parts. Two mountain locomotives from Millstone Hill appeared on the Barre trolley tracks to pull muck and stone. In the State House, Governor John Weeks set up a rehabilitation committee headed by Fred Howland, president of the National Life Insurance Company, whose monumental granite headquarters at river level below had also been visited by the Winooski.

Governor John E. Weeks, an old Vermont Yankee, was finding it hard to admit that maybe he was going to have to look outside the state borders for help. The conflict that tormented his mind boiled to the surface when he overheard a remark that Vermont had gone to hell and could never come back. Weeks, regarding with frosty disdain the reporter who had made this crack, stated that Vermont would not only come back, but would do it on her own. The newspapers made a big play of this, declaring that the governor was going to do it all by himself.

Since the damage totaled about $25,000,000 and the Winooski valley was without telephones, electricity, mail, roads or railroads, Governor Weeks found it necessary to telephone, as soon as a trunkline went through, his friend Calvin Coolidge, who was sitting in the White House wondering what had happened to his native state. Weeks asked Coolidge if he would mind sending up "your man Hoover" to survey the wreckage. Coolidge said he would see about it and early next morning wired the governor: "Your man Hoover is on his way." Hoover, after checking the devastated river towns for a few days, reported: "I have seen Vermont at its worst—but I have also seen Vermonters at their best."

The legislature met in a special session on November 30 and authorized an $8,500,000 loan to finance long-range reconstruction—over $24 for every man, woman, and child in the state. Private concerns such as the American Woolen Company at Winooski, which suffered a million-dollar loss, were taking care of their own.

On February 4, 1928, three months after the flood, a special train of the Central Vermont Railroad rolled up the valley on a jubilee tour. Among its passengers were Sir Henry Thornton, president of Canadian National Railways, to which the C.V. is affiliated, and Governor Weeks. It is not known if the disparaging newspaper reporter was aboard. Crowds cheered the engine as it steamed into each town. Bands played and factory whistles blew.

Long after the flood scars had healed the valley was still preoccupied with the river. Though meteorologists had described the deluge as a hundred-year flood, the next one could plausibly occur tomorrow. Army engineers had made an exhaustive survey of the Winooski and its tributaries and reported to Congress on February 26, 1931. By 1935 two thousand CCC workers had begun a flood-control project in the hills above Waterbury on Waterbury River. At the same time the corps was building dams on two other Winooski tributaries, at Wrightsville and East Barre. The upper portion of the once-thriving village of Wright's Mills had to be erased when the 1,500-foot barricade of earth began to rise from the river bed, for upon its completion spring waters would pile up 90 feet above the old stream.

It was Medad Wright, nearly a hundred years before, who originally dammed the river there. He had first built a sawmill in Calais but there wasn't enough water to run it. Townspeople had told him so, but Medad built a dam, put up the mill, and let the water through to the wheels. They say that the saw started rapidly, as if it were saying, "Me-dad, Me-dad, Me-dad," but that the water soon ran out and the saw began to labor: "Me . . . dad, Me . . . dad, Me . . . *Dead.*" Wright subsequently moved to Wright's Mills where he built another dam and harnessed the water to millstones, which ground as many as 14,000 bushels of oats a year. At that time up-and-down saws were the thing, but Medad installed a circular one in his lumber mill.

As the years passed he began to make machinery for other New England mills—looms and cider presses and granite-polishing machines. And so the village of Wright's Mills grew around the dam—houses, a store, a church. The young people formed "The Young Ladies' and Gentlemen's Lyceum" and gathered in the church to debate such questions as

Resolved:

"That it is for the general good of society that all classes of men should be educated.

"That war is in no case justifiable and ought to be abolished.

"That Indians have suffered more at the hands of the Whites, than the Africans.

"That profanity is a greater evil than intemperance."

Medad Wright was happy at his work and Scotch airs like "Come Boat Me Over to Charlie" followed him around his mill and his town. When he died his children took over. When they died, the business moved to Waterbury and the village of Wright's Mills languished. Upon completion of the flood-control dam in 1936, waters of the Winooski's North Branch rushed in behind the embankment and submerged the north end of the village.

It had taken three years to complete the dam. At times people of the valley wondered if it would ever be finished. There was the morning when they saw several railroad freight cars stacked high with nothing but wheelbarrows. Washington planned to turn its back on the machine and use wheelbarrows— the more wheelbarrows the more men employed.

The largest earth-filled dam east of the Mississippi was growing on Waterbury River. Near the site of the dam a village of barracks had sprouted, complete to a movie theater. Two thousand men, engaged in the largest CCC flood-control project in the country, were clearing the forest and pasture and excavating 450,000 cubic yards of earth and rock, to build a dam 2,000 feet long, 900 feet wide, and 175 feet high of 2,200,000 cubic yards of clay, rock, and rip-rap. It was to make a lake six miles long out of Waterbury River and tame for certain the ravages of its spring flow.

On the morning of July 30, 1936, there was quite a stir in the valley of the Winooski. A special train was due along the tracks of the Central Vermont. Every bridge, every switch in every railroad yard, and forty-two grade crossings over which the train would pass were heavily manned by New York and Vermont police, immigration patrolmen, customs officers, and the railroad maintenance force. Possibly secret service agents feared the president's entry into a "furrin" state. There was a big crowd at the Waterbury station when the special train rolled in a few minutes before nine. If, as reported, "there was more hand clapping than cheering—and there wasn't much hand clapping," it must be remembered that these were people who had never put a Democratic governor into the State House nor sent a Democrat to Congress since the birth of the Republican party. Besides, Vermonters are not demonstrative.

The president left Waterbury for the dam at Waterbury River. There, as he viewed the immense gully with its anthill activity, he commented: "It's a great sight—a great sight." The chief executive descended the steep valley to Waterbury, and,

winding upstream along the river road, next visited the completed
dam at Wrightsville. There he called the metropolitan reporters
to his car and told them he had "some educating to do." He outlined the history of the project, said that the last flood had come
within eight feet of the top of the dam, which saved Montpelier,
and concluded: "That is a very excellent illustration of co-operation between the government and the state in boondoggling!"
After posing with the flood basin in the background, the president
returned to Montpelier, where he participated in a flood-control
conference at the capitol. He then re-entered his open car and
started east along the river toward New Hampshire. Franklin
D. Roosevelt was leaving the Winooski valley.

3

The flood dams at Wrightsville and East Barre occupied
great numbers of men, who, in the height of the depression, had
perplexed Washington by marching in force upon it in a bonus
army. When, in late 1934, officers of the Army Engineers Reserve Corps began to visualize the end of their work at Wrightsville and East Barre, they started to cast about for a third project
in the Winooski valley that would keep their large force of
CCCs intact and working.

Near Waterbury in the valley of the Waterbury River tributary they studied a location that promised to be the most effective flood-control point in the whole river system, but they found
that most of the land in the valley was owned by the Green Mountain Power Corporation. Officials of the power company, however, after conferring with the army engineers, offered to give the
land to the state in return for power rights at the dam beyond the
requirements of flood control. Charles Smith, governor of Vermont, saw something for everybody in the new site. The lawless
Winooski, which had cost the people of Waterbury and the valley
below intermittent fear and suffering, would be incapable of rising
to harmful flood heights. The federal government would keep the

unemployed busy, and the power company would get the hydro-electric rights. An agreement was reached between the corporation, the state, the army engineers, and the national director of the CCC, and work began on the largest flood-control project of its type in the country.

When Roosevelt visited the partially completed dam in 1936 he apparently was not aware that the Green Mountain Power Corporation had the hydro rights to the dam. Engaging in the flood-control parley at Montpelier, his mind's eye saw a vast, government-sponsored TVA embracing the New England valleys.

Upon becoming governor of Vermont in 1936, George D. Aiken looked into the agreement for the Waterbury River Dam and was not pleased with what he found—he did not believe that power corporations should control the natural resources of the state. The Vermont legislature started an investigation and thoroughly aired the whole original agreement. The governor announced that he did not think Washington would finish the dam unless the Green Mountain Power Corporation made certain concessions. The concessions were made, new contracts were drawn up, and the completion of the dam was assured.

Meanwhile in Washington, though the army engineers had known all the past and present arrangements with the state and power company, the president apparently had not. When he found out, he was reported to be furious. He felt that where the federal government put money into flood-control projects *it* should have the power rights. The Democrats in Congress soon sponsored a bill which would give the government the authority to take in New England any lands that it saw fit for flood control. The bill furthermore stripped the army engineers of the privilege of saying whether power facilities should be installed in government-built dams. This was because of the unholy alliance at Waterbury River between the government and a private corporation—and the Administration was determined not to have it happen again. The authority to determine whether dams were suited for power was given to the Federal Power Commission, staffed with Roosevelt appointees. In the proposed bill a number of sites in the valley of the Connecticut River were earmarked for federal dams, and a principal one was in Vermont at Union Village.

Shortly before the Flood Control Bill emerged from the Congressional hopper for a vote, George Aiken, the intractable Yankee governor, declared at Plymouth, the birthplace of Calvin Coolidge, that he would not surrender the natural wealth of the state of Vermont to anyone. He pointed out that the state had entered into a flood-control pact with the other New England states, but this did not give the federal government blanket permission, as the bill before Congress contended, to take any Vermont lands it wanted without the formal agreement of the state.

> What Vermont asks is . . . the right to handle purely local affairs in our own way . . . to enter into agreements with any of our sister states on such matters as may concern our states alone; to continue, without interference, adhering to the principles of industry, self-reliance and self-respect, and to remain solvent. These things are our desires, to the attainment of which our efforts will be directed.

On June 15, 1938, Senators Ernest Gibson, Sr., and Warren Austin determined in the United States Senate to "talk as long as we can" to prevent acceptance of the Flood Control Bill. Despite their efforts the measure came to a vote, and with a 51-to-32 majority the government possessed the power to take lands for dams and reservoirs without the consent of the states. Only the Congressional delegation of Vermont voted solidly against the measure. The other New England states felt it hopeless to continue the fight. The Vermont senators resolved, however, that they would "resist this federal aggression with every legal means." "We are a small state," declared Austin in the senate,

> . . . We have a small population, 365,000 people, but they are attached to the land. On one highway, where my grandfather's farm was located, there are now five farms contiguous to each other, occupied by the direct lineal descendants of the first settlers of those farms . . . It was bred in us to fight for the integrity of the state.

President Roosevelt signed the Flood Control Bill at Hyde Park, June 29, 1938. He approved eleven million immediate dollars to start six dams on the Merrimack and Connecticut— including the one in Vermont at Union Village, and called for further flood-control plans on the Winooski, the Otter, and other Green Mountain rivers.

"The loss of a battle does not mean the loss of a war," rationalized Governor Aiken in Vermont. Warning that the basic issue was not power or flood control but one of maintaining a balance of power between the state and the federal government, he launched a campaign of rallying all the New England governors behind the States' Rights banner.

The dedication of the immense CCC dam on Waterbury River took place on October 29, 1938. Since this dam was state-owned, it was not involved in the controversy, and the ceremony proceeded in an atmosphere of amity. Roosevelt wrote that he was "delighted with what has been achieved in the Winooski valley," and when the commanding general of the First Corps Area handed the governor an immense key signifying the transfer of the site to the state, Aiken commented: "From the size of this key I would say that it would open the Panama Canal."

For months, however, the governor had been vigorously reiterating that the state of Vermont, despite the passage of a bill by Congress, would not give up any land to the federal government except by the formal agreement of the state legislature. On October 30, Aiken received notice that the War Department was willing to negotiate with the state for the flood-control lands. On January 8, 1939, the secretary of war had a mysterious change of heart. He informed Aiken that the War Department would proceed with the dam at Union Village, and there would be no contract with the state.

"I wouldn't want to question the faith of the president," commented Aiken, "but something has changed the mind of the War Department." On January 11 the governor convened the legislature of Vermont in a special session. A strange quiet pervaded the crowded House chamber as the governor reviewed the stand he had taken. He asked the legislature whether he should back down or continue the fight. "It is almost beyond belief that the federal government should consider the taking of our lands of so little importance that it doesn't even require a written agreement," Aiken declared. The legislature of one of the poorest states in the Union briefly considered the matter, then voted $67,500 to carry the fight through to the Supreme Court.

The next day the secretary of war announced that the blame for the delay in the flood-control work "lies squarely with the governor of Vermont." The secretary said he proposed to follow the same procedure in Vermont as he had in New York and in other states.

The newspapers reported that the "difference between 'giving' land and 'taking' it today precipitated New England into the latest battle in the old, old war of states' rights."

On January 13, 1939, the governors of all five of the New England states supported Aiken's point of view and demanded federal co-operation. The secretary to the president, Stephen Early, said: "If Vermont doesn't want the protection it doesn't have to have it. Other states want and can use the money."

"We are a little state in wealth," the Vermont governor at once asserted, "but there are some things more important than money . . . We ask that the agreement drawn up by the War Department—and we didn't write a word of it—be signed by them as well as by us. In refusing to do this, they have admitted that federal domination and not federal leadership is the secret purpose of the government at Washington."

Representative John Rankin, Mississippi spokesman for the Administration in the House, said that the power trust was behind Aiken in the controversy with the government. Aiken answered this by referring to his early comment about the CCC dam at Waterbury River: "I strongly recommend if any more so-called flood-control dams are constructed in Vermont, where power development is deemed likely or probable, that the title to such dams be held by the public for the benefit of all our people. No more entangling alliances with utility companies should be made."

In Congress, Rankin, a member of the House Appropriations Committee, suggested that Vermont "be given the right" to match the federal funds for repairing the damage that the hurricane of 1938 had done in Vermont—and that the federal appropriation be accordingly cut $2,000,000. To this Aiken replied: "The reasons given for this action were petulant and unworthy of Congressional committeemen. If they think they can impose their will upon New England by bribes or threats to induce us to give up to them our heritage and means of livelihood, they had better spend a little time reading New England history."

On January 17, 1939, Roosevelt at a press conference called the fight a tempest in a teapot. He said he didn't think the government had ever tried to take land from Vermont without the state's consent. The president indicated that he would try to reach a settlement in the dispute.

Democratic leaders held a series of conferences, and on May 10, 1939, the government announced that it was ready to go ahead with New England flood control pending permission from the state legislatures for the federal government to proceed.

On June 14, Governor Aiken announced: "The government has conceded the justice of our position."

The fight over New England rivers—in reality one for the control of hydroelectric power—continued. On July 15, 1939, when the New England flood-control project was well under way, Representative Rankin announced in the House that he would make every effort to have a little TVA in New England as soon as possible. The Supreme Court of the United States, overruling federal, district and circuit courts, and the attorneys general of forty-one states, decided late in 1940 that the federal government had authority not only over navigable rivers but over all waters which might be made navigable. Five of the justices reporting in the majority of the 6-to-2 decision, were appointed by President Roosevelt. The Second World War stalemated, for the time being, the advance of federalists up the rivers of the country.

The Winooski is not navigable today, and it is not federal— it is a Vermont river still. The dam at Waterbury River rises in massive dignity to the height of a 10-story building. It is the only dam ever built as the result of an agreement between the state, federal government, and private power company. The whir of turbines is not yet heard at Waterbury River—because the powerhouse has not yet been built. In the eventual circumstances of its building lies, perhaps, the key to the power riddle that faces Vermont and the country.

Today, proponents of state power, government power, and private power are still carrying on their three-cornered fight. Champions of state power distrust the encroachment of the federal government, point to the gross mismanagement of the private utilities during the 1920's and their control by the banks. They are not any more willing to have the private utilities dam up Vermont valleys than they are the federal government, and they are fighting the expansion of the utilities in Vermont despite the fact that there is no other agency to meet the rising demand for power. The New Deal is dead—but there are today many vigorous proponents of government power. They see, the country over, tremendous regional flood-control, irrigation, and power developments along the lines of the TVA. The point of view of the private utilities is expressed by the man who started it all, Thomas Edison:

There is far more danger in public monopoly, than there is in private monopoly, for when the government goes into business it can always shift its losses to the taxpayers. If it goes into the power business, it can pretend to sell cheap power and cover up its losses. The government never really goes into business, for it never makes ends meet, and that is the first requisite of business. It just mixes a little business with a lot of politics and no one ever gets a chance to find out what is actually going on.

30

MONTPELIER-ON-THE-ONION

$\mathcal{T}$HE dome of the Capitol has been staring into the Winooski since 1808 and the river has been staring back. There is no indication that both are not satisfied with what they see.

The first dome was over a belfry, perched on a three-story wooden building with front porches on the second and third floors. By 1832 representatives had whittled away most of the pine seats and the floors were incurably stained with tobacco juice. They voted a new State House, and by 1836 its fine granite features deserved the pride of the lawmakers who gathered in it for the first time that year.

On January 5, 1858, the janitors stacked the furnaces with four-foot wood to heat the State House for a Constitutional Convention scheduled for that day. They went home to supper leaving the cold air intakes closed and by seven o'clock flames from the windows showed orange in the river. From every direction men ran to the classic structure to save what could be moved. Several appeared with a large portrait of George Washington. The state librarian heaved books out a window into the snow. Firemen charged to the river with the intake hose, while others built a fire in the boiler of the steam pumper. But it was too cold for the engine, which quickly froze. The State House was presently an inferno and it remained for the unfortunate lawmakers to stand by only for whatever there was in it as a spectacle.

The bleak shell of granite that remained the next day caused a flare-up of one of the most persistent political skirmishes ever waged in the town of Montpelier. Lasting about ninety years, it has proved nothing so much as the stubborn resolution of the Vermont brand of Yankee. The fight was over the location of the capital. Burlington wanted it at Burlington; Montpelier wanted it where it was. The burning of the State House gave new hope to Burlington adherents, who had been agitating for a change since 1808, and when the governor called a session of the General Assembly to plan for a new State House on February 18, 1858, the battle was spiritedly resumed. During a seven-day exchange of insults every possible argument was set forth.

Unhealthful situation: Burlington claimed Montpelier was a pothole on a foggy riverbank and that lawmakers became sick immediately upon arrival. "If the State House had not been there, no man who was not fit for a place in the insane asylum would believe that its location in Montpelier could be thought of."

"The north and northwest winds," countered Montpelierites, "carry all the vapor and dampness of the lake from Plattsburg and throw them directly at Burlington." In order to keep warm, they said, residents of Burlington sealed their houses with double windows in November, which were never once opened until April.

Lack of Scenery: Montpelier had no beauty. How would Ethan Allen's monument look pushed up against a stony hill? . . . Montpelier had just enough scenery. It would be wrong to plant the capital on a spot with choice vistas of the mountains. "Even the temple of Jerusalem would look inferior against such a setting."

"Burlington has a fine view of the water; but there is water enough at Montpelier for a man to drink, or to drown himself in if he becomes melancholic, and what more is wanted?" Montpelier was the place for the capital since a handsome new building would show off by contrast.

Lack of Military Advantage: Burlington was dangerously situated. A capital there would be an excellent target for cannon balls of British ships coming up the lake.

Lack of Morals: Montpelier utterly disregarded the state prohibition law. Everybody drank in Montpelier . . . Had anyone forgotten the case of the pickpocket when the state fair was held at Burlington? If any liquor did come to Montpelier, it came from Burlington. On this subject Representative J. Door

Bradley from Brattleboro arose and stated: "It seems hardly fair to me to lay all our sins to the door of the town where we assemble. As a matter of fact the representative from Burlington and I had some brandy and water together, and the Senator from there gave me some gin. What is more it was an excellent article—and what was worst of all, he brought it from Burlington."

Mr. Woodward of Westford jumped up and announced

hotly: "I am authorized to state by the senator from Burlington that Mr. Bradley asked him if he had any gin and when he said he did that Mr. Bradley followed him into his room and didn't leave until every drop was gone."

The final vote was Montpelier—138; Burlington—80. The new State House would be built in Montpelier and the matter was closed, for the time being. Construction began. The Doric pillars for the portico were hauled over the ice of the river from the Barre quarries and the burned-out shell was rehabilitated. The result was an uncommonly handsome building which Stanford White, the eminent and widely traveled New York architect, judged the finest specimen of Greek architecture he had seen.

Even so, Burlington did not give up. A bill to move the capital appeared in nearly every session until 1900, and all the old accusations and counteraccusations were heard anew. Rare is the heated session of Vermont lawmakers without undercurrents of humor. An atmosphere of industry and dignity, however, usually prevails. Representatives from the state's eight small cities and 238 towns go to Montpelier to the detriment of their own farms and businesses. Their pay is slight and, since they desire purely to serve, graft is scarce in Montpelier. A story is told about a representative who had to make a considerable sacrifice to attend the legislature. After he had been in the House a week and not much had happened beyond organizing the business of the session, he leaned over and said to his seatmate: "I been here a week and they ain't asked me to do anythin' yet. My board and room has been costin' more than I figgered, so yestiday I took a job cuttin' ice down the river. I figgered if they need me, you could send fer me."

A session of the legislature is an object lesson in unvarnished talk and straight thinking. Whether they have had much formal education or not, representatives share an ability to get to the real issue of even a complex matter and make a fair-minded decision. They cannot be led, bulldozed, or propagandized. Those who try it have their projects backfire in their faces. Just where this clearness of vision comes from is somewhat a mystery, considering that many representatives live in isolated hill community towns. Certainly a true perspective of life and its problems is best learned near the land, and in Vermont Nature never allows men to forget her.

From the townships, represented every other January within the classic granite walls of the State House, men have gone out to become leaders in many fields of endeavor. Vermont has supplied forty railroad presidents, one hundred and three congressmen from twenty-seven states, and forty-nine college presidents. New York City has sixteen times as many people as the entire state of Vermont, yet two mayors of New York were Vermonters, another built its first elevated railroad, two others were president of the New York Stock Exchange and the New York Life Insurance Company. The Winooski valley has been the home of the country's greatest living philosopher, an editor of the New York *Times,* presidents of the American Telephone and Telegraph Company, the Western Electric Company, and the Baldwin Locomotive Works, and the first man to drive an automobile across the United States.

There is a man down the valley in Burlington who, whenever he is in town, prefers to work on the rare apple trees he is growing in the back yard. He grew up in Missisquoi river farm country and went to law school. He became mayor of the town of St. Albans, scene of the Civil War's northernmost Confederate raid, and gained attention as a negotiator in cases prominent in the affairs of the state and country. Even so, Warren Austin says he could not give a good extemporaneous talk. When he campaigned for the United States Senate in 1931, he memorized all his speeches. After fifteen years of quiet perseverance on Capitol Hill he received a telephone call from the White House—and the members of the Senate arose in spontaneous ovation. The lawyer from the valley of the Missisquoi and of the Winooski had become the first United States ambassador at the seat of the United Nations.

Montpelier's most famous citizen was probably George Dewey, who added to America's historic quotations by saying; "You may fire, Gridley, when ready." George was born in a small house on the riverbank almost opposite the capital. The admiral's first experience in navigation was at the age of thirteen when he undertook to drive a horse and wagon across the Winooski at high water in the spring. The wagon overturned and floated downstream while George, clinging to the horse, managed to make the bank safely. He frequented the swimming hole at the head of Main Street, and on other occasions while skating fell through air holes in the ice. He was acquainted with the water of a river at least by the time he went to Annapolis. He was one of fourteen men to finish the course in 1858, in time for action in various naval battles of the Civil War. By 1865 he was a lieutenant commander, and by 1888 a commodore, in charge of Bureau Equipment and Recruiting. In 1897 Redfield Proctor, Vermont senator and later secretary of war, suggested to President McKinley that Dewey would be a good man to command the Asiatic Fleet. McKinley agreed, and Dewey became an admiral. Not long after this he received orders to destroy the Spanish squadron at Manila, and with shouts of "Remember the Maine" rising from the throats of his men manning the guns, he did so.

This was an abbreviated type of war that could appeal to the country—all the excitement and glamour with few of the heartaches. Dewey was a hero. Congress passed an act to promote him to the rank of admiral and he therefore became the ranking officer of the Army and Navy of the United States. It also voted to present him a sword and accepted the design submitted by Tiffany and Company of New York. The hilt and certain other details were 22-karat gold. The guard of the hilt was an eagle whose claw grasped the handle. "The Eagle's expression is defiant, but a wreath of laurel in its beak indicates it is peacefully inclined." In the design were an admiral's oak leaves, the arms of the United States and the arms of Vermont with a scroll bearing the Vermont motto, "Freedom and Unity." The sharkskin grip was inlaid with stars and bound with gold wire. There was a monogram with the letters "G.D." and "U.S.N." in diamonds. The scabbard of fine steel damascened in gold, had a pattern of rosemarines, dolphins, Phoenician galleys, frequent Ds and an inscription to Dewey from the nation, in memory of the victory at Manila Bay, May 1, 1898.

A local boy had indeed made good. When he landed, New York's two-day celebration with guns, whistles and lights, spelling DEWEY on the Brooklyn Bridge, scarcely outdid that which had been held in Montpelier, where ten thousand people assembled. Flames two hundred feet high rose from a bonfire, bunting was everywhere, and lights on the dome of the Capitol shone in the river like a jeweled tiara.

> Oh, dewey was the morning
> Upon the first of May,
> And Dewey was the admiral
> Down on Manila Bay;
> And dewey were the regent's eyes,
> Them orbs of royal blue—
> And do we feel discouraged?
> We dew not think we dew.

Montpelier's Dewey celebration was somehow out of character. There had never been one like it before with the possible exception of Lafayette's visit in 1825, and there has never been one since with the possible exception of the visiting aviatrix, Amelia Earhart. As a rule Vermont does not go in for pomp and ceremony for prominent individuals, even if they are native sons. If a governor develops symptoms of ostentation, he is not likely to last long. One recent governor lived in a rooming house near the Capitol on State Street, and all governors within memory have eaten either at the Pavilion Hotel or in the restaurant at the Montpelier Tavern. The average Vermont Yankee would suffer deportation before he would "put on airs" for any reason, and hicks from the city who have tried it have experienced quick and devastating deflation.

The passion for balloon pricking in Vermont sometimes hurts—and it sometimes goes a little too far. In 1902 the D.A.R. decided to perpetuate the memory of General Lafayette's visit to the capital by attaching a bronze plaque to the Pavilion Hotel, a porch-encrusted brick landmark adjoining the State House. The first Pavilion was built in 1808 and the present one in 1876, on the foundation of the other. The hotel has always been Republican headquarters and today its mansard roof gazes into the river with the same Victorian reserve as it did the day it opened, when it was feted by all the governors of the New England states.

By February, 1903, the bronze tablet ordered by the D.A.R. had arrived. It bore the words: "The Marquis de Lafayette was entertained here on June 28th, 1825. Erected by the Daughters of the American Revolution." The unveiling was scheduled for February 23, and on the preceding night the tablet was riveted to the building and obscured by an American flag, which, in turn, was covered with a black cloth.

About noon the next day a stealthy figure approached the tablet, slipped something underneath the black cloth, and departed unnoticed by anyone. The band soon appeared, the ladies of the D.A.R., townspeople, and Joseph A. De Boer, spirited orator of the occasion. He delivered a high-toned address and closed with the words: "When the American flag is lifted, you will see words to be read by generations yet unborn."

The cloth was whisked away, the flag lifted, and on a card that just covered the tablet were these words: "Wilson's Whiskey —That's All."

Montpelier is today a town of eight thousand people, whose homes are perched on terraces carved from the banks of the Winooski at the junction of the Little North Branch, passing underneath the streets, and the main stream entering from the east. It is a Vermont town in every way except that it is larger than most. The green hills rising on every side are rampant with color on fall days and deep with snow in winter. The capital is as steadfastly Republican as ever and gives no indication of being shaken from this tradition, shared by no other state in the Union. Not that Democrats are alien to the town. Burlington, a city more along metropolitan lines, has sent many to the legislature and Montpelier through the years has had a few of its own. Democrats in Vermont post their candidate for governor purely as a matter of form. Republicanism is an immovable object and Democrats waste little money or time trying to be an irresistible force. Issues are fought out in the Republican primaries. From time to time there have been some warm controversies under Montpelier's gold dome, but there has been room enough within the Republican party itself to resolve the varying shades of opinion.

The recent Green Mountain Parkway dispute cut a wide swath through the Republican party. A mountain highway would have bisected the state had there not been more Republicans against it than Republicans for it. The river probably took more than casual interest in the parkway fight since Washington wanted to build a road from south to north over the highest ridges. The highway would have minimized the Winooski's importance as an east-west artery. Surrendering its sovereignty as the most-traveled route in the state comes hard even to a river.

"Many people," wrote Leon Gay, the president of the Vermont Historical Society in 1935 at the end of the dispute,

seem to feel that Vermont has nobly done its duty in not hitching her mountains together so that the tourist can go up and down all our peaks in one day, or quicker if super-powered cars are used. It would now seem that New York and Boston bus companies will not display the sign "Ride to Vermont over the top of all the Green Mountains and return for twenty dollars. We provide the lunches, give you five minutes on each mountain. Enjoy Vermont scenery while you ride" . . . Vermont has given a greater share of her young people to the nation than any other state and these native Vermonters have gone on to fame and fortune all over the country. The simple, rugged, independent life, with its church background, is the

reason . . . We are living in a fast-moving age. Good roads, the telephone, radio and automobiles are rapidly changing the habits of our
people. In many ways these inventions are a blessing, but they have
brought evils undreamed of by our forefathers . . .

Some of the arguments used in the battleground of the legislature were reminiscent of the fight to locate the capital. Unprece-
dented crowds pressed into the Senate and House chambers during
the hearings, which turned out to be a "regular Roman holiday of
oratory." There was shaggy-haired Representative Charles A.
Shields, who asked "rhetorical questions of the farthest corner of
the hall," Charles B. Adams, with his thumbs hooked in his vest
pockets and eyes squinting over the top of his glasses, Jeremiah
Evarts, with a pile of legal books stacked beside him to support his
arguments, and Representative Hale of Lunenberg, the 80-year-
old patriarch of the General Assembly, who made his arguments
against the parkway with almost religious fervor.

Every argument—economic, recreational, historical, aes-
thetic, legal, and religious—was thrown in.

"We desire freedom from the very things this parkway will
bring. Why should we spend $500,000 and give away 50,000
acres of land to get the people to come to Vermont when they are
coming anyway . . . ?"

"The legislature has no right to cede land to a 'foreign
sovereignty.' "

" . . . The grand old traditions of Ethan Allen want Vermont to remain as it is . . . "

"Of all men of Vermont Ethan Allen was unhampered by
tradition . . . Ethan was a revolutionist. If Ethan Allen were
here today, he would be for the parkway."

"If the Lord had wanted a parkway along the Green Mountains, the Lord would have put one there."

"My first drink from the spring in Smuggler's Notch was
taken from my cupped hands when there wasn't even a cracked
timber to suggest that others had been before me . . . I got

within a few rods of a fox before he saw me, for the wind was blowing from him to me . . . "

The Green Mountain Parkway was defeated, and the legislature went home. The golden dome of the Capitol stared into the Winooski and the river stared back. There was no indication that both were not completely satisfied with what they saw.

31

THE QUEEN CITY

$\mathcal{G}$RASSE Mount was the dream of Captain Thaddeus Tuttle whose sharp trading as a lawyer-merchant in Burlington at the turn of the nineteenth century made him rich. The first-growth logs of pine crowding the Winooski on their way to the lake and Canada further swelled Tuttle's fortune and that of his lumber partner, Ira Allen. In 1804, aged forty-six, Thaddeus watched his house take form at the crest of Ira's pine plains. Just above its solid masonry the University of Vermont was graduating its first class. From Pearl Street, two blocks away, sounded the hoofs of 8- and 10-horse teams drawing heavily laden canvas-covered "landships" to the river. Beyond the hill under the Falls, sloops exchanged cargoes of salt and molasses and rum for iron and potash.

By 1805 Grasse Mount's spacious rooms echoed the footsteps on the handsome curved staircase in the main hall—the Tuttles had moved in. The master of the house was busy charting the Winooski turnpike which would follow the river east to join the north end of Elijah Paine's turnpike at Montpelier. And he was also concerned with putting his erstwhile partner, Ira Allen, out of business. Though Tuttle had probably swindled Allen out of the land for Grasse Mount, his conscience did not prevent him from evicting his associate from his river home with forged documents. He wrote Ira:

> You will . . . take notice that the dwelling house wherein you now live . . . tract of land, tenements, mills, forges, the north half of the mill dam with all appurtenances and privileges . . . are now all owned by us

—as you may more fully discover in the Records in the Town Clerk's office . . . wherefore you are hereby required to quit the possession of said premises immediately and suffer us to enter in the peaceful enjoyment and occupancy—and on your refusal so to do we shall proceed to take such measures to force your compliance, as the law and our best discretion shall appear to justify.

From your most loving friends
Thaddeus Tuttle

——————————
——————————
——————————
——————————

Tuttle was destined to taste poverty himself, and justly so. By 1824 he, too, had overextended and was forced to sell Grasse Mount to Cornelius Van Ness, a Dutchman from New York. Tuttle moved to the small house on the corner of his estate, where he had carried on his mercantile trade, and there died in absolute poverty at the age of seventy-eight. Grasse Mount's new Dutch owner, who had come to Burlington to practice law, was shortly appointed district attorney for Vermont by President Madison. His greatest political achievement was the governorship of the state. Thus shone from the windows of Grasse Mount candlelight that reflected the gowns and jewels and crystal of state dinners.

There had been that evening in 1824, perhaps most memorable of all. The courtyard was bright with lamps of many colors suspended from the trees, and light came from every window of the mansion. The miniature of a hero was stamped on the gloves of the ladies now arriving. Old soldiers of the Revolution had come. The governor's elegant coach with its two footmen had gone up the turnpike along the river with a horse company to meet the procession from Montpelier. The great man and great moment arrived together. Applause greeted him as he entered the courtyard and passed through the graceful doorway. General Lafayette was within the walls of Grasse Mount!

Cornelius Van Ness, completing his second term as governor, aspired to the United States Senate. Since the incumbent senator, Horatio Seymour, did not intend to run again, Van Ness threw his hat into the ring. Seymour did run again and won by a small majority. Cornelius was ruined in Vermont politics but Andrew Jackson appointed him minister to Spain.

When the Van Ness family moved out of Grasse Mount, Heman Allen, Ira's nephew, moved in. With the death of his father, Heman had gone to live on the river with his uncle, who treated him as a son. Heman, in turn, stood by through the last disheartening years of Ira's life, salvaging what he could of the Onion River Land Company and fighting his legal battles. James Monroe appointed Heman the first minister to Chile and when he returned in 1828 "Chili" Allen went to live in Grasse Mount.

The seemingly endless timber of the Vermont hinterland was still tumbling down the Winooski in 1828. Burlington was already gaining a reputation as a hustling lumber center. Though river transport had established the first settlement in town near the Falls, a thriving colony now grew on the bay at the lake, where piers stretched into the water to service the lake steamboats. Midway on the hill between the river and the lake the occupants of Grasse Mount could observe the activities of both lake and river communities.

One day in 1834 there appeared these lines in the newspaper: "Died: at Grasse Mount, in this village on the evening of the 1st inst. Mrs. Elizabeth L. H. Allen, wife of the Hon. Heman Allen, late minister of the U. S. to the Court of Chili."

Henry Leavenworth, a Burlington lawyer, bought Grasse Mount in 1845 and opened streets through the vast acreage of the grounds, but he did not live there long. In 1853 Charles Marvin, a retired sea captain, who struck it rich in the California gold rush of '49, looked upon the face of Grasse Mount and was captured by its beauty. They say he paid an artist $10,000 to decorate the front rooms with a French design of cupids and garlands, a proper

background for the statuary he placed in niches of the walls. The grounds were an Eden of flower gardens and fruit trees, and the Marvins yielded as abundant a crop of children—there were five in Grasse Mount's new family. The friendly fireplaces which on winter nights over the years had warmed raconteurs of river and lake stories, now lent atmosphere to Captain Marvin's tales of the sea.

Grasse Mount, now fifty years old, still reigned as patriarch of Burlington mansions, but recent changes in the surroundings damaged its reputation. A steep, wooded ravine which ran from the Winooski through the center of town to the lake shore below bisected Burlington. In the upper town on the river, merchants in knee breeches entertained customers over glasses of grog in their small counting rooms, living a life almost apart from the people on the bay. As the colonies grew, they squeezed the ravine until the cleavage between the communities disappeared. When the railroad came through in '49, it displaced the brook along the bottom of the ravine. The soot from the engine blew up the hill toward Grasse Mount. Who knew when a spark would end the career of the stately edifice, by setting the town ablaze? The local newspaper took a more philosophical view: "In the summer the frogs and in winter the boys with their sleds had almost undisturbed possession. Now the railroad runs through the hollow and with its hurried stream of life crowds out of its bed the muddy brook. And so it goes. The changes crowd us as we write . . . changes in the men . . . and the children who play around the corners . . . and changes in the churchyard . . . "

Around the roof of Grasse Mount the urn-shaped finials of the white railing were poised in classic contrast to the smoky railroad and the

variety of nasty weatherproof, fat, lousy and lubberly hogs that have thrown themselves through the liquid mud of the streets. We noticed one of those shameless animals on Saturday, half as big as a barn, lying in the middle of the street, his eyes partly closed, his dirty ears slowly flapping, his fool of a tail just moving lazily in the mud, and his organs of articulation giving occasional birth to a self-satisfied grunt . . . If the selectmen, hog-heywards or Constables . . . don't put an end to it, let us have the cows and hogs counted as inhabitants, enjoying equal privileges with us all . . .

Standing at the head of a street four blocks below Grasse Mount is the Unitarian church, only twelve years younger than the old house. Paul Revere cast its bell and Charles Bulfinch, it is probable, proportioned its fine tower. A controversy now raged within its parish. After John Brown was hanged for trying to free the slaves in 1859, they brought his body north to Vermont. The Reverend Joshua Young, pastor of the Unitarian church in Burlington, accompanied it to its final resting place in the cold Adirondacks. There he gave John Brown's funeral sermon. It was the old, old story of the prophet's fate, said Joshua Young.

"Truth forever on the scaffold, wrong forever on the throne."
Paradoxically, the people of the largest town in the state, which
was first to prohibit slavery, did not see it that way. They called
Young "an anarchist, a traitor to his country, a blasphemer and a
vile associate of Garrison and Phillips." For delivering John
Brown's funeral sermon, the Burlington Unitarians dismissed him
from his pulpit.

In 1868, Lawrence Barnes, a Burlington lumberman,
bought Grasse Mount from Captain Marvin for $35,000. The
Winooski had given up most of its accessible timber. If the Burlington lumberyards were to keep alive, more lumber had to be
brought to feed them—and quickly. The new master of Grasse
Mount began bringing in logs from Canada by way of Lake
Champlain. Endless piles of dressed lumber mushroomed along
the lake front and were shipped out by rail and boat all over the
world. Burlington was soon the largest lumber center in New
England—in the entire country it was exceeded in size by only
two other ports. Although the Winooski had lost its lumber trade
to the lake, it found other industrial tasks. At the Falls the mills
around the site of Ira Allen's old shipyard grew to a great size
and the mill town of Winooski, directly across the river, developed apace. Kerseys, cassimeres, billiard cloths—a river's water
wheels could be infinitely resourceful.

At Grasse Mount Lawrence Barnes was adding a wing and
a glass spheroid conservatory. A cupola capped the alterations.
Barnes's wife, who found Captain Marvin's gardenias and cupids
on the walls distasteful, had the rooms done over in a geometric
pattern. Large black carpets with red roses and green leaves
covered the floors, a gilded B now graced the top of every window, and white Italian marble mantels rested over the five fireplaces on the first floor, and the four on the second. There was no
hope in trying to stem the tide. Even the proposed fountain in the
City Hall Park failed to escape. "The fountain will occupy the
center of the park and will be principally of iron from the orn-

amental works of Beebe and Company of New York. The principal figure will be a Neptune from the points of whose trident three streams will rise and fall into a spacious circular basin surrounded by a suitable grouping of stone tritons and dolphins in diverse attitudes . . . "

By 1880 street after street of fine homes with stained glass, gabled roofs, carriage houses, and expanses of tailored lawns evidenced the prosperity of the lumber barons. On the back of the mahogany directors' chairs of the Bank of Burlington were paintings of the directors' residences. The $100,000 Howard Opera House with its plush and gilt was not equaled in Washington or surpassed in Boston, and contributed to the lovely ordered life of the rich on the hill. Laborers could be owned for a dollar a day. There were enough inventions to ease life but not enough to hurry or change it. The telegraph had come to town in '48, then gaslights, a central water system, and the telephone. The Winooski and Burlington Horse Railroad Company would soon be replaced by the first electric trolley line in the state. The Barnes Hose Company had just won the great National Tournament in Chicago. On a local parade day the champions of the United States, bearing the name of Grasse Mount's squire, ran 900 feet to the hydrant, screwed on the nozzle, and raced 300 feet with the hose—time: 55⅞ seconds.

Lawrence Barnes's wife outlived him but when she died in 1894, Edward Wells purchased Grasse Mount. A patent medicine called Paine's Celery Compound made several distinct fortunes and built as many fine mansions on the hill for the various members of the Wells family. Paine's Celery Compound, "a Vermont Medicine that has the largest sale of any medicine in the world," was not all they manufactured in their Burlington drug firm, Wells & Richardson Company. There were Diamond Dyes, Lactated Food, Kidney-Wort and Improved Butter Color. "A lady uses some of their Diamond Dyes," explained promotional literature, "and finds that they do even more than she expected. This gives her confidence in the manufacturers and when she is looking for a food that will make her baby healthy and strong and hears that Wells and Richardson Co. make Lactated Food, she naturally tries that. Then if she is nervous and weak and learns that the firm who make Lactated Food, also prepare Paine's Celery Compound, she has confidence that this is a reliable remedy, and purchases a bottle."

Wells did not live in Grasse Mount but further divided the land, and, reserving a large lot for himself, sold the old mansion to the University of Vermont in 1895. The college made the house the first girls' dormitory. Grasse Mount has served well during its 50-year tour of duty as housemother to countless college girls. There have been times, as a dormitory, when the mansion has risen to the heights of the days of Cornelius Van Ness—years, for example, when the college presented plays on the wide wooded lawn.

Two arc lights, fastened up between the trees, gave the necessary illumination to the plot of ground which served as a stage, and its forest background of cedar and elm. During the evening the moon rose and its light showed up the outlines of the great old house, close by, and made the illusion of "a lawn before the duke's palace" complete. The close shrubbery, the low hanging evergreens and the huge elms, whose boughs fairly made a canopy over both audience and stage formed as close a resemblance as possible to the Forest of Arden and when Touchstone asserted, "Aye, now am I in Arden" his hearers could believe him without the slightest hesitation.

Main Street today is the principal thoroughfare in a well-painted city of thirty thousand people. It still rises from the lake to the crest of the hill by the college green, where it joins with the river road to Montpelier. The view to the east, of the rolling green hills and high mountains of the Winooski valley, is one of Burlington's permanent resources. So is the picture of blue Champlain with the Adirondacks beyond, a view which William Dean Howells considered superior to that of the Bay of Naples. There are human resources too—the French Canadians, the Italians, the Irish, and the old Yankees, whose northern-clime vitality have produced a handsome modern city far up in the cow country where you wouldn't expect to see one; a city which on occasion supplies the country with a John Dewey, an Atwater Kent, or a Warren Austin.

The lumber industry has waned. Rubberized fiber pads for automobile seats crowd from an extended row of machines in a factory where they used to make wooden iceboxes by hand. The trolley car and steam roller have gone the way of the watering trough and the hitching post. On Saturdays farmers from the far corners of the Winooski valley come into town to shop—but not behind a horse, as they did during Grasse Mount's first hundred years. And Main Street is far too busy to be roped off for "coasting," as it once was in the long leisurely winters of the nineties.

Change has come even to Grasse Mount's cellar. What was once a dining room for the help is now the laundry. The furnace is where the kitchen used to be and the once-spacious icebox, where hams and beef hung, is now a coal bin. But the face of the mansion is the same and its gold mirrors are as stately as ever. Today Grasse Mount shares with Main Street the traditions of 142 years. Such a privilege comes only to a river, a street, or a sturdy old house.

32

FOR THE GENIUS OF THE STUDENTS

*T*HE pupils, aged six to ten, arrive with their lunch boxes at 8:15. At 8:25 Mildred Bullock rings the bell whose clear tones announce the start of school. Standing behind their desks, the children first pledge allegiance to the flag. The Lord's Prayer is followed by a Bible verse or story and a song. Nineteen small pupils in the first three grades then explore the mysteries of the three R's. Meticulous planning by Mrs. Bullock enables her to carry on the work of all three grades in the same room. Somehow she manages to salvage time for slower pupils who need individual instruction.

On winter noons the Parent-Teacher Association of Calais provides hot dinners. In spring and fall the children carry their tin lunch boxes out under the trees in front of the school. Some of them report to Mrs. Bullock to dust the desks or carry water from the spring across the street. They do their chores agreeably and with the knowledge that the work is equally parceled out. This is accomplished by their club, to which each child pays dues of one cent a month. The president of the club, a third-grader elected by ballot, presides over weekly meetings which determine who will be the teacher's helpers for the following week. In one such meeting the children decided to store the school football, purchased by club funds, under Mrs. Bullock's desk for safekeeping.

Recently they voted to buy a clock for their schoolroom. When the motion was put, all but two girls voted for it by raising their hands. These two were first-graders who had apparently not quite understood the business before the meeting.

"Sandra, don't you want a clock?" asked the nine-year-old president. Sandra nodded. "Then raise your hand." Sandra did so.

"I guess you don't want a clock, Brenda."

"Yes, I *do!*" said Brenda.

"Well, raise your hand."

Triumphantly the president turned to the teacher. "What's that you say when everyone raises their hands, Mrs. Bullock?"

"It's unanimous."

"Unanimous," said the President. "We get the clock."

During the winter the children sell scrap iron and old paper to swell the club fund. Halloween and Christmas parties with their booths and grab bags, songs and plays, provide further revenue so that there is enough money for a present for each pupil on his birthday. Activities of the club prepare children to enter 4-H work, with its animal husbandry and forestry, its cooking and sewing.

Into all these activities parents enter wholeheartedly, for it is part of the heritage of Vermont that a child, however isolated his home, shall receive as much schooling as possible. It is a matter of pride to the people of Calais that most of Mildred Bullock's pupils graduate from high school, and some go on to college.

In rural areas during the past decades richer states have constructed district schools to which buses deliver hundreds of children from miles around each morning. But in recent years, some educators have decided that such mass training deprives the child of the third dimension of education—a dimension possessed in abundance by small schoolrooms.

For twenty-five years, in the afternoon when the sun makes yellow patterns in the schoolyard, she has watched the children start up the dirt road away from school. As in their parents, there will be in these children the strong democratic spirit that seems to dwell in the hills—for that spirit dwells in Mildred Bullock.

2

In the town of Northfield-on-the-Dog is a small plateau, elevated from rolling terrain and fringed in the distance by mountains. On the plateau is a quadrangle of buildings which flank the green carpet of the parade ground. The flagpole and two old caissons present to the visitor final and unmistakable evidence of the existence here of a military college, even if he has not seen the bronze plaque at the gateway to the reservation: "THIS INSTITUTION WAS FOUNDED UPON THE PRINCIPLE THAT A CITIZEN SOLDIERY IS ESSENTIAL TO THE MAINTENANCE OF FREE GOVERNMENT . . ."

In 1819 one of the early superintendents of West Point, Captain Alden Partridge, founded at Norwich, on the Vermont bank of the Connecticut River, the "American Literary, Scientific and Military Academy." For many years it waged a valiant if desperate struggle for existence. In 1866 it moved inland to Northfield on the Winooski's Dog River tributary. There it resumed the effort to procure an adequate staff, enough students, and buildings where they might be taught. The weariness of war that pervaded the country very nearly caused the school to close its doors, but it was able to limp along with the aid of a rich alumnus.

The visit in 1899 of Admiral George Dewey '55 to lay the cornerstone of Dewey Hall proved a lasting stimulus to the north-country academy, one of eight universities recognized as essentially military by the War Department. The physical plant on the Quadrangle began to grow. Below the plain a polo field was carved out of flat ground along the banks of the Dog River, and adjoining stables were built to house cavalry mounts.

The prospective cadet today does not have to pack two bunches of quills, candles, snuffers or shoe blacking, nor does he consider the old regulation prohibiting whiskers and beards, a hardship. But the Spartan life of cadets under Alden Partridge, who marched them about New England early in the nineteenth century, still typifies Norwich. Though Norwich is a liberal arts college, military trappings—drills and inspections—are the heart and substance of life on the Quadrangle. The six hundred cadets are organized into companies commanded by student officers. Military courts, presided over by cadet captains, deal with infractions of the rules. The commandant of the academy, a cavalry colonel bearing the title Professor of Military Science, is assisted by a teaching staff of regular army officers and enlisted men.

Though the United States abandoned cavalry training in the historic sense a number of years ago, the oldest military-collegiate institution in the country retained its horses until the summer of 1948. As in years past, when the entire army moved by horsepower, the cadets could until recently be seen riding their cavlary mounts about Vermont. The War Department recently sent $100,000 worth of modern war implements, ranging from tanks to skis, to set up at Norwich a Mountain Training Unit, the first of its kind in the country.

Near Dewey Hall on the Quadrangle stands, strangely enough, the United States Weather Bureau, which frequently announces temperatures colder than any other station in New England—sometimes 40 below. And yet reveille is sure to sound at 6:00 A.M. The Dog River is asleep then under its heavy casing of ice. The first rays of light have not yet illumined the mountain fringe, deep with snow. But the day on the Norwich plain has begun.

The valley of the upper Winooski lies from north to south, facing the winter sun. Sunlight drenches the land in summer, for the river has sculptured a wide, rolling valley that favors the sky. Here is a land, with its mosaic of planted fields, its red silos, and occasional white villages, that lives up to the eyes of the imagination. Plainfield is a town in this country. Its five hundred people work on the land, or in the two sawmills, or at trades, or in the stores.

On the outskirts of the town, a tree-bordered drive leads to a large house, once the manor of "Greatwood," a 200-acre estate. As you approach, the roar of a motor announces a tractor drawing a hayrack. Several young men, wearing blue-jeans, drive the tractor off into a field beyond the house. Near you, at the left of the entrance, a boy and a girl about eighteen years old are raking leaves. From somewhere come the faint strains of a violin selection from Mozart. Inside, in the room to the right of the front hall, a group of young people are seated in discussion. In the room to the left of the front hall is a library, and on the table are copies of *The Nation,* the New York *Times, Theatre Arts,* and the *National Geographic.*

This is Goddard College, whose ancestor, the liberal "Green Mountain Central Institute," was founded in Barre by Vermont Universalists in 1863.

The boys on the tractor and the boy and girl raking leaves are Goddard students. The college believes that too many young people today do not know how to use their hands. In the fields around the college they are required to learn. Between the first and second semesters students must hold down a job of some kind. For two months they become day laborers, store clerks, factory hands, waitresses, and nurses' aides.

The college conducts its affairs in the manner of its own community, the village of Plainfield. Every student, teacher, and employee has an equal vote in the College Community, and it is the community that manages the school. Visitors express astonishment at the informality and apparent lack of discipline, so completely different is Goddard. Each summer the college conducts its New England workshop. Farm and business prospects of the hill country, the region's arts and crafts are among the subjects that receive, in forums, the attention of teachers, industrialists, farmers, labor leaders, and students.

Goddard is one of Vermont's two educational experiments. The other, in southern Vermont, is Bennington College, established in 1932 on a plateau cupped by the Green Mountain and Taconic ranges. There, three hundred girls pursue art, literature, science, and social studies in an educational atmosphere unclouded by hour exams and finals. That such radical concepts of education should appear in a state so concerned with tradition proves the eternal enigma that is Vermont.

Through the years there have been a number of sectarian seminaries along the river. There is the Episcopal school at Rock Point, Mount St. Mary's Academy, and upstream at Montpelier there is the Vermont Junior College, formerly Montpelier Seminary, the oldest Methodist school in the country. Today, directly on the banks of the river at the gorge stand the buildings of the only 4-year sectarian college for men in the state.

Not many years after the death of Ethan Allen, his daughter, Fanny, a renowned beauty reacting perhaps against her father's Deist teachings, became a nun and entered Hŏtel-Dieu in Montreal, where she planned to spend her life taking care of the sick. She died in 1819 at the age of thirty-two. In 1894, six sisters from Hŏtel-Dieu journeyed to Winooski Park, the site of Ethan's old farm, and there founded the Fanny Allen Hospital. For ten years little further change occurred on the high, quiet promontory over the river at the gorge, but in 1904 a group of Catholic priests, suffering from nostalgia for their celebrated Mont-Saint-Michel, left France for Winooski Park to start a college. The French government had seized the schools they had established in Brittany and it had been necessary for most of them, members of the Society of St. Edmund, to journey to America and begin again. In Vermont, at Winooski Park, their sole possession was some land and one small building, which they had acquired from an old resident. Since they had little money, they lived largely off the land.

The strictly classical course of instruction, patterned after the lycée and taught by men trained in the universities of France, included our high school and two years of college. There were twenty-seven and a half students at St. Michael's on its opening day—a grammar school youngster accounting for the fraction.

By 1921 the number of students had increased many-fold and by 1931, when the high school was abandoned and St. Michael's became a college according to the American plan, the future of Winooski Park was assured. Today, the scene of intense activity on the promontory above the river matches that of other colleges which strive to feed and house the rush of GIs receiving an education under their Bill of Rights. Barracks moved from Fort Ethan Allen, a mile up the road, have become dormitories, classrooms, a mess hall, a library, and an auditorium. Carpenters and masons are occupied with permanent structures. The Sisters of St. Martha are busy in the household, true to their Biblical heritage, doing the things that keep more than seven hundred men housed and fed.

There are both Catholic and non-Catholic students at Winooski Park. Nineteen fathers and twenty-seven laymen teach St. Michael's courses in the various arts and sciences, and among the professors there are several who are not of the Catholic faith. This is unusual and is a tribute to the French fathers whose broad influence is still felt at St. Michael's. In a large frame building set in the midst of converted army barracks, the college last year helped to sponsor a summer stock company, the Ethan Allen Players, whose varied productions drew large audiences to Winooski Park. Throughout the season priests holding retreats and actresses rehearsing their lines shared the college paths.

Up the street, the hospital founded in memory of Fanny Allen still ministers to the sick with quiet efficiency, as she might wish. The colonial buildings that are rising above the river to complete the vision of the founders of St. Michael's should please even the bombastic frontiersman who was Fanny's father, for Winooski Park is, in a way, still a frontier.

A short distance downstream, on the opposite crest of the sand terraces that the river sculptured in glacial times, rises the brick tower of the Ira Allen Chapel. The high land between the lake and river has been the seat of the University of Vermont since 1800—but there were then few indications of academic life in Burlington. President Sanders was out felling pine trees in order to make room for buildings, and when he was doing that the wheels of learning ceased to turn; for Sanders was the whole faculty. He taught Latin and Greek, chemistry and mineralogy, anatomy, surgery, and belles-lettres.

The War of 1812 was the University of Vermont's first major pitfall. The prelude occurred on July 4, 1811, in the middle of the college green where five hundred people were attending a barbecue. As soon as they had devoured a large stuffed ox, which had been roasted in a nearby pit, the speechmaking began. One man called the officers of the government scoundrels, supported by knaves and fools. In a scene of utmost disorder partisans of war against England nearly mobbed him. The next morning a straw image ten feet high, swinging by a rope at the site of the barbecue, testified how political feeling was running. In the evening the dummy was ignited. The flames glared against the sky and cast their fitful image down College Street. When war came, the government seized the buildings President Sanders had laboriously erected, and the university had to dismiss the faculty and pack the students off to other colleges. The government did not pay for the use of the buildings during the war, and since many prospective students had gone or planned to go elsewhere, the college opened its doors in the most abject poverty in 1815. Poverty did not compromise its high principles one whit. There were thirty-two paragraphs of misdemeanors and criminal offenses, a violation of any item of which might cause a student to be "rusticated" (separated from the rest), or even expelled.

It is curious that the oldest university in the state should have failed to graduate a student before Middlebury College, founded at the turn of the eighteenth century on the Winooski's neighboring Otter Creek to the south, had done so. While the Burlington college was founded in 1791, it did not start functioning until 1800, because its benefactor, Ira Allen, was mixed up abroad in the affair of the muskets. This gave Ira's political enemies a chance to establish their own college in Middlebury. The founding fathers had the advice of Timothy Dwight, president of Yale, who had slogged down the banks of the Otter Creek to Middlebury in the fall of 1798 at the very time discussions about the new college were going on. When the miller and two doctors, conversing with Timothy Dwight, told him that the Burlington college had "relinquished both exertion and hope," he agreed that a college at Middlebury was desirable. Chartered shortly thereafter, Middlebury soon graduated its first student. There were thus, at the beginning of the nineteenth century, two colleges of the same type within thirty-eight miles of each other. Neither, of course, was coeducational, but there were "female seminaries" in both towns—and the one in Middlebury was conducted by the fiery champion of the oppressed sex— Emma Willard.

During its first decades Middlebury gained notably in prestige and size until, in 1836, it was almost as large as Harvard. In that year, however, a cyclone of radical evangelism blew over the campus in the person of Jedediah Burchard, past master of oratorical hell-fire and brimstone. The students and most of the townspeople started to brood about their souls and the town was presently embroiled in religious dissension. Within three years two-thirds of the student body had left. The Univeristy of Vermont, which had discarded theology and was pursuing Truth with scientific fervor, regarded the plight of Middlebury with amusement and interest, for the Burlington college, waging a spirited year-to-year fight to stay alive, had been clearly the underdog since the War of 1812.

Progress, however, was evident. It had been some time since the Vermont campus was a woods. With the advent of the 1820's students at Commencement wore ruffled shirts and wristbands, white gloves, standing collars, white cravats, black coats, "small clothes tied with ribbons at the knee," and slippers with silver buckles. Undergraduates who found it difficult to make ends meet wore woolen hose and powdered their hair with white flour. By 1823 the college had seventy students and a handsome, if scantily furnished, building. Colonel Buel's parlor carpet, however, was always available to hide the rough planks during public exhibitions. "It was of noble size and more than covered the area of the stage, and many an oration and poem . . . and colloquy was delivered from that carpet to an admiring audience." Fire reduced the fine building to rubble in 1824, a disaster that drove President Haskell out of his mind. The citizens of Burlington pledged a substantial sum for a new building, and when Lafayette visited the town in 1825 he laid the cornerstone.

During the administration of James Marsh, in the years that followed, the University of Vermont ascended heights of radicalism unscaled by any other college in the country. In 1829 Marsh published Coleridge's *Aids to Reflection,* with explanations and an introductory analysis. Transcendentalism—a philosphy that motivated Emerson, Thoreau, and a whole generation of American writers—was thus born at the university. Evaluating Coleridge's concept of the role of Imagination in the poet, as contrasted with that of Reason, Marsh's book proved to be, in the era's immutable pool of thought, the dropped pebble whose widening circles disturbed not only the country's literary, but its academic minds. The University of Vermont was the first American college with a department of English literature. Developing the idea of the "partial course," as in the sciences, it established a chemistry laboratory as early as 1832. Less than two decades after the death of Ira Allen it presented, as he had hoped, "the French and other languages of the present day and such other studies as might be most useful and applicable to the genius and views of the students . . ."

Middlebury, still prostrate from the blow administered by the radical evangelist in 1836, was reduced in faculty a decade later to the president and one professor. It was suggested that "Middlebury had done its work, nothing remained for her now, but calmly to fold her robes around her and lie down to her long repose." At the semicentennial celebration adrenalin was administered by loyal alumni who promised a program of financial revival. With one hundred students by 1860, the school was once again in cheerful circumstances—only to be rendered once again desolate by student enlistment in the Union Army. But Middlebury's severest years had passed. When, after decades of hot controversy, women were cautiously admitted in the fall of 1883, the college entered a new era of relative stability.

Fame in the hierarchy of colleges was, nevertheless, reserved for Middlebury until the twentieth century. It came more or less by way of a strange character named Joseph Battel, friend of the Morgan horse, archenemy of the horseless carriage, newspaper editor, rustic, scientist, and hotel proprietor. Battel had started an inn named Bread Loaf in the midst of the Green Mountains not far from Middlebury and had built up a large clientele of summer people who enjoyed his nature sermons and fist-shaking incompatibility with the motorcar. Battel wrote two large volumes called *Ellen, or The Whisperings of an Old Pine,* in the text of which everything that Battel or, seemingly, anybody knew about the world of physics, astronomy, biology, mathematics, medicine, architecture, et cetera—was revealed in a series of conferences between the beautiful Ellen and an old pine on the top of Lincoln Mountain. Battel bought the mountains within sight of the inn—about 30,000 acres worth—all of which passed in due time to Middlebury College. Thus began the

Bread Loaf Summer School of English, conducted now for a quarter of a century by luminaries of American letters.

Today, both Middlebury and the University of Vermont are prominent among the colleges of New England. The Burlington university is half under private and half under state auspices, with agriculture and technological schools and a fine medical college in addition to its liberal arts course. The large temporary classroom building and three new brick dormitories on the east campus, and the trailer colony by the baseball diamond on the banks of the river, are testimony of the housing shortage occasioned by the increased enrollment following the war. Similarly crowded are the sororities and fraternities, located in many of Burlington's old homes on the hill toward the lake.

As in all the other colleges along the river, the specter of bankruptcy has periodically stalked the campus of the University of Vermont during the past hundred years. President Guy Bailey died before the Second World War, leaving the college with a staggering debt. But he left it with fine new buildings and a heritage of service to the youth of Vermont, many of whom he financed out of his own pocket. There was an old lady named Winnie Bell Learned, who lived in Williston on Cherry Hill Farm. She wore high button shoes and dresses that hung down to the ground. On her farm she raised flowers, which for twenty-five years she brought into town in her Model T touring car. Few people knew that the money she made from her gladioli was putting young people through college. Those who knew considered that there was good reason for the University of Vermont sticker on the windshield of Miss Winnie Bell's Ford.

33

IN ITS TRUE COLORS

ℱARMERS' carts, 8-horse "landships," traveling vendors' wagons, and horses of itinerant preachers did not raise all the dust from the winding river road in the early days. Occasionally there rumbled from town to town carriages of traveling portrait painters. These men called at river farmhouses and for modest sums crudely represented on canvas the faces of housewives and children. Evidently the painters carried a number of "torsos" in stock—juvenile and adult, fat and thin. It was necessary only to attach the head to the prefabricated body and the painting was complete.

Itinerant painters fascinated Thomas Waterman Wood, who as a youth in Montpelier resolved to follow in their footsteps. By the time he reached his late twenties in the middle nineteenth century, he had outdistanced them; he had done portraits of wealthy patrons in Washington, Baltimore, and Canada and had embarked upon a series of "genre" pictures of life along the Winooski. For a study of a vendor by firelight, "The Yankee Pedlar," he used as a subject a Calais character known as Snapping Tucker. A Williamstown store became "The Village Post Office." "The Drunkard's Wife" depicted a tearful, shawl-draped woman holding a baby and belaboring a fat bartender outside a grogshop where her husband had passed out in the gutter. "Truant Gamblers" was a scene of boys with dice in a barn, and a man approaching with a pitchfork. "White Mice" was a portrait of a Negro child holding the rodents in an atmospheric barn. An old woman with her sewing basket became "A Stitch in Time."

Other titles were "A Pinch of Snuff," "The Glorious Fourth," "Coffee, Sir?" "The Faithful Nurse," "Raffling for the Goose" and "A Cogitation," which showed a Montpelier resident leaning on a pitchfork. *Harper's Weekly* bought this picture and published it with the caption "Is Greeley a Fool or a Knave?" Paradoxically, the Montpelier model, a man named Ripley, was an ardent supporter of his neighboring Vermont journalist, Horace Greeley.

Wood painted faithful reproductions of a number of European masters. Portraits of Americans like Andrew Carnegie, DeWitt Clinton, and Admiral Farragut financed his experimentation in techniques of drawing and etching. He paid the attention of a craftsman to composition, lighting, perspective, and detail, and his pictures were much admired in national exhibitions by his fellow artists as well as the public. They elected him vice-president of the National Academy of Design, a post which he held for eleven years. For eight more years, until 1899, he served as its president.

Many of Wood's pictures are as good as those of any artist of the romantic school, but in an age which scoffs at provincialism, bald-faced sentimentality, and painting things photographically, Wood has been largely forgotten.

Another early artist of the Winooski valley was Vermont's first Episcopal bishop, the father of thirteen children, John Henry Hopkins. He established a school near the mouth of the river, designed Gothic churches, wrote a great deal of poetry, composed hymns, and produced, by lithograph and water colors, America's first set of flower prints. His skill in meticulously reproducing the structure of the plant and imparting delicate gradations of color to its leaves and petals, dated from the days he had helped Alexander Wilson with his birds of America prints.

The pastoral quality of the countryside and the variousness of the hills and valleys have dominated the canvases of artists who have chosen to portray Vermont through the years. Today,

Paul Sample's pristine paintings of red barns and green hills, Luigi Lucioni's preoccupation with the infinite configurations of tree trunks, and Norman Rockwell's studied faces reflect little more inclination to experiment with the Vermont image than did the flower prints of John Hopkins and Thomas Wood's realistic sketches of rural life.

34

VOICES OF THE VALLEY

> Ho—all to the borders! Vermonters, come down,
> With your breeches of deer-skin, and jackets of brown;
> With your red woolen caps and your moccasins, come,
> To the gathering summons of trumpet and drum.

*V*ERMONT'S most celebrated poem was written incognito by a Quaker who feared that he had no business dealing with a warlike subject. The 17-stanza "Song of the Vermonters" therefore appeared in the *New England Magazine* in 1833 under the name of J. T. Buckingham, a friend of the author. But in 1877 John Greenleaf Whittier admitted in a letter to a Burlington friend that he had written the poem. The early struggles of a handful of men who waged war with human nature at large had for the moment triumphed over the Quaker in Whittier.

> Yet we owe no allegiance; we bow to no throne;
> Our ruler is law, and the law is our own;
> Our leaders themselves are our own fellow-men,
> Who can handle the sword, or the scythe, or the pen.

An admirer of Vermont, Whittier seemed to have learned well its geography and history.

> We've sheep on the hill sides; we've cows on the plain;
> And gay-tassled corn-fields, and rank growing grain;
> There are deer on the mountains; and wood-pigeons fly
> From the crack of our muskets, like clouds on the sky.

> And there's fish in our streamlets and rivers which take
> Their course from the hills to our broad-bosomed lake;
> Through rock-arched Winooski the salmon leaps free,
> And the portly shad follows all fresh from the sea.

Like a sun-beam the pickerel glides through his pool;
And the spotted trout sleeps where the water is cool; .
Or darts from his shelter of rock and of root
At the beaver's quick plunge, or the angler's pursuit.

Far from Michiscoui's wild valley to where
Poosumsuck steals down from his wood-circled lair,
From Shocticook river to Lutterlock town—
Ho—all to the rescue! Vermonters, come down!

America's first dramatist, Royall Tyler, for a time professor of law at the University of Vermont, was in the vanguard of the large company of writers who have tramped up and down the valleys through the years. Literary ministers like Nathan Perkins and Timothy Dwight jogged over the rough trails to record pioneer living. In the nineteenth century there came Walt Whitman and R. W. Emerson.

In his diary for August 12 and 13, 1868, Emerson wrote: "Traversed the banks and much of the bed of the Winooski River much admiring the falls, and the noble peaks of Mansfield and Camel's Hump . . . and the view of the Adirondacks across the Lake." He climbed Mansfield and looking down on a shimmering mountain pool, Lake of the Clouds, remarked: " . . . the party which reached the height a few moments before us had a tame cloud which floated by a little below them." Emerson stayed overnight at the hotel on the mountaintop.

The next morning a man went through the house ringing a large bell and shouting "Sunrise" and everybody dressed in haste and went down to the piazza. Mount Washington and the Franconia Mountains were already visible, and Ellen and I climbed now the *Nose,* to which the ascent is made easy by means of a stout rope firmly attached near the top, and reaching down to the bottom of the hill, near the House. Twenty people are using it at once at different heights. After many sharp looks at the heavens and the earth we descended to breakfast.

During the latter 1800's Vermont lost great numbers of her young people to the city's crescendo of disorder. But Rudyard Kipling chose the pastoral environment of the Green Mountains to write *The Jungle Books* and *Captains Courageous.* During the early years of the twentieth century, John Dewey—who had been born in Burlington in 1859—was pointing out that the artificiality of industrial life had severed people from a small community's "sharable situations" of living. The knowledge of vast numbers of people had become "spectator" knowledge, which was of small value compared to the knowledge of cause and effect gained by "doing." The foremost American philosopher has lived to see his ideas about occupational instruction woven into the country's fabric of education. How much Dewey's universal system of philosophy owes the experience he gained as a young man in Vermont may not be measured; but it was quite likely the proving ground of his thinking.

Contemporary writers have found in the Vermont hills a mental climate suitable to their labors. Sinclair Lewis, Dorothy Canfield Fisher, Ludwig Lewisohn, Robert Frost, Stewart Holbrook, Arthur Guiterman—the list is a varied one. The poet laureate of England, Robert Bridges, had a "Vermont Window" in his home at Oxford. The Winooski flows past birthplaces and homes of author, critic, and publisher unroiled. If Charles Edward Crane felt so inclined he could slingshot a stone into the river from his Montpelier office window. For his nature articles in the Metropolitan newspapers, Arthur Wallace Peach has tramped practically every square yard of the valley of the Dog. R. L. Duffus was born in Waterbury and Publisher John Farrar in Burlington, in which town the patriarchal Henry Holt built a Georgian mansion with a clover-leaf swimming pool, terraced gardens, and Mount Mansfield framed in his dining-room window.

Since the days of the Allens' "beech seal" war there has appeared from time to time poetry written by local bards who reached the periphery of national literary prominence. The work of others remains unsung outside the borders, yet this whole group has aptly distilled the flavor of Vermont. Barty Willard, a wheelwright in Burlington before the turn of the nineteenth century, could compose a jingle quite literally at the drop of a hat. The proprietor of a haberdashery one day scoffed at Willard's old hat and declared that if Barty could at once compose a rhyme about a hat he would give him a new one. Barty threw down his hat and began:

> There's my old hat
> And pray what of that,
> 'Tis as good as the rest of my raiment,
> If I buy me a better
> You'll make me your debtor,
> And send me to jail for the payment.

John G. Saxe, editor of a Burlington newspaper, gained considerable recognition with several published volumes of poems, most of them about Vermont.

> 'Tis here the Morgan horses and Black Hawk
>   steeds abound,
> For grace and beauty, strength and speed, their
>   equals can't be found;
> They will always "go it fleetly" and always
>   "come it strong."
> 'Tis my delight on a summer's night to sing
>   the Farmer's Song.

Rowland Robinson, a distinguished Vermont folklorist who lived in Ferrisburg, between the valleys of the Winooski and Otter Creek, drew his material from the environment about Rokeby, his home. In the words of his Sam Lovel:

"The air o' the woods tastes good to me, fer 'Thain't been breathed by nuthin but wild creatures. I luffter breathe it 'fore common folks has. The smell o' the woods tastes good tu me, dead leaves 'n' spruce boughs 'n' rotten wood, 'n' it don't hurt none if it's spiced up a lettle bit wi' skunk an' mink 'n' weasel an' fox p'fum'ry. An I luffter see trees 'at's older 'n any men, an' graound 't wan't never plauwed ner hoed, a-growin' nat'ral crops. 'N I luffter hear the stillness o' the woods, fer tis still there. Wind a-sythin, leaves a-rustlin', birds a-singin', even a blue jay a-squallin' haint noises. It takes folkes an' waggins an' cattle an' pigs an' seech to make a noise."

Dan Cady traveled about the Winooski valley in the early 1900's meticulously noting down the sights, sounds, smells and institutions of country life, preserved in several atmospheric volumes.

A house without a suller wall
Is jest no kind of house at all;
A mud, or Calafornie, sill
Would be taboo in Underhill;
They always excavate the spot
Beneath a building in Charlotte;
You find, jest as you' s'pose you would,
Vermont foundations pretty good—
But here's the gall inside the cup,
They every one need banking up.

No less moved to portray the Vermont handiwork of nature and men have been great numbers of citizens whose writing has found its way into various state publications. Of the origin of *Tah-wah-bede-e Wadso*—The Saddle Mountain—which became Lion Couchant, then Camel's Rump, later Camel's Hump; and its companion, Mount Mansfield, the Reverend Perrin B. Fiske speculated:

The Camel's Hump is there on high,
His head the sages think,
Is by the river's brink, where once
He ran to kneel and drink.
But stumbling in his thirsty haste
He threw his rider high,
And there lies Mansfield as he fell
A-staring at the sky.

Just who invented the lines by which thousands of New England school children learned their state capitals may never be known, but the words still echo in the back rooms of the memory:

Maine, Augusta on the *Kennebec*,
New Hampshire, Concord on the *Merrimac*,
Vermont, Montpelier on the *Onion* . . .

In 1926 the proprietor of the general store in North Montpelier, Walter Coates, suffered the loss of his only son. That year Coates published the first edition of *Driftwind—from the North Hills*, a wallpaper-covered, handset magazine of poetry and verse and homilies which proved the literary wealth that had been locked in the minds of Vermont farmers, clerks, and schoolteachers. A people sufficiently endowed with the art of the metaphor to comment of one of their state officers: "He's a fifteen-watt bulb but he burns all the time"; or, without benefit of metaphor: "It's going to take the country a long time to get over the good Roosevelt's done," merited such a vehicle of expression as *Driftwind*.

No contributor outstripped the farmer, teacher, minister, health officer, moderator, school director, justice of the peace, merchant and editor, whose own facile pen chronicled many a tale of the country and people about the Little North Branch.

PARDON JANES

The Mystery Man of Calais

Of Pardon, son of Solomon Janes, my story
    Will tell—this scion of a race whose sire
Once ruled the Puritans—whose rising glory
    Was blasted by an unfulfilled desire.

Four generations of red blood wrought him:
    His father, son of Irene Bradford Janes
Whose grandfather was William Bradford, taught him
    To prize this legacy within his veins.

Old Pardon Janes? These East Hill folk will tell you
    What Pardon was, though few may tell aright
The bitter disillusionment that fell to
    His lot, to blast the world within his sight.

Mere woman-hating crank, love-cracked he surely
    Was not, though that has been a common guess:
What wrecked his latter years is matter purely
    For inference,—he never would confess.

Old Janes was simple "Pardie" once—the dandy,
    The debonair of many a joyous dance
And husking where red ears and maids were handy
    And love walked arm in arm with young Romance.

A rising man was Pardon—yes, his neighbors
    Saw talent there; they thought his judgement sound:
On matters that concerned their town and labors
    They sought him, by his keen decisions bound.

To legislative halls his genious guided
    Him twice; distinction followed where he led;
And in forensic argument who sided
    With Pardon Jane's side came out ahead.

Cozened by men, an evil genious whirled him
    Up to what dazzling heights, what cherished goal?

Then what ill chance, chicane or misstep hurled him
    Down where mistrust of man ate out his soul?

Who knows? Who cares? Blight fell, bright eyes were
        clouded
And souls embittered then no less than now,—
    Back to the hills of home he went unshrouded
    In gloom, the maker of a cynic's vow.

"Whatever craft can steal true merit loses,"
    We hear him mutter; "faith in friendship dies;
He can put trust in humankind who chooses;
    I find them, men and women, vile with lies.

"I'll wear no clothing venal hands pernicious
    Have toucht (Fresh bolts of cotton, torn in strips,
He fashioned into robes); no taint of vicious
    Humans shall soil the things that pass my lips."

In dealings with the world the self-willed hater
    Bore his short-handled pitchfolk iron-wrought
And double-pronged, which served him as dumb waiter
    Working as hands, counting things sold or bought.

The wind-swept hill, the house, the restless spirit
    That trod its pine-board floors in robe of white,
The square box stove, the barrel, the spider near to
    The eerie pitchfork and the anchorite!

There on the hill his bones rest, but his spirit
    Haunts the town's rumor with an untold woe,
And the sunk grave mutters to such as hear it
    The tragedy that lies lip-locked below.

35

ECHOES AND OVERTONES

$\mathcal{T}$HE Mad River, which enters the Winooski at Middlesex, winds for miles from the south through a narrow cleft in the mountains. A tillable field at river level occasionally breaks the rhythm of hills but the theme of this land is its forests. As if challenged by the leaf trees' fall symphony of color, the evergreens permeate the air with fragrance, and on windy days with a chorused dirge. The smokestack's plume of steam above buildings clustered around the millpond, piles of uncut logs and dressed lumber, and a windowful of wool plaid shirts in Moretown's general store testify to the eye (as does the whine of saws to the ear) that trees dominate the villages as well as the fields.

Beyond Moretown's general store and its schoolhouse is a rise of ground on which stands a rather large frame house of nondescript architecture. At twelve o'clock noon any day of the year except Sunday, a well-worn pickup truck rattles up the street and swings into the driveway. A man of seventy, with gray hair and a face marked with the lines of outdoor life, gets out and enters the house. After dinner he may loosen his scuffed, high-laced shoes and lie down on the settee; but Burton Ward is soon off down the road again in his truck. In the summer of 1946 a spark from a distant flaming roof ignited his farm, about three miles from town, and burned the house and barn to the ground. He could have let the land grow up to trees because he didn't need the farm, but he could not imagine the land without buildings. He is just now finishing the new 125-foot barn and the house, which with a few men he built last year. When the buildings are completed he will sell them for a modest sum, as he did the land

245

for the large skiing development at Mad River Glen. Then he will have to find some other project to keep productive now that his son Merlin is running the two lumber mills and the general store.

Burton Ward's father, Hiram O., built a dam on the Mad River in 1842 and set up a sawmill in which he made shipping crates out of the million feet of lumber he cut annually from the hills around Moretown. Today, Hiram's great-grandsons, who work around the mills summers, have prospects of going into the lumber business. The reason is that for every tree cut down by the Wards over the past four decades they have planted one. A husky grove of trees below the town, set out years ago by Burton Ward to pay for his grandsons' college educations, will do just that. In thirty years he has planted nearly a million trees on the 22,000 acres of land he owns in fourteen townships.

Burton Ward's headquarters is his general store and post office, the nerve center of Moretown. His son, Merlin, is postmaster and manager, and Merlin's wife, whom the people recently sent to the legislature—and who is chairman of the Board of School Directors on the State Education Committee—helps dispense the mail and wait on trade. Villagers frequently telephone Mrs. Ward to ask if they got a postcard, and if so, would she read it over the phone. Those who want goods from the Sears, Roebuck catalogue are also accustomed to calling in. Mrs. Ward writes the money orders, adds the sum to their bills at the store, and phones them when the Sears, Roebuck merchandise arrives. There are not many items that cannot be bought right in Moretown. Ward's store offers underwear, roller skates, nail polish, toasters, Wampole's Cod Liver Oil, birthday cards, suspenders, ice cream, dresses, flashlights, detective mysteries, shoes, horse collars, hair nets, glue, rubber balls, flit guns, yarn, beef, grass seed, wallpaper, mousetraps, and root beer. On Monday nights the store opens at 7:30 and is soon filled with townspeople and the men who come down from the lumber camps in their woolen shirts and overshoes. They quickly dispose of the week's events, current lumber operations, the political situation, and the weather.

The store, the two mills, and the various projects in the woods tax the energies of the Wards. Burton had another son, Kenneth, who went to Dartmouth College and for some time served as mill superintendent. One day, while playing with his boys, he was struck on the side of the head by a baseball. During the weeks that followed a haunting, almost moribund expression

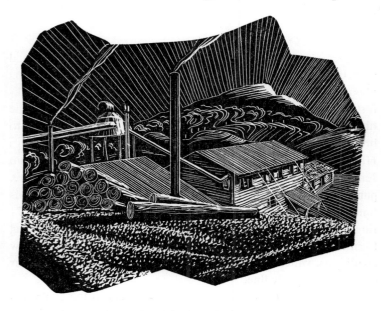

appeared in his eyes. He complained that in the plays put on by the village he could not commit his part as he used to. A brain surgeon in Montreal found a tumor, perhaps aggravated by the blow he had received. Nothing could be done and the strapping, tireless young man was soon dead. Burton Ward's impassive Vermont face became somewhat more deeply lined. There are still, of course, his other son and his five grandchildren, and there is consolation such as only the people of a village like Moretown can give—the people whom he has in turn sustained through prosperity and depression.

There are also the trees. Not so many years ago he seeded a distant field choked with wild grass. During the next two years whenever he studied it from a distance he could see no indication of new growth of any kind. But at the end of the second year one day when frosts had killed the grass and weeds, and there was a fresh snowfall, he looked across the hills to his field and saw the green heads of thousands of young pines above the snow.

2

Before the sky over the rim of mountains to the east is tinted with the cold pink of a new skiing day, Jenny Gale is moving about in her tidy kitchen firing up the range and preparing breakfast for a bulging household. She sets up one long table in the dining room and one in the living room. A stampede down to breakfast occurs about 8:30. The skiers get cooked cereal, eggs (from Jenny's hens), bacon, all the milk they can drink (from Jenny's cows), homemade doughnuts, and every other morning, pancakes and maple syrup (from Jenny's sugar bush). About this time the crank-type telephone on the kitchen wall (number 57–ring 5) rings five times. Ski-tow manager Charlie Lord is calling from the top of the mountain with a report on weather and snow conditions, which Jenny passes on to the skiers and to the four others on the party line.

At 9:30 the bus arrives to take the skiers to the cable lifts that transport them to the mountaintop. Before they depart Jenny has probably lent one of her boarders her husband's old raccoon coat or his mittens. Jenny, a spry gray-haired woman, whose grandmother's uncle arrived by pack horse to clear the trees in 1791, then washes the dishes and makes beds in the nine rooms occupied by skiers. On a farm of 90 cows, 100 hens, two horses, and two dogs there are farm chores to do. To occupy her spare time she is treasurer of the Stowe-Mansfield Association, clerk of the School Board and associate editor of the *Mountain News,* which prints information about the town's extensive ski project.

She first took in skiers in 1934. At that time Mansfield was simply the highest mountain in Vermont. Since 1921 summer tourists had been able to climb by road up 4,300 feet to an old hotel at the summit, where they could view the valley of the Winooski, Lake Champlain, and the Adirondacks forty miles away. But after the first snow flew, the mountain was abandoned to the natives. A few residents recall skiing as early as 1902 on thin homemade slabs with toe straps. It was not until about 1931 that skiers appeared along the logging trails. Sensing that a new era was at hand, the townspeople, headed by lumberman Craig Burt, set out with axes and picks to clear the first ski trails.

In 1934 the first ski train arrived from New York via the Central Vermont Railroad. Since the skiers had each paid a lump sum for all expenses, everybody in town was supposed to provide identical meals.

"There was friction between the two inns and the private houses during the first years," Jenny recalls. "The inns thought we might feed better than they could afford to. Worst of it was we were supposed to have exactly the same meals. Supposing you'd put up more raspberries than strawberries—then what?" Ski instructor Sepp Ruschp, a pupil of Hannes Schneider, arrived from Linz, Austria, in 1936, having critically examined our eastern mountain ranges, and plumped for Mansfield, which has a snowfall equal to that of most of the Rockies.

In the summer and fall of 1946 you could hear the tapping of hammers along the main street of Stowe. The smell of paint wafted from doorways. Some houses were annexing ells. A few residents, having reappraised their houses, were tearing off front verandas and giving the 125-year-old bricks a fresh coat of white—all they have to do to produce colonial facades that people pay thousands to reproduce today. Booth's restaurant, which has murals of ski characters of all ages gliding down the walls, including an old gent with a beard, pipe, and swallowtail coat, was freshening up its dining room. Silas Stebbins was stocking up his meat market and grocery store. Gale Shaw was rationing time between his dry goods emporium, the Stowe woodworking plant, and the new ski lift. McMahon's general store was getting in a stock of sweaters and mittens to supply New Yorkers who come underdressed. Milkman Carroll Pike was arranging to step up his daily 400-quart milk supply. A. Clovis Couture was fixing up his taxi. Edmund Wells, blacksmith, was ready for his annual bout with broken ski bindings.

The Stowe-Mansfield Association, whose members accommodate skiers, surveys its mountain and its township of sixteen hundred people in the valley with a now-practiced eye. Since the start it has had to deal with operators from the outside who would turn Mansfield into a hot-dog stand. "If they'd put up big hotels, we might have let our farms go, hired out to the hotels, and during the war would have been on our uppers," Jenny declares. Stowe's experience with big hotels is still fresh in its mind. Nine men from New York, Boston, and Montreal built one with two hundred rooms on the town's main street in 1863. It had a big lobby, parlors, livery, bowling alley, a park, and a pond for fishing and boating in summer and skating and curling in winter. "Hall's Band" of Boston furnished music for the opening in 1864. High society from all over the East was brought to Stowe from the Waterbury railroad station in 4-horse Concord coaches —the Pullmans of the stagecoach era. As went the hotel, so went the village for twenty-five years until one brisk day in early October, 1889, it caught fire. Though farmers from miles around dropped their tools and rushed to the scene, there was no saving the wooden rambler. Flames were soon shooting from a thousand windows. Next morning the big hotel era in Stowe was over. Since the operators chose not to rebuild, Stowe suffered a painful period of reorientation as a small Vermont town without benefit of tourist trade. Today its citizens would rather not be dependent on hotels, skiing, or other conditions beyond their control. The town will expand as it can, adjust carefully.

"Craig Burt puts it this way," says Jenny. "We mustn't sell skiing by the yard—like cambric cloth." The Ranch Camp, a rustic lodge in the woods where trails come together and where supplies are delivered by dog team, is more the Stowe idea. It used to be a camp for lumberjacks. In 1933 a series of historic bean dinners were held there during which five bushels of beans and 248 pounds of potted beef and salt pork were consumed. The camp hasn't changed much except that skiers stay there now. Each guest makes his bed. Recently, former guests were asked if they wished to suggest changes in the Ranch Camp. All except one wrote back, "No changes." The one exception suggested several improvements and added, "But this would change the camp and I wouldn't like it."

Having lived in an atmosphere of schusses and Christies for the past ten years, there is little, at least theoretically, that Jenny doesn't know about skiing. On bad days skiers pound the upright piano in the living room, play cards, visit their friends up and down the road between the mountain and town, or try their hand at milking cows. Before he died in 1945, Ed Gale, who was born in '68, occupied their idle time with stories. There was Ira Allen's exploratory expedition to Mansfield, Nathan Robinson, Esquire, who moved into town in 1798 to start a hotel with a thousand silver dollars hidden in a barrel of beans, Smuggler's Notch and Dead Horse Hill; and more recently there were the visits of the Vanderbilts in coach-and-four, as well as Henry Ford, Thomas Edison, and Harvey Firestone on one of their camping trips. "Ed could tell the yarns."

A certain number of Stowe's guests come decked out in sweaters trimmed with antelopes, just to stand around. "Ski clothes and equipment run into money," says Jenny, looking over her glasses. "Hardly worth it if they don't intend to ski."

The Blue Laws have only recently been lifted in Vermont.

There is some feeling, particularly among older residents in Stowe, against hilarity on Sunday or any other form of moral laxity. This is understandable in a town during whose history upwards of 175 couples have been married fifty years or more. The people of Stowe, it has been observed, do not consider marriage an experiment. One Sunday evening the skiers lodged at the home of Arba Pike, an old-time resident, decided to move the chairs back and play leapfrog. Unable to do much to break up the game, Arba pulled down all the curtains so at least the neighbors wouldn't see. Entering into the spirit of this, the skiers put the curtains back up. Arba pulled them down. The skiers put them up—and so on into the evening.

The over-all impression made by Stowe on outsiders from everywhere is positive. Even the Swiss are not strangers to Rocky River Farm. Jenny had a group of twelve one Christmas. "They cooked Swiss dishes on the range and sang Swiss songs. They mixed a drink made from bags of nuts, spices, and sour wine which they brought with them. The odor was good but we couldn't agree on the taste."

Toward evening, after the skiers dive into her good round farm supper and she washes and puts away her dishes, Jenny is apt to go to the window. The sky over the mountain looks pleasantly threatening.

"Feels like snow," she comments buoyantly. "Guess I'll go down and fire up."

3

Across the valley from Jenny Gale, high on a wild road that follows Miller Brook, a rushing stream that drains Lake Mansfield into the Winooski's Waterbury River—lives Clyde Brink. His farmhouse could stand painting and the barn a little shoring up, but the roof doesn't leak and he's stacked plenty of wood for the winter.

"Not much of a farm right now," admits Clyde, "but

they's two hundred acres of timberland and prob'ly fifteen to twenty acres of tillable land more'r less. My wife's mother's lived on the place fifty-five years come this fall. She's an aged lady now—'twould be a shame to move her. PLACE SUITS US, DOESN'T IT, MA! (She's a little hard a hearin'.)"

"Ma," declares Leola Brink, "was a Russell. Her grandfather, my great-grandfather, was Byron Russell, born up here in 1821 before it was Stowe when 'twas the town of Mansfield. When he was twenty-seven he led a bear hunt through Nebraskie Notch; they was four of 'em on the hunt. They walked all night and come mornin' Byron Russell flushed two bears. Well, he only had an ax and by the time he'd hollered fer the others the bears had a head start. They followed the tracks toward West Cambridge and all of a sudden they come to the end of the tracks—no brook, no cave, no bare rock—nothin'. Back a ways was a ledge and By says to 'em, 'Bar's'll do that. They stopped dead, then walked back'ards, steppin' in their own tracks till they come to this ledge. Then they jumped sideways over the ledge an jes' walked off.' Well, they got the bears anyways and collected the bounties."

"Them people," says Clyde Brink, "would go into the woods with an ax, hew 'em out a house and put it together with wooden pins—cut their own shingles with shingle trees. They's a man lived up here on Hedgehog Hill—jest ledges—name was William Pratt. Had gray hair and a beard—remember him well. He built a house up there and raised fourteen children—some of 'em livin' now. Did it with hard work. The Pratts'd go to bed when 'twas dark and they was up at the first peep of day. He only bought five gallons of kerosene a year, ten pounds of white sugar—because he had his own sugar bush—sodie, a little salt; had his own cider mill, hen house, and blacksmith shop. They made their own snowshoes, tanned their own hides, and made their own lacin's. Melvina—she was his wife—would milk cows and make butter —pack it in tubs. She'd drive the geese back and forth to pasture

and go hayin' with William up on the hill that heads toward Hard-
wood Flats. They'd roll the hay right down the hill. William had
a yoke of red steers—drove either one just as you would a horse.
Course he had to put the collar on upside down. When he was
young he got into his mother's lye—she was goin' to make soap.
Well, he ate the palate right out of his mouth, couldn't speak
good. Never got mad, never swore—he'd jes' say, 'Doy all hop
up!' or 'By jolly.' Used to go round to the neighbors with an
auger borin' pump logs before they was any pipe around. Can see
'em goin' by now. Went to town once in a while. Had an old-
fashioned buckboard—middle was bellied right down to the
ground, no springs—jes' slats."

   " 'Bout two Sundays a year," says Leola, "they'd go by in
their best wagon. Melvina'd have on long skirts, tight waist, and a
strawberry hat set right down on top of her head with elastic."

   "Really went to town when they started," agrees Clyde.
"They had more fun than the Indians. Them old people was
sincere—if they liked you they liked you. Today they like you if
you'll tote 'em around somewheres."

   "Don't seem to me," says Leola, pouring water into the hot-
water trough hitched to the coal stove, "that people live any more
—seems if they don't stop to live. Today you got to get a car and
go somewheres. We've always stayed put right here—plenty of
work and plenty of fun too. I've got six hundred quarts canned
down cellar and I'm not through either. Fruits and vegetables,
jams and jellies, peaches and plums—our own beef and pork, and
cure our own hams. We don't have to go to the store every night
for our feed—never had to. Why, Ma used to make her own soap
here—set up barrels full of ashes, put water in it, and let it drip
through. When it drains out—that's lye. They'd save their fats
and bones and boil it with lye in a big caldron outdoors. ALWAYS
HAD A BARREL OF SOAP DOWN CELLAR, DIDN'T YOU, MA?
Owned their own sheep and sheared 'em, spun their wool and
made the boys' mittens and the girls' stockin's. They had one day

set aside to make their own tallow candles, enough for a year's supply. Dried their own beans and corn and ham for succotash. Ev'ry so often they had quiltin' or apple-parin' bees. Some would pare, some would slice, and some would string. Look at the girls today—why, they ain't one in twenty-five that can sew or cook! We're old-fashioned and you won't believe it but we never had a radio till two years ago come Feb'uary and we don't like all the talk on it now."

"Never owned but one car—bought that last year," Clyde says. "We always had a horse, and a good one too, and I don't mean presume so, either. She was thirty-three years old but she'd make the village in fifty-five minutes—that's seven miles of hills. That mare would skim the ground jest like a swallow. Short legs and a heavy chest. Didn't weigh no more'n nine hundred and a half, but more horse per pound than any you ever see. Course, she was a little might notional—there was usu'lly some trick or other they'd do. She'd stand all day with a blanket over her but when you backed her out you wanted to be in your seat, mister. If I had my mare now—she was a Morgan—you could drive that car away and do whatever you was a mind to with it. You need a bushel of nerves to work on them things—always somethin' 'bout 'em that ain't quite right."

"All that wants to live in the city can live there," declares Leola. "A lot of 'em is in that time-payment plan pretty heavy, tryin' to keep up with the Joneses. And they's a lot more that never done a tap of work in their lives. This handout business ain't doin' the country any good. Of course," says Leola, turning up the wick in the Aladdin lamp, "a lot of people try to make out we're pretty hicky up here. Mebbe so."

"Mebbe not, too," says Clyde. "Mister—we've got things up in this country!"

4

The hardest time for Lucette Varin to get up is in winter at six o'clock in the morning when it is not yet light. A tall, dark, rather slight girl, she is already on her way to work at 6:15 when the whistle blows at the American Woolen Company a few blocks away from her home at 6 West Street in Winooski. Often, the plow has not yet cleared the sidewalks and cars have not made tracks in the street, so she has to wade through snow almost up to her knees.

She crosses the bridge over the ice-stilled river and is outside the Chase Mills plant at 6:30 when the night shift quits. She climbs the stairs to her machine on the third floor and is ready to start her 160 bobbins at a given signal, as are hundreds of others on the same shift. In the three factories on both sides of the river are twenty acres of floor space loaded with machinery run by two thousand Lucette Varins, who turn raw wool into finished cloth, dyed, shrunk, and ready for the market. During the war they made material for 4,841,200 GI blankets, 4,000,000 GI overcoats, and 2,300,000 GI uniforms, as well as cloth for overcoat linings and sleeping bags. History in the mills repeats itself. Built in 1835, one of them produced goods for the Union Army during the Civil War, and two of them made clothing for dough-boys in the First World War. They are making some gabardines and plaids now, but orders for khaki are still heavy.

"I will be glad when we get off khaki," Lucette says. "There has been hardly anything but khaki, khaki, khaki for seven years." She hears they are going onto green dye. Even so, her work cannot change since her machine operates the same way whatever the color of the wool.

Each floor of the three factories is a sea of machinery, and each ceiling a maze of belts and wheels. Every machine has its specific place in the drawn-out process of cleaning and combing the raw wool, of sorting and grading it, twisting it and drawing it into strands, of spinning, winding, and weaving it into fabric, and washing, rinsing, dyeing, shrinking, and drying the cloth. Though the machines have changed, they have been doing the

same general work since 1835, as has the river that powers the
machinery of the mills and washes, rinses, and dyes. Once, the
Winooski turned wheels directly belted to the machinery, then it
supplied water for the huge steam engines, and now it spins electric turbines in the powerhouse; but the pattern of its work at
the mills is the same.

The day is long for Lucette Varin. The work is not hard—
it is monotonous. "You watch the bobbins go round and round,
and spend most of your time smoking." But she would not do anything else. She takes home over $30 a week, and that is much more
than the girls who work in the five-and-ten are getting. It is not
so much the work she likes, it is the money, and she considers she
gets pretty good pay for a girl who has not had the opportunity
for much education.

When the whistle blows at the end of her shift she joins
the rush for the staircase and is soon out in the cold winter air on
her way home. With her are men and women of many nationalities, some of whom have worked in the mills since they were
twelve years old.

Lucette's boy friend, Arthur Liberty, may stop by to see her
or, if the weather is good, take her out on his Indian motorcycle.
Every Sunday they take a trip on it to Montpelier, Barre, Plattsburg, or some place like that. She wants someday to bail out of a
plane in a parachute, but she likes to ride on Arthur's motorcycle
because it is the nearest thing to an airplane. They are both members of the Champlain Motorcycle Club, which meets every
Thursday night and every so often stages a "blowout."

Lucette finds it hard to hold onto her pay. She likes nice
clothes and trades in the best store in Burlington, across the river.
She has bought a phonograph combination and has records made
by most of the good bands. When she was in Kentucky last year
she bought a large plaster of Paris frog with a baby frog on its back,
a plaster of Paris Spitz dog, and a deer about two and a half feet
high, which cost her two weeks' pay. The conductor told her that

no animals were allowed on the train, but she got back to Winooski with them all right, except that one of the deer's horns was cracked. She has them in the living room in the house on West Street where she lives with her sister and mother.

She is not sure but that she was happier on the farm in Colchester where they grew up. Life in the fields was free and at the end of the day they felt as if they'd done something. But her family did not own the farm and when the man who did, sold it, the Varins had to move to Winooski. In their Winooski home they are much better off, Lucette feels, than a lot of people. There are many families who were out of work when the mills closed during the last depression, and they had to get in debt to keep going. The Varins have almost everything they want—except possibly a front-room set.

On the wall in the most prominent place in the living room is a picture of Paul Varin. Paul was nineteen when he was killed on the beach in Normandy. They never received his beads or prayer book or dog tags from the army, but the chaplain who wrote seemed to think he was killed on the beach. Five miniature American flags border Paul's picture above the inscription: "In our Country's Service . . . that Liberty will be preserved." Hanging below the picture is a transparent case with a Bronze Star and a Purple Heart.

"My mother still thinks he's coming back," Lucette says, "but it's been three years. When we're in a store Mother still says, 'This is something Paul would like.' "

It is not so strange that Lucette Varin would be glad if they changed from khaki, in the mill, to green dye.

36

DOWNSTREAM

$\mathcal{M}$ACHINE and granite works, sash, blind, box, furniture, shoe, butter and cheese factories, saw, cider, grist, cotton, woolen, and paper mills—these were legion on the river a hundred years ago. The rush of water from the mountains to the lake provided the only source of power, and every village of consequence in the valley was located on the Winooski or one of its tributaries. To-day you may still see in numerous valley towns the familiar dams with their overflow of clear water, the red mills with their multi-paned windows, handhewn beams, and wide leather belts, which connect the cider press, millstones, or lathes with the rumbling water wheel below.

Covered bridges that the floods by chance left unmolested are other spans to the past. Nearly two dozen of these hardy structures still bridge the Winooski and its tributaries, reminding travelers to keep their horses at a walk. Ancient signs attached to the stout beams inside advertise the cures of earlier generations:

Dr. B. J. Kendall's
Quick Relief for all
Aches and Pains
Internal & External

Dr. G. S. Green's
Blood Purifier
NERVE TONIC
Ask your Druggist for it

Kendall's spavin cure for all lameness.

Prof. Flint's Powders
for
Horses and Cattle

Ayer's Pills
For Billious Disorders and
For all the purposes
of
Purgative Medicine

The bridges creak and grumble under the abusive wheels of trucks and cars. Days when the iron-supporting rods served as chinning bars, the beams as tightropes, the latticework in the side as niches for propping fish poles are ended.

The river has changed. A hundred years ago thousands of sheep grazed on its banks, but when, after the Civil War, railroads invaded the West, Vermont's legion flocks of merinos began to disappear. During the latter decades of the nineteenth century the Winooski valley and all of Vermont became a vast butter tub and cheese factory. In 1869 the state produced 5,000,000 pounds of cheese and in 1879, 25,000,000 pounds of butter. This business, too, went to the West, which vied with eastern cities in attracting an even more vital product—young Vermonters. The old people left on the homestead could justly remark: "The only place that's growin' is the graveyard." The cities repaid their debt. As they grew in the twentieth century, they demanded of the Vermont hills immense quantities of fluid milk and eggs. To supply these perishables the Green Mountain State, only a night's haul from the densely populated seaboard, became a broad milkshed with more cows than people. Thousands of Jerseys and Holsteins replaced the merinos at the river's brink.

The Winooski valley is different now, and yet it is in many respects the same; it is a mosaic of all the varying patterns of 175 years. There are the old mills and the new ones, hoary covered bridges and modern steel spans, Diesel tractors and oxen, proprietary general stores and co-operatives, night-lighted egg factories, and the unsupervised hens scratching in front yards.

Waters which well from the hills of Cabot to form the main branch of the Winooski are joined, outside eastern Berlin, by Stevens' Branch. A few hundred yards before the Little North Branch enters the main channel in the heart of Montpelier, the river is held back by a dam at the site of the old clothespin factory and the Bailey Grain Company. On the north side of the millpond is the manufacturing section, threaded by railroad spurs. Since one freight car may be loaded with granite and the next

with Montpelier crackers, the main track—along with the river—
is the only common denominator of this cluttered area.

The water wheel under the clothespin factory turned machinery that fashioned clothespins when they first appeared in the
United States and, although this old plant is a storehouse now, the
activities of its early years may be identified by the gigantic
weathered clothespin on the roof. With two factories on the other
side of the river, Montpelier is still the clothespin capital, having
diversified its line to meet changing conditions. New England prefers the slotted type, presumably because the spring pin is liable
to freeze to the line, while the people of the South will have
nothing but the spring type, which ensures laundry against wind-
storms. After generations of making the traditional white-birch
or beech pin, Montpelier has added plastic numbers in bright
colors.

A grain elevator of the E. W. Bailey Company rises on the
opposite side of the dam from the old clothespin factory. E. W.,
the father of George Bailey, the present owner, extended his
operations throughout New England and became an influential
member of the Chicago Board of Trade. By 1891 the mercurial
grain business caught him off balance and he was wiped out.
Within a decade he was on his feet again. E.W. is said to have invited all his creditors, who had long since written off his obliga-
tions, to a Chicago dinner at which they found on their plates
checks for the full amounts due them, plus interest. In a comfortable wooden building near the bridge, George Bailey, a spry,
wry octogenarian, who carries the nickname of "Vermont" on his
Rotary Club badge, has continued the substantial business, now
one of the oldest of its type in the country.

Below the dam, the wide lawn of the State House, flanked
on one side by the granite home office of the National Life Insurance Company and on the other by the granite State Office Building, is only a stone's throw from the river. In 1927 the Winooski
imparted a special watermark to the books of the Vermont His-

torical Society, whose rooms house a wide variety of items such as the Stephen Daye Press, the first in North America, Ethan Allen's shoe buckle, and the Gorham silver from the battleship *Vermont,* three-stacker flagship of the navy in 1909.

State Street clings to the banks of the river as far as the Montpelier cemetery on the eastern edge of town. This is not the capital's only cemetery but it is the largest. As travelers enter Montpelier, the forest of tombstones deepens their impression that Vermont has perhaps more than its share of cemeteries. This is true only to the extent that Vermonters have been dying longer than people farther west. Vermont graveyards, despite their abundance, are not necessarily depressing. The tombstones of two young women prematurely laid to rest down the valley in Stowe offer a poignant lesson to living generations.

In memory of

Betsey, consort of
Capt. Elias Bingham
who died Sept. 10th
D 1805
in the 20th year
of her age

In memory of

Abigail, consort of
Capt. Elias Bingham
who died Sept. 14th
D 1804
in the 25th year
of her age

THIS DOUBLE CALL IS LOUD TO ALL
LET NONE DESPISE AND WONDER
BUT TO THE YOUTH IT SPEAKS A TRUTH
IN ACCENTS LOUD AS THUNDER

Upstream in Plainfield a marker serves warning to those who would imprudently swim in the river:

Abial Ledoyt son
of Jacob and Polly Perkins
who was drowned August 17, 1826
aged 13 years and 14 days

THIS BLOOMING YOUTH IN HEALTH MOST FAIR
TO HIS UNCLE'S MILL-POND DID REPARE
UNDRESSED HIMSELF AND SO PLUNGED IN
BUT NEVER DID COME OUT AGAIN

Toward the west for a few miles beyond Montpelier the Winooski flows slowly through a country of dairy farms. Enlarged by waters of the Dog River, it becomes more turbulent as the mountains begin to restrict its channel. The Mad River, which flows through some of the wildest country in Vermont, enters the main channel at Middlesex. In 1897, 120 acres of forested land slid 2,416 feet off the mountain at Fayston with a roar that convinced inhabitants it was the millennium. The Mad River, conspiring with the elements to loosen the precipitous terrain on its banks, was responsible. A similar landslide of 100 acres had occurred near the same spot in 1827. Settlers once farmed some of the high land above this tributary but abandoned it with the opening of the West. Forests reclaimed the fields, and the farmhouses, gnawed by porcupines, rotted and fell into their cellar holes. Today at Mad River Glen, where the snow stays until May or June, steel towers of the most powerful ski lift in the country have risen among the trees. The silence of this wilderness is disturbed elsewhere only by the stealthy bobcat, the nimble deer, or the lumbering black bear. The wolf and panther have withdrawn into the forests of Canada, yet the mink, fox, and beaver are here, the raccoon, the marten, and the rabbit.

On logging trails you may occasionally happen upon the cabin of a trapper or the ramshackle hut of a hermit. Such strange men have, through the years, coveted the isolation afforded by the wooded and mountainous land between Middlesex and Waterbury. Alexis Mead, grandson of the first settler of Middlesex, lived here alone for three or four decades as did white-haired Jim Roberts, who withdrew into the Middlesex mountains when a freshet destroyed his up-and-down sawmill in 1902. Jim was fastidious about his hermitage, which had a French roof and was filled with flowers. Nearby were the 30-foot falls of a mountain brook that flows through towering ledges to empty the Notch. Roberts lived alone but could occasionally be seen on the road wearing a black suit, gloves, and a high silk hat.

Edward Judd, the Hermit of Bear Swamp, was an Irish refugee from the grueling road-gang days when the tracks of the

Vermont Central were laid. His eldest daughter, born in Ireland, came to America upon her mother's death and soon announced her intentions of marrying a man of whom her father did not approve.

"Es' I went along down to th' widdin," said Edward Judd, "I cuts me a good thick shtick, en waits aroun' out in th' other room till th' widdin's over. Thin whin it's over I axes someone to tell me son-en-law will he stip out and shek hans wi' his faether? Mind now! I give him me left han' ta shek and brings out th' shtick wi' the other an' lathers him good. Aye, sir. 'Tek that fer a widdin' present,' sez I."

With the addition of the Mad River at Middlesex the Winooski has received the waters of all but one important tributary. By the time it reaches the outskirts of Waterbury it has broadened its channel perceptibly. At this point, a stone's throw from the river on the left bank, the trees and a group of buildings hugging the side of the mountain look dusted with talc—and they are. A river, which has helped expose the granite of Millstone Hill and the hard mottled green and red "Winooski Marble" near its mouth, has here cut through a rich vein of the softest of all minerals, running through the mountains from Canada to Georgia. From the buildings beside the rocky escarpment, an electric train run by storage batteries follows a narrow-gauge track through a tunnel three-fourths of a mile long, and six hundred feet from the surface. In a temperature of 40 degrees Fahrenheit, regardless of the season outside, men blast the flaky stone from the vein where, thousands of centuries ago, heat and pressure and solution transformed igneous rock into talc. Chunks are loaded on the small train and brought to the plant at the mouth of the tunnel, where machines saw the rock into slabs or dry, pulverize, screen, and purify it. Slabs of the stone, which Indians fashioned into pipes and ornaments and which the first settlers used for making fireplaces, are now made into washtubs, foot warmers, griddles, and fireless cookers. Powdered talc is necessary to the mixing of

paints, lubricants, and insecticides, and the manufacture of dynamite and paper, pottery and hot-water bottles. Of all the talc
shipped from this plant and one other in Vermont a few miles
across the mountains, only 4 per cent becomes face powder, which
by a complicated process of flotation, is refined to a degree where
it will hardly settle in the air.

The river flows languidly across the plain upon which
spreads the town of Waterbury. It passes, on the right bank, a
group of buildings, some of which have bars on the windows.
New brick additions testify that Vermont has more than its share
of the mentally sick. Merrill Howard Bennett is one of the many
patients who gaze through the bars toward the railroad tracks, the
river and fields beyond. For twenty-four years prior to July,
1942, this anemic figure paced the floor, promising himself he
would escape one day. His chief pleasure was to watch the coming
and going of Central Vermont trains. After the entry of the
United States into World War II, herculean freight locomotives
hauled train after train loaded with boxes marked "Ford" from
Canada; and in the night special trains from Washington to
Montreal roared down the valley. Bennett liked the fleet *Washingtonian* best. It arrived at Waterbury at midnight drawn by an
American mountain-type locomotive. He had drawn detailed
sketches of it and liked to show an angry cloud of smoke billow-
ing from its stack.

On Saturday, July 4, 1942, Bennett could hardly contain
his excitement, for he had been able to obtain the key to his ward
and it was necessary only to await the proper time to slip out. At
9:30 that night he turned the key, quietly closed the door after
him, and making his way quickly through the corridors and out of
the building, he disappeared in the shadows. In a few minutes he
was in a field in Duxbury, watching with fascination as the flames
of a $30,000-barn he had ignited mounted higher to the sky. But
he had more important business. He was soon hurrying along the
river in the darkness with an ax and a shovel. Before midnight he

had reached Slip Hill, upriver and on the opposite bank from the talc mine. Here the tracks of the Central Vermont perch on the top of a lofty embankment built after the flood. In the middle of this embankment Bennett began to dig and chop at the ties and the track, and as he did so he pictured in his mind the coming disaster. The *Washingtonian*—engine 602—was due in a few minutes. After stopping at Waterbury, it would gain headway enough by the time it reached here so that when it struck the break in the track the engine would plummet into the river, pulling the cars after it. He dug furiously and hacked at the ties with his ax. A whistle announced 602's departure from Waterbury. Sweat stood out on Bennett's sickly forehead. With great effort he tried to pry the track away from the damaged ties, then set to work again with his shovel. The yellow light of the engine flickered down the track. The cough of the cylinders was fast and regular. As the engine bore down upon him, Bennett withdrew to the side to drink in this moment for which he had long dreamed. Number 602 roared over the approaches to Slip Hill, the bright embers of its firebox gleaming in the river. In a moment it reached the point where Bennett had been working. With scarcely a tremor it passed over the track, followed by the brightly lighted cars, and disappeared toward the east into the night. The dark figure by the tracks plunged into the woods.

They found Bennett aboard the *Washingtonian* at White River Junction five days later and took him back to Waterbury, where they learned that he had burned down the barn. By proceeding to Slip Hill on a handcar, railroad officials verified his admission that he had tried to wreck the *Washingtonian*. Bennett was once again behind bars in the somber building by the river. "But I'll get out!" he grimly warned his attendants.

Waterbury River is the Winooski's next large tributary. On the crest of a hill near Stowe in the Waterbury River valley, there is a structure which is in striking contrast to the Vermont farmhouses around it. And yet in an environment of mountains the large chalet with its flowers and filigreed balconies is at home. Here, in the dark, early hours of a May morning in 1947, Baron Georg von Trapp lay dying. The son of an Austrian navy captain, he had been born sixty-seven years before in Zara, Dalmatia. At the age of nineteen he fought in the Boxer Rebellion, and in the World War he became the almost mythical commander of the German submarine fleet, famed for his surprises and unorthodox tactics. He went back to his large villa in Austria after the war, wrote a distinguished book about navy operations, and raised nine children. One summer day before the Second World War, Mme. Lotte Lehmann heard the von Trapp children singing folk songs in the Salzburg Festival and, impressed by the clarity and sweetness of their voices, suggested that the baron allow them to enter the professional concert field. He was reluctant, as he had plans for taking the family around the world in a yacht, but presently consented to their appearance in an amateur folk-singing contest. They won first prize over forty choral groups. Soon they were performing before Chancellor Schuschnigg in the palace at Vienna. A young priest, Dr. Franz Wassner, organist at the Austrian Salzburg Seminarium, had decided to become their full-time instructor. Soon the von Trapp family was singing concerts in Italy, France, Belgium, Holland, and England.

At this juncture the Brownshirts marched into Austria. Hitler offered von Trapp command of the Nazi naval forces, but the baron declined. He gave up his fortune and villa, and with his wife, Dr. Wassner, and his large brood sailed for America. The problems of life in a new land at once presented themselves at Ellis Island, where, handicapped by poverty and almost insuperable language difficulties, the baron, baronness, and Dr. Wassner could be sustained only by hope. They rented a house in Germantown, Pennsylvania, where the large family made their own clothes, shoes, furniture, and pottery. Almost at once they began a series of concerts in this country and were received with enthusiasm as great as that of their European audiences. At length, in 1942, they accumulated enough money to buy 660 acres of farm land in the Winooski valley on the side of a mountain above Stowe. With hammers, saws, and drills the entire family went to work renovating some abandoned CCC barracks where they might hold their Sing Weeks during the summer. They were also building a villa hundreds of feet above the music camp on a high field from which they could look out over six mountain peaks. Under the baron's direction the children—boys and girls—pushed wheelbarrows heavy with cement and laid the foundation. Within the family there were hands skilled at carpentry and shingling, weaving and decorating, and the house was largely a product of their own labor. The animals of their farm—the cows, pigs, and hens, which they themselves tended—supplied the meat and dairy products for their table.

In a few years the von Trapps had come to be the most heavily engaged attraction of concert history in America—performing 125 concerts a year. The freshness of their voices, perhaps instilled by life in the Tyrol, had, as the baron expected, been sustained by the simplicity of life in the Green Mountains. To thousands of New Yorkers the von Trapps annually convey in their Christmas service at Town Hall something of the spirit that prevailed during the eve of the Nativity on the rim of the Waterbury River valley. Locked for several days, the door of the living room was thrown open on that night. The tree, bright with lights and ornaments, laden with cookies and fruits and hand-made presents, cast its radiance upon the entire family. Before midnight, the baron and baroness arose and dressed, and carrying lanterns went to the bedroom door of Rupert, their eldest son. Together they sang "Hirten auf um Mitternacht." Rupert joined them, and the three proceeded to the door of the next eldest child, and the next, until the entire family had arisen and joined in the singing. Holding their lanterns, they proceeded down the snowbanked path through the crisp Vermont night to their chapel, which they had converted from a barn, and there held their Christmas service.

Five short years after they had arrived in the Waterbury River valley, at 3:30 on the morning of May 30, 1947, Baron von Trapp died. In the field outside the villa his family fashioned a cross to which the funeral procession marched. From the throats of his ten children there arose into the air above the mountain field his favorite lullaby.

The von Trapps are not the only musicians in the valley. The Vermont Symphony Orchestra, a native product, gives housewives, students, farmers, and bankers from all corners of the state the same satisfaction as that gained from the Vermont Poetry Society by those who like to write, and from the summer art schools by scores of amateur artists. Switching engineers and granite workers, who help to compose the incredible mosaic of the 165-piece orchestra, come down from the hills to rehearsals and concerts with enthusiasm rarely exhibited by grownups—a zeal which matches that of the girls and boys of the high school bands, gathered together yearly in the Vermont Music Festival in Burlington.

West of the mouth of Waterbury River, where the Winooski cuts the Green Mountains in two, the Long Trail, a footpath on the crest of the wooded peaks from south to north, is broken. But the 4,000-foot descent from Camel's Hump and the greater climb to the peak of Mansfield on the north side of the river is the most striking part of the hiker's trek. Near Mansfield is Sterling Mountain with its crystal pond spreading out thirty acres under the clouds. Here the water lily, the yellow-flowered spatterdock and the bladderwort are seen, scarcely less interesting to botanists than the Alpine saxifrage, the Greenland sandwort, and the three-toothed cinquefoil that inhabit the highest slopes of Mansfield. The waters from Sterling Pond wander through deep crevices in the rock and gush forth clear and cold into Smuggler's Notch at the rate of two hundred thousand gallons a minute.

In the heart of the Narrows at Bolton, the Winooski shows how intimidating a mountain river may become—particularly a river that during its flood poured forth more feet of water per second, for its drainage area, than any stream in the history of the nation. With the sound of thunder the water plunges over the old power dam at Bolton Falls and spills out on the widening valley below.

Rainbows that live in the spray above the foot of the dam are no more elusive than the rainbows that live within the roiling water. Many prize trout still inhabit deep holes such as this, rising on occasion for the angler's fly. The Winooski is the home of most kinds of fresh-water fish. Hundreds of years ago even the lively salmon came up from tidewater to stay, but this fish could not withstand the dams with which the first settlers plugged the river. The yellow perch, the green pickerel, the brown trout and the black bass, the fierce northern pike and the lazy sheepshead, the wall-eyed pike, the catfish and the mullet are in the river. There are fish as small as chubs and smelt and as large as sturgeon. Old men recall Sundays when they grappled for the last-named on the intervale below the Winooski mills. From the back of a rowboat they raised and lowered strong poles strung with sash cord and cod hooks. The cord went taut, the boat began to slosh up and down and was shortly off on a giddy tour, provided the man with the pole could hold on. When the battle was over (sometimes the men lost when their boat overturned) the sturgeon was pulled ashore if he was too big to be hauled aboard. Specimens of this strapping fish sometimes scaled 150 pounds and were nearly six feet long.

In centuries past, fish served as a staple in the Indians' diet and focused their life on the river. From the lake far into the mountains, the banks periodically yield testimony of this. In Bolton during the mid-nineteenth century, an Indian jar twenty inches in diameter with a capacity of fourteen quarts was found. Another urn was discovered in a rock shelter in Bolton Falls in

1895. The famous Colchester jar, acknowledged to be the finest specimen ever uncovered in New England, was taken in almost perfect preservation from under the roots of a tree on the river in Colchester. Below Bolton in Richmond, a half mile up the Huntington River from its junction with the Winooski, a birch tree three feet in diameter, found growing in 1809 in one of the mounds of an Indian encampment, gave evidence of long years of Indian occupation.

Today, in the thick wild woods above Bolton, whiteskins—as intractable as any Indian—forage for game. At the end of the deer season, when sportsmen have stopped hunting, the natives start. Wardens assigned to this area, adjoining the 12,000-acre army artillery range where paratroopers and cavalry regiments trained during the war, are accustomed to dismissing rifle shots in the woods after deer season as target practice. One warden on the trail of an illegally killed deer lost his pipe when a bullet took it from his mouth. After fruitlessly trailing hunters who had walked backwards to make confusing tracks in the snow, other wardens have returned and found maple syrup instead of oil in the engine of their car, so that when they started up the syrup sugared off and burned the bearings. The Bolton Outlaws, descended from generations of woodsmen and trappers, kill deer out of season in order that their children may eat. Wardens who do not understand are invited to stay out of Bolton.

A small colony of similar people, not, however, of native but of foreign stock, live at the mouth of the river in shacks on stilts over the water. They still make their living by fishing and trapping.

The climax of the river's journey through the Green Mountains comes at Bolton Falls. Beyond, it relaxes as it winds out of green foothills across the plain on which is situated the town of Richmond. On the eastern outskirts of this town it passes, on the right, a small white freshly painted building. In this hut over corncob and maple fires, Luke Harrington smokes a ton of ham, bacon, and sausage a week, and cures the meat in a pickle that is an old family recipe and his own closely guarded secret. Luke's tearoom nearby serves as a trap for summer travelers who, when they savor the meats, join his scattered clientele. In order to leave the tearoom they must pass through his display of Vermont products and are tempted by woodenware, hooked rugs, cheese, honey, and maple sugar.

In the center of the town, on the left bank, is the pride of Richmond—the Round Church. It has sixteen sides, capped by a bell cupola, and was built in 1812 by four religious societies according to a church-sharing plan. Sixteen men, the story goes, agreed to construct a side each, and the seventeenth man the cupola. The balcony and elevated boxes, where sat the tithers to scrutinize weekly contributions to the plate, poise today in all their rigid puritanism. Henry Ford wished to buy, dismantle, and reconstruct the church in Sudbury, Massachusetts, as part of a colonial exhibit, but the town of Richmond guessed it wouldn't sell. The Round Church annually receives the Universalists of New England, and at other times serves as a well-lighted town hall.

As it leaves Richmond the Winooski flows across an expanse of bottom land as productive as any in the valley, despite periodic inundation. The river rose to flood stage in 1936 and 1938 and was high in the spring of 1947, but the storage dams in the hills, barricading millions of cubic feet of water, allowed no such catastrophe as that of 1927. Even so, Gordon Quinlan's herd of fifty-nine $200 cows were isolated one morning when the rise of land in the lowlands below Richmond where they were grazing suddenly became an island. At 7:00 A.M. the neighbors gathered at Quinlan's, speculating as how best to retrieve the herd, now separated from the mainland by 150 feet of water. They crossed this intervale in a boat, tied the end of a rope around the neck of one of the cows, and returned to the shore, paying out the rope. The men all took hold and pulled the cow off the fast-submerging island. The unhappy animal was under water more than on top during her involuntary excursion, but was finally hauled ashore intact. Two others received the same treatment. Seeing this, the other fifty-six on the island decided they would rather swim and all entered the river together. With $7,200 worth of anxiety, Quinlan watched as they paddled against the current, ultimately reaching the shore much farther downstream.

On the lowland farms beyond Richmond the trees with which nature binds the soil on a riverbank have long been cut down. Here by 1936 open wounds of erosion were threatening between five and twenty acres on each of several farms. In August, 1936, as the result of an appeal by local farmers, the United States Department of Agriculture inaugurated the Winooski River Soil Conservation Project, the first of its kind in the country. Since there was no precedent to serve as a guide, men from the Soil Conservation Service arrived in Vermont merely with instructions to control the erosion the best way they could.

On the old Governor Chittenden farm a chute had opened which threatened 180 acres of bottom land if the river changed its course. The men went to work and laid whole trees one on top of another at the entrance to the chute until they had a barricade 10 feet in diameter and 1,000 feet long. Wire cables bound the trees together and were fastened to the ground by eight 3-ton concrete anchors. A rock-filled crib held the northern end of the barricade in position, while the southern end was attached to a "dead man"—a log buried deep in the ground. The high water of 1938 broke the cables attached to the dead man and swung the barricade aside. The soil-conservation experts, then working on other farms nearby, returned to the Chittenden farm, moved the 1,000-foot barrier back into position, and anchored the southern end to a rock-filled crib similar to that at the northern end. Inside the barricade along its entire length they planted willows and hybrid poplars, which would help to hold the silt and gravel deposited by the water flowing through and over the diversion wall. These measures were successful. A decade later the river was still in its old channel and the gully was filling up.

To keep the Winooski from dissolving acres of land from its shores each year, the men laid rock rip-rap up to the average low-water mark, then brush-matted the rest of the bank above the rip-rap, and planted basket willow, hybrid poplars, and osier dogwood on a 50-foot strip next to the banks to discourage any farmers from plowing the last few furrows. Lessons learned in the Winooski conservation project have been applied with success on the Missouri and the wide rivers of the Middle West.

On land cleared nearly 175 years ago by Vermont's first governor, stands the handsome brick house built by One-Eyed Tom, for his son Martin Chittenden. The brick, laid in a mosaic of large diamonds, lends lacy adornment to the exquisite proportions of the house. Some of the boards of the pine flooring inside are nearly two feet wide, and all of them are two inches thick. The arched doors, the staircase, the recessed windows, the fireplaces upstairs and down, are perfect examples of colonial design. An interesting, if third-rate, picture of a maiden, a child, and a husky grapevine hung until recently over the mantel in the large room to the left of the front entrance. The legend about the picture was that One-Eyed Tom had remarked to a carpenter that it would be nice to have a picture over the fireplace, and the carpenter volunteered to paint it. But the Philip Hasbrooks, who bought and restored the house, decided to take the picture down. When they did so the legend of its origin vanished, for underneath it, painted on the wall and framed by a gold-leaf wood roping, was the seal of the state of Vermont with its pine tree, cow, and mountains. On the left was the French liberty cap, and on the right an American flag with sixteen stars and stripes.

When the Hasbrooks moved in they discovered that the original front door was missing. A Mr. Roberts of Williston, talking with the new owner of the house one day, said that his great-grandfather and all the rest of the family, perennial residents of Williston, had been carpenters, and that he had saved about fifty of his great-grandfather's molding planes. The planes were produced, and one of them matched exactly the recessed work on the doors. The problem of making a new front door was solved and the fact almost certainly established that Roberts's great-grandfather had helped build the Chittenden house.

On the ridge above the old Chittenden house is the Vermont Research Forest. There are trees on the sunny river slope that have never before grown in Vermont. The men at the experimental station have no idea what will happen to some of them, but can see no reason, if a Douglas fir will grow in Oregon, why it won't grow in Vermont. Here, growing in a few acres, are Austrian and Scotch pines from Central Europe, ponderosa pine from Idaho, Japanese and European larch, and English walnut. The new varieties may become as valuable to the economy of Vermont as the pine and sugar maples. If the larch trees find the climate agreeable, they will become the fence posts around future Vermont pastures. And if the English walnuts grow well, they may bear a new and salable product.

Out of the seventy different kinds of maples in the world, there are seven growing in Vermont, and of these the sugar, or rock, maple is called upon to provide not only the country's largest supply of syrup and sugar, but a substantial portion of its maple furniture. Growing along the rivers, there are maple trees which were of considerable size when Indians roamed the valley, and which, on their weathered trunks, exhibit scars made by blunt axes, large holes made by 1¼-inch augers, and small holes bored for the spouts in use today. The farther north the rock maple grows the better the flavor of the syrup boiled from its sap. Vermont farmers tap over five million maples yearly, few of them less than forty years old. The number of trees old enough to be tapped is steadily lessening because of demands of the furniture and woodenware markets. For this reason the state hopes that the experiments at the tree farm will be fruitful. For some of the projects it will take sixty years to find out.

On the southeastern slope of the Research Forest, looking out to mountains ranged on the horizon, is the newly chosen site of a Vermont 4-H recreational camp to which, presently, will come children from around the state. Today you may see on rounded valley knolls occasional small buildings. Some are painted white, some are of logs, and some of stone. Most of them are shuttered and capped with snow in winter, but in summer, during the months they shelter their city owners, they come alive. The past decade has witnessed the shoring up and rehabilitating of scores of old farmhouses on marginal valley land, for the tide toward the city has turned. The harried people who come to Vermont, even if only for a few summer weeks, have displayed an incontestable longing to take root. In an unstable world they find stability among people who, while they may not know the answers to the atomic bomb or the perennial and gloomy threat of war, go about their business as if they did.

The turning of city people toward the country is a repudiation of the tinsel and chromium of urban behavior. The new immigrants thirst for the time-tested fundamentals of living, and they may find them in a state that has shown it will not sacrifice the simplicity of its ways on the altar of Progress. Scores of factories have come to the valley and have adjusted comfortably in the small towns. Yet the Winooski is a country river and a country river it will remain, for this is its heritage and its promise.

Below the Research Forest and the high slope of the Vermont 4-H camp, the river gathers impetus for its descent to Lake Champlain. At Essex Junction, the home of a much-maligned railroad station, the river leaves the flat bottom lands and cuts again through ledges of rock that lower it by gradual stages to the lowlands below Winooski. The station at Essex Junction has a smoky brick porte-cochere under which the trains pass, and

presents a somber picture in the half-light of a February morning
when passengers waiting for the train are confronted by the
tombstones of a cemetery just across the track. E. J. Phelps,
Vermont senator and minister to England from 1885 to 1889,
composed a four-stanza poem called "The Lay of the Lost Traveler," which the station deserves, if the town of Essex Junction
does not.

> With saddened face and battered hat
>   And eye that told of black despair,
> On wooden bench the traveler sat,
>   Cursing the fate that brought him there.
>   "Nine hours," he cried, "we've lingered here,
>   With thought intent on distant homes,
> Waiting for that elusive train
>   Which, always coming, never comes,
>   Till, weary, worn,
>   Distressed, forlorn,
> And paralyzed in every function,
>   I hope in Hell
>   His soul may dwell
> Who first invented Essex Junction."

A dam at the site of the largest hydroelectric station within Vermont makes a 3-mile pond of the river at Essex Junction. During
the flood 116,000 cubic feet of water roared over the dam per
second, boiling along the deepening channel leading to the gorge.

A short distance downstream, on the crest of its high right
bank, are the buildings of the Champlain Valley Exposition.
Each year, between August 25 and 31, these acres swarm with
fairgoers from all over the valley. There are the livestock, fish
and game, arts and crafts, and 4-H exhibits, the horse races and
the garish widway.

"HELL DIVERS! Where the girls race the boys and the
boys race the girls. Loop the loop upside down a mile a minute.
Say, this show goes on all the time, riding, racing and driving
together!" . . . "You don't have to wait, Ladies and Gentlemen. Enter right here, Marie the Baby Ape! You'll see her
roller-skate and ride bicycles. It's children's prices today. There's

no waiting—EVERYBODY—plenty of room. Just starting now— another big show. One purpose—that's to make you laugh!"

Fort Ethan Allen is on a continuation of the same sandy plateau that was the river's delta thousands of years ago when the sea invaded the valley. As a cavalry post it has come very near being declared surplus by the army in the years following its strenuous World War II training schedule. Though horses prance and caissons roll no more in Memorial Day parades, mechanized armies must still maneuver in winter, and of this season the civilian-populated fort has abundant raw materials.

The adjacent sand plateau above the opposite bank of the river has become the Burlington airport, with six scheduled daily flights to New York and Boston. Beyond the revolving searchlights and the winking lights on the wings of planes lifting from the field is the crest of the hill at Burlington, with its red-lighted radio tower, and the bright solitaire above the belfry of the Ira Allen Chapel at the University of Vermont.

Below the Winooski Gorge the river passes on either side of an island around which local sportsmen once raced horses on the hard winter ice. In summer, work horses swam the river and machinery was rafted across to harvest the island's thirteen acres of hay. The boys of the neighborhood had a baseball diamond there, but the 1927 flood covered it with sand and stone. It has since become a jungle of trees and sumac and wild blackberries. On the left bank at this point the river has cut off the pioneer road down which, in 1789, moved the funeral cortege of Ethan Allen.

The countless lights of the woolen mills show in the night water like bright beads. On a summer's evening during prosperous times, if the river is not spilling over the dam, the clacking machinery may be heard on the intervale below the old "log-rolling place." A few miles beyond the memorial tower at Ethan Allen Park the Winooski leaves the open lowlands and moves slowly through a dense marsh inhabited by fish hawks and frogs.

Near Colchester Point, after passing under a bridge of the Rutland Railroad, it joins the waters of Lake Champlain, flowing north to the St. Lawrence and east to the sea.

Acknowledgments

$\mathcal{T}$HE following people have made vital contributions to this book: the editors—Mr. Hervey Allen, Mr. Carl Carmer, Miss Jean Crawford and Miss Faith Ball; Professor Jeremiah K. Durick, of St. Michael's College, and Mrs. Ruth Perkins, of the Wilbur Library, University of Vermont.

I am also grateful to Professor William R. Adams, of the University of Vermont, Ambassador Warren R. Austin; Mrs. William Barclay, of Barre; Mr. M. E. Barnes, of the Central Vermont Railway; Mrs. Lena Bizzozero, of the Vermont Department of Health; Mr. and Mrs. Clyde Brink, of Stowe; Mrs. Mildred Bullock, of Calais; Mr. John Clement of the Vermont Historical Society; Miss Gladys Flint, of the Billings Library, University of Vermont; Mrs. Jenny Gale, of Stowe; Miss Helen Hale, of the Plattsburg (New York) Public Library, Mrs. Doris G. Harvey, of the Wilbur Library, University of Vermont; Mr. and Mrs. Philip Hasbrook, of Jericho; Mr. J. A. Healy, of Jones Brothers Corp., Barre; Miss Muriel J. Hughes, of the University of Vermont; Professor Elbridge C. Jacobs, of the University of Vermont; Mr. Dorman B. E. Kent, of the Vermont Historical Society; Professor Julian I. Lindsay, of the University of Vermont; Mr. Gene Magnus, of the Eastern Magnesia Talc Company; Mr. William Muir, of the American Woolen Company, Winooski; Mr. Earle W. Newton, of the Vermont Historical Society; Mrs. Mary Greene Nye, of the Vermont Historical Society; Mr. Bernard O'Brien, of Montpelier; Miss Marguerite Olney, of Middlebury College; Mrs. Proctor Page, Jr., of Burlington; Professor Arthur W. Peach, of Norwich University; Miss Mildred I. Phelps, of the Aldrich Public Library, Barre; Dr. Royce S. Pitkin, of Goddard College; Mr. Robert Polworth, of the American Woolen Company, Winooski; Miss Winifred Prior, of Burlington; Miss Fanny Rothman, of the Fletcher Free Library, Burlington; Mr. Harold Rugg, of the Baker Library, Dartmouth College; Mr. Philip Shutler, of the Vermont Water Resources Board; Dr. and Mrs. M. C. Twitchell, Jr., of Burlington; Miss Lucette Varin, of Winooski; Mr. Sylvester Vigilante, of the New York Public Library; Mr. Burton Ward, of Moretown; and Mr. Ruben Zile, of the United States Soil Conservation Service.

The details and dialogue in the chapter "Land of the Onion" are based on Ira Allen's own account of his exploratory trip in his *Autobiography*.

Ethan Allen's discourse with Parson Aminidab Robinson on the hereafter in the chapter "Darkness at Noon" was taken from "Theology of Ethan Allen in a Dialogue with Amminidab Robinson," in the book *Letterz, Moral and Theological,* by Jonathan R. Forest, Winooski, Vermont, 1859. The account of Ethan's death in the same chapter is based upon a sworn statement to John N. Pomeroy, in 1852, by Hawley Whitten of Milton, Vermont, who was a hired boy on Allen's farm when Ethan's mulatto man, Newport, brought the general home to die. The statement is to be found in the John N. Pomeroy papers at the Wilbur Library, University of Vermont, and is substantial evidence, in the face of much controversy and speculation, as to the exact manner and day of Ethan's death.

In the chapter "To a Man of Spirit," the details of the capture of the ship *Olive Branch* and Ira Allen's misfortunes in Europe are to a considerable extent based upon the meticulous findings of James B. Wilbur, published in his two volumes, *Ira Allen, Founder of Vermont (1751-1814).*

The dialogue in the chapter "Taking the Snake" is drawn from *The Trial of Cyrus Dean for the Murder of Jonathan Ormsby and Asa Marsh, before the Supreme Court of the State of Vermont,* Burlington, 1808.

The Millerite ballad in the chapter "Judgment Day" is from the Helen Hartness Flanders Collection, Middlebury College.

BIBLIOGRAPHY
Books

Allen, Ethan, A Narrative of Colonel Ethan Allen's Captivity. Walpole, N. H.: Thomas and Thomas, 1807.

Allen, Ira, Particulars of the Capture of the Ship Olive Branch. London: J. W. Myers, 1798.

————, Natural and Political History of Vermont. London: J. W. Myers, 1798.

————, Autobiography, in Ira Allen Founder of Vermont. James B. Wilbur—Vol. I. Boston: Houghton Mifflin Company, 1928.

Adams, James Truslow, New England in the Republic (1776-1850). Boston, Mass.: Little, Brown and Company, 1926.

Bigelow, J., History of Stowe, Vermont. Hartford, Conn., 1934.

Brayley, Arthur W., History of the Granite Industry of New England. 2 vols. Boston, Mass.: A. M. Hunt Company, 1913.

Burnett, Edmund C., Letters of the Members of the Continental Congress, 1774-1784. 8 vols. Washington, D. C., 1921-1936.

Cady, Daniel L., Rhymes of Vermont Rural Life. Rutland, Vt.: Tuttle Company, 1919.

Champlain, Samuel de, Les Voyages de la nouvelle France occidentale, dite Canada, faits par de Champlain—et toutes les descouvertes qu'il a faites 1603-29. Paris, 1632.

Child, Hamilton, Gazetteer and Business Directory of Chittenden County for 1882-1883. Syracuse, N. Y.: Hamilton Child, 1882.

————, Gazetteer of Washington County for 1783-1889. Syracuse, N. Y.: Edited by Wm. Adams, 1889.

Chipman, Daniel, A Memoir of Thomas Chittenden, the first governor of Vermont . . . Middlebury, Vt.: 1849.

Coates, Walter, and Frederick Tupper, Vermont Verse, an Anthology. Brattleboro, Vt.: Stephen Daye Press, 1932.

————, Land of Allen, and Other Verse. Athol, Mass.: W. Paul Cook, 1928.

Colburn, Zerah, A Memoir of Zerah Colburn. Springfield, Mass.: G. and C. Merriam, 1833.

Congdon, Herbert Wheaton, Old Vermont Houses. New York: Alfred A. Knopf, 1946.

Crane, Charles E., Let Me Show You Vermont. New York: Alfred A. Knopf, 1937.

Crockett, Walter H., Vermont, the Green Mountain State. 5 vols. New York: Century History Company, 1921.

————, Vermonters, a Book of Biographies. Brattleboro, Vt.: Stephen Daye Press, 1932.

Davenport, Walter Rice, Biography of Thomas Davenport. Montpelier, Vt.: Vermont Historical Society, 1929.

Davis, W. T., The New England States, Vol. III. Boston, Mass.: D. H. Hurd Company, 1897.

DePuy, Henry W., Ethan Allen and the Green Mountain Heroes of '76. New York: Phinney, Blakeman and Mason, 1860.

Dewey, Adelbert M., Life and Letters of Admiral Dewey. New York: Woolfall Company, 1899.

Douglas, Paul F., Yankee Tradition. Burlington, Vt.: Jacob B. Abbott, 1941.

Ellis, William A., History of Norwich University (1819-1911). Montpelier, Vt.: Capital City Press, 1911.

Emerson, Ralph Waldo, Journals of Ralph Waldo Emerson, 1864-1876. Edited by Edward Emerson and Waldo Emerson Forbes. Boston, Mass.: Houghton Mifflin Company, 1914.

Fiske, John, The American Revolution. 2 vols. Boston, Mass., 1891.

Flanders, Helen Hartness, The New Green Mountain Songstress. New Haven, Conn.: Yale University Press, 1939.

————, Vermont Chap Book. Middlebury, Vt.: Middlebury College Press, 1941.

Footpath in the Wilderness—The Long Trail in the Green Mountains of Vermont. Middlebury, Vt.: Middlebury College Press, 1941.

Force, Peter, American Archives, Vol. II, 4th Series. Washington, D. C., 1837.

Graham, John A., Descriptive Sketch of the present State of Vermont. London: Henry Fry, 1797.

Hall, Benjamin, H., History of Eastern Vermont. New York: D. Appleton Company, 1858.

Hall, Hiland, History of Vermont from its discovery and admission into the Union 1791. Albany, N. Y.: J. Munsell, 1868.

Harlow, Alvin F., Steelways of New England. New York: Creative Age Press, 1946.

Hemenway, Abby Maria, The Vermont Historical Gazetteer (1868-1891). 5 vols. Montpelier, Vt.

————, Poets and Poetry of Vermont. Brattleboro, Vt.: W. Felton, 1860.

Holbrook, Stewart H., Ethan Allen. New York: The Macmillan Company, 1940.

Jones, Matt B., Vermont in the Making. Cambridge, Mass.: Harvard University Press, 1939.

Lamb, Wallace E., The Lake Champlain and Lake George Valleys. New York: American Historical Company, 1940.

Lee, John P., Uncommon Vermont. Rutland, Vt.: Tuttle Company, 1926.

Lee, W. Storrs, Father Went to College, the Story of Middlebury. New York: Wilson-Erickson, 1936.

Levasseur, A., Lafayette en Amerique en 1824 et 1825 . . Paris, 1829.

Lewis, Theodore G., History of Waterbury, Vermont (1763-1915). Waterbury, Vt.: Harry C. Whitehill, 1915.

Linsley, D. C., Morgan Horses Today. New York: C. M. Saxton and Company, 1857.

Ludlum, David M., Social Ferment In Vermont (1791-1850). New York: Columbia University Press, 1939.

McLaughlin, James F., Matthew Lyon, The Hampden of Congress. New York: Wynkoop, Hallanbeck and Crawford, 1900.

New York, Guide to the Empire State (American Guide Series). New York: Oxford Press, 1936.

Nye, Mary Greene, Vermont's State House, Montpelier, Vt., 1936.

Pell, John, Ethan Allen. Boston, Mass.: Houghton Mifflin Company, 1929.

Perkins, Nathan, A Narrative of a Tour Through the State of Vermont from April 27 to June 12, 1789. Woodstock, Vt.: Elm Tree Press, 1920.

Perry, Dean H., Barre in the Great Flood of 1927. Barre, Vt., 1928.

Rann, W. S., History of Chittenden County. Syracuse, N. Y.: D. Mason Company, 1886.

Sanborn, A. J., Green Mountain Poets. Claremont, N. H., 1872.

Sheridan, P. H., Memoirs of P. H. Sheridan, Vol. I. New York: Charles L. Webster Company, 1888.

Slade, William, Vermont State Papers. Middlebury, Vt.: J. W. Copeland, 1823.

Smith, Justin, Our Struggles for the Fourteenth Colony. New York: G. P. Putnam's Sons, 1907.

Sparks, Jared, Life of Colonel Ethan Allen. Burlington, Vt.: C. Goodrich & Company, 1858.

Stong, Phil, Horses and Americans. New York: Garden City Publishing Company, 1946.

Stone, Arthur F., Vermont of Today with its Historic Background, Attractions and People. New York: Lewis Historical Publishing Company, 1929.

Thompson, Charles M., Independent Vermont. Boston, Mass.: Houghton Mifflin Company, 1942.

Thompson, Daniel P., History of Montpelier, Vermont. Montpelier, Vt.: E. P. Walton, 1860.

Thompson, Zadock, Gazetteer of the State of Vermont. Montpelier, Vt.: E. P. Walton, 1824.

Trial of Cyrus B. Dean for the murder of Jonathan Ormsby and Asa Marsh, before the Supreme court . . . of the state of Vermont. Burlington, Vt.: Samuel Mills, 1808.

Van de Water, Frederic, The Reluctant Republic. New York: The John Day Company, 1941.

Vermont, a Guide to the Green Mountain State (American Guide Series). Boston: Houghton Mifflin Company, 1937.

Walter, Charles T., Lights and Shadows of the Flood of 1927. St. Johnsbury, Vt.: Cowles Press, 1928.

Wilbur, James B., Ira Allen, Founder of Vermont (1751-1814). 2 vols. Boston: Houghton Mifflin Company, 1928.

Williams, The Reverend John, The Redeemed Captive. Northampton, Mass.: Hopkins Bridgeman Company, 1853.

Williams, Samuel, The Natural and Civil History of Vermont. Walpole, N. H.: Isaiah Thomas and David Carlisle, 1794.

Wilgus, William J., The Role of Transportation in the Development of Vermont. Montpelier, Vt.: Vermont Historical Society, 1945.

Wilson, Harold F., The Hill Country of Northern New England (1790-1930) New York: Columbia University Press, 1936.

Manuscripts and Pamphlets

Abair, Joseph G., The Flood of November 3rd and 4th, 1927. Montpelier, Vt.: Capital City Press, 1928.

Allen, Ethan, Manuscripts. Burlington, Vt.: Wilbur Library, University of Vermont.

Allen, Ira, Journal of Surveys, 1773. Photostats. Burlington, Vt.: Wilbur Library, University of Vermont.

————, Diary of 1796. Burlington, Vt.: Wilbur Library, University of Vermont.

————, Calendar of the Ira Allen Papers. Burlington, Vt.: Historical Records Survey (Montpelier, Vt., 1939), Wilbur Library, University of Vermont.

Allen, Levi, Manuscripts. Burlington, Vt.: Wilbur Library, University of Vermont.

Atwood, R. E., Stories and Pictures of the Vermont Flood. Burlington, Vt., 1927.

Auld, Joseph, Picturesque Burlington. Burlington, Vt.: Free Press Association, 1894.

Barclay, William, Manuscript: Brief History of the Scottish Pioneers During Their First Decade in Barre, Vermont (1880-1889). Barre, Vt.

Baptist Church of Christ, Essex, Vermont, Manuscript. Burlington, Vt.: Wilbur Library, University of Vermont.

Biennial Report of the Public Service Commission of the State of Vermont. Dec. 31, 1931, to Dec. 31, 1933. Springfield, Vt., 1934.

Dawn Valcour Community Circular, published by the Dawn Valcour Community, Winooski, Vermont, 1875. Montpelier, Vt.: Vermont Historical Society.

Evans, Llew, Mount Mansfield Capstone of Vermont. Boston: Appalachia, 1944.

Flanders, Helen Hartness, Ballad Collection. Middlebury, Vt.: Middlebury College.

Forbes, Charles S., 20th Century Burlington, Vermont Double Souvenir Number. St. Albans, Vt., 1900.

Forbes, Kenneth V. A., Typescript: Chapter from the Story of Early Vermont Music; thesis for Master of Arts degree in the Department of Music, University of Iowa, Iowa City, 1927.

Forest, Jonathan R., Theology of Ethan Allen In A Dialogue With Amminidab Robinson; in Letterz, Moral and Theological. Winooski, Vt., 1859.

Goodrich, J. E., Burlington, Vermont, Clipper Souvenir, Burlington, Vt., 1893.

Granite Quarries in Vermont, Vermont Department of Public Health, Division of Industrial Hygiene, Barre, Vt.

Historical Souvenir of Barre, Vermont. Barre: Nickerson and Cox, 1894.

Hooker, George E., Manuscript: Labor and Life at the Barre Granite Quarries. Brief Survey of Social Conditions on Millstone Hill, Barre, Vermont, in the Autumn of 1895.

Jacobs, Elbridge C., Report of the State Geologist of Vermont 1935-36. Also 1941-42. Burlington, Vt.: 1936, 1942.

Kinnison, H. B., The New England Flood of November, 1927. Geological Survey Water Supply Paper 636c, U. S. Department of the Interior, Government Printing Office, Washington, D. C., 1929.

Kimball, F. M. and M. P., When the Water Came to Waterbury, Vermont; edited by Lloyd E. Squier. Waterbury, Vt., 1928.

Kent, Dorman B. E., Annals and Antics of Earlier Montpelier, Vermont. Montpelier, Vt., 1947.

La Fargo, Cosette Louise, Typescript: Thomas Wood, American Artist of the Nineteenth Century; A Dissertation Submitted to the Faculty of the Division of the Humanities in Candidacy for the Degree of Master of Arts. Chicago, Ill.: University of Chicago, 1947.

Magnus, Gene, Manuscript: In Regard to the Talc Industry in Vermont. Waterbury, Vt.

Middlebury College Bulletin. Vol. XXXII, No. 5. Middlebury College Press, 1935.

Mould, Willis P., Manuscript: Granite, Its Origin, Age, Structure. Barre, Vt.: Rock of Ages Corporation.

Nicolle, The Reverend Victor F., Historical Sketch of the Society of St. Edmund, Winooski Park, Vt.

Pomeroy, John N., Manuscripts. Burlington, Vt.: Wilbur Library, University of Vermont.

Putnam, Ralph W., Manuscript: Medad Wright of Montpelier, Vermont. Waterbury, Vt., 1945.

Raising Morgan Horses Today. The Morgan Horse Club, New York, 1929.

Records of the Winooski Turnpike Company, Treasurer's Book, April 22, 1808, to November 16, 1830; Vol. 2, February 8, 1830, to January 1, 1849. Montpelier, Vt.: Vermont Historical Society.

Rowell, Gail E., Manuscript: Justin Morgan and the Breed He Founded. Tunbridge, Vt., 1946.

Sanderson, H. R., Typescript: A Review of the Winooski Valley Flood Control Project. Thesis for the Degree of Civil Engineer, University of Vermont, Burlington, Vt., 1939.

State of Vermont Water Resources and Electrical Energy. Published by authority of the General Assembly of the State, 1941.

Stevens, Henry, Manuscripts: Papers of Vermont Miscellany, Vols. I-III. Office of the Secretary of State, Montpelier, Vt.

Trapp Family Singers. New York: Program Publishing Company.

Vermont Maple Sugar and Syrup. Department of Agriculture,

Bulletin 38. Published by the Vermont Department of Agriculture, 1941.

Wilbur, James B., A Letter of Levi Allen, 1789. An Address Before the Massachusetts Historical Society, October, 1923.

Williamson, Chilton, Typescript: Vermont in a Quandary, 1760-1820. Vermont Historical Society, Montpelier, Vt.

Winooski River, The. Report of the Chief Engineers. House Document No. 785, 71st Congress, 3rd Session, Washington, D. C.

Newspapers and Periodicals

Allen, Leslie H., The Story of Grassmount. The Vermonter, Vol. 11, Nos. 12 and 13, 1906.

Bailey, Harold L., Vermont State House, Being a Narrative of the Battle Over the Location of the Capital and Its Construction. Vermont Quarterly, Vol. XII, Proceedings of the Vermont Historical Society, Montpelier, Vt., 1944.

Bancroft, Ernest H., Why People Should Favor the Green Mountain Parkway. The Vermonter, Vol. 41, Nos. 1 and 2, 1936.

Barre Daily Times: Nov. 7, 1927, August, 1936, March, 1937, June, 1938, October, 1938, January, 1939, Mar. 23, 1940.

Boston Globe: Nov. 10, 1927.

Buckham, Matthew H., One Hundred Years of the University of Vermont. In The Ariel, Yearbook of the University of Vermont, 1905.

Burlington Daily News: March, 1937, April, 1937, August, 1937, September, 1937, June, 1938, October, 1938, January, 1939.

Burlington Free Press: Nov. 10, 1848, July 23, Nov. 20, Dec. 20, 1849; June 25, 26, 1850; Jul. 17, 29, Aug. 1, 1854; Aug. 18, 1856; Feb. 18, 23, 25, 1857; May 15, 21, 24, June 3, 8, 9, 11, 19, 1858; Dec. 5, 13, 1859; Dec. 24, 1863; Nov. 29, 1865; Dec.

12, 1867; Sept. 1, 3, 11, 1874; Mar. 5, 15, 1875; Nov. 3-20, 1927; Nov. 1, 1930; Mar. 20, 27, 1935; Apr. 5, July 30, Aug. 1, 3, 1936; March, 1937, April, 1937, August, 1937, September, 1937; June, 1938, October, 1938; January, 1939, Feb. 2, May 10, June 14, 15, July 15, 1939; Dec. 18, 1940; Feb. 16, 1944.

Burridge, Pauline E., Glimpses of Grasse Mount. In Vermont Alumni Weekly, Vol. X, Nos. 9, 10, 11, 12.

Chapin, J. A., Hermits of Middlesex Notch. The Vermonter, Vol. 14, No. 12, 1909.

Coates, Walter John, Driftwind. Edited, printed, published at North Montpelier, Vt. (1926-1942).

Crockett, Walter H., Dedication at Winooski. In Yearbook and Roster of the Vermont Society, Sons of the American Revolution, Burlington, Vt., 1915.

————, Ira Allen and Colchester. The Genealogical Quarterly Magazine, Vol. II, No. 4, 1900.

Cummings, Charles R., The Green Mountain Parkway Plan. The Vermonter, Vol. 38, No. 8, 1933.

Davenport, Walter Rice, Thomas Davenport, Pioneer Inventor. Vermont Historical Society Collections, Montpelier, Vt., 1929.

Gay, Leon W., Keeping Unspoiled Vermont, Unspoiled. The Vermonter, Vol. 40, No. 8, 1935.

Jones, Walter E., The Village Bridge. The Vermonter, Vol. 42, No. 4, 1937.

Kent, Dorman B. E., Address at the 125th Anniversary of the Birth of Thomas Davenport. Vermont Historical Society Collections (1926, 1927, 1928).

Lindsay, Julian I., To the University of Vermont: 150 Years of Growth and Service. University of Vermont Alumnus: Vol. 20, No. 8, 1941.

Lossing, Benson J., Ethan Allen. Harper's Monthly Magazine. Vol. 17, No. 102, 1858.

Montpelier Evening Argus: Dec. 14, 1936; June, 1938; October, 1938, January, 1939.

Morgans as Cavalry Horses. The Vermonter, Vol. 14, Nos. 10 and 11, 1909.

New England Telephone and Telegraph Company: Vermont Flood Hit Us Hard; How We Rallied. In Telephone Topics, Vol. 21, No. 8, 1927.

New York Times, Nov. 6, 1927.

Peach, Arthur W., The Proposed Parkway a Threat to the State's Well Being. The Vermonter, Vol. 41, Nos. 1 and 2, 1936.

————, Breaking the Black Silence. The Vermonter, Vol. 32, No. 10, 1927.

Plaisted, Edgell R., Nature Improved and Otherwise. The Vermonter, Vol. 38, No. 10 and 11, 1933.

Rife, Clarence R., Ethan Allen, an Interpretation. New England Quarterly, October, 1929.

Robinson, Rowland, What's In a Name? Contributors' Club, Atlantic Monthly, October, 1892.

Root, Eliza W., Reminiscences of Early Days. In Vermont Antiquarian, Vol. 3, June, 1905.

Rutland Herald: March, 1937.

Swasey, Della Le. B., When Waterbury Was Under Deluge. The Vermonter, Vol. 32, No. 8, 1927.

Thomson, Allen W., Famous Vermont Morgans. The Vermonter, Vol. 14, Nos. 10 and 11, 1909.

Twynham, Leonard, Early Community Church Ideas in Vermont. The Vermonter, Vol. 38, Nos. 6 and 7, 1933.

Vermont and Farm Bureau News, April, 1941.

Ward, Burton S., Vermont Forestry. The Vermonter, Vol. 36, No. 10, October, 1931.

INDEX

Abnaki Indians, 4, 7, 8, 15, 19, 54

Abolition of slavery in Vermont, 219

Adams, John, 95, 96

Adirondack Mountains, 5–7

Advertisement in Hartford *Courant,* 33

Age of Reason, The, by Tom Paine, 140

Age of the river, 5

Aiken, Governor George D., 196–98, 200

Algonquin Indians, 3, 4, 6–8, 10, 15, 18, 28

Allen, Ebenezer, 45, 88

Allen, Ethan, 4, 20, 28–39, 44–48, 65, 212
  captivity, 51, 57–58
  daughter, death of, 88
  death of, 89
  defiance of court, 61–62
  defiance of New Yorkers, 39
  "gods of the hills," remark on, 29
  land project. *See* Onion River Land Company
  life, post-Revolution, 82–90
  loss of command of the Green Mountain Boys, 45
  negotiations with the British over possible alienation of Vermont, 64–73
  plan for taking of Montreal, and his capture, 45–48

Allen, Ethan, *Continued*
  Reason the Only Oracle of Man, 140
  religion, 85–88, 138–40

Allen, Mrs. Ethan, 82

Allen, Ethan and Ira, contest in woodsmanship, 29–30
  land purchase by, 28–39. *See also* Onion River Land Company

Allen, Fanny, 228

Allen, Hannibal Montressor, 82

Allen, Heman (brother of Ethan and Ira), 20, 31, 45, 74, 83, 216
  death of, 59

Allen, Heman ("Chili" Allen), (nephew of Ethan and Ira), 109, 216

Allen, Ira, 4, 29, 45, 51–57, 59, 65, 67, 214–15, 231
  arrests in France, 100–06
  college founded by him. *See* University of Vermont
  death of, 112
  expedition to Europe, for purchase of muskets, 92–106
  imprisonment at Burlington, 108–09
  land project, 20–27. *See also* Onion River Land Company
  life, post-Revolution, 83–84, 91–112
  part, in surrender of Burgoyne, 57

Allen, Ira, *Continued*
portrait, 37
sale of property, 109
Suez Canal project, 102
Allen, Ira and Ethan, contest in woodsmanship, 29–30
land purchase by, 28–39. *See also* Onion River Land Company
Allen, Ira (son), 110
Allen, Mrs. Jerusha, 96
Allen, Levi, 33, 74–77
Allen, Zimri (brother of Ethan and Ira), 31
death of, 59
Allen, Zimri (son of Ira), 110
Allen family, 28, 31
control of Vermont government, 59
Allen's Rock, 30
American Woolen Company, 192, 256
Animals, 263
Army headquarters at Burlington, 133
Arnold, Benedict, 28, 54, 66, 133
Artists, 235–37
Atrocities, Indian. *See* Indians
Attempt by the British to detach Vermont from the other colonies, 63–73
Audacious, 94
Austin, Senator Warren, 197, 207–08, 222
Authors, 238–44

Bailey, E. E., Company, 260, 261
Bailey, Guy, 234
Baker, Remember, 20–27, 29, 31, 33, 34, 36, 38, 40, 42, 48–51
Baldwin, Matthias, and Locomotive Works, 160
Barnes, Lawrence, 219–20

Barras, Vicomte de, 101, 104–06
Barre, 141, 157
flood of 1927, 186
history of the quarries, 175–84
naming of, 123–24
"Stovepipe City," 181
Battel, Joseph, 233
Battle of Lake Champlain, 133–38
Bear hunt, story of, 253
Belknap, Suel, 158, 159
Bell, church, saved from Deerfield, 13
Bennett, Merrill Howard, 265
Bennington, 20, 29, 57, 68, 70
Bennington College, 228
Berlin, 36, 134, 135, 260
Black Swan, taking of, 127–32
Blue laws, 251–52
Bodies kept in cold storage, tale of, 168–70
Bolton, 5, 36, 159, 271
Bolton Falls, 270, 271
Bolton Narrows, 5, 158, 159, 270
Bolton Outlaws, 271
Bread Loaf, and the Summer School of English, 233–34
Bridges, covered, 259
Brink, Clyde and Leola, 252–55
Brown, John, 218–19
Brown, Joseph, 115–17
Bulfinch, Charles, 218
Bullock, Mildred, 223–24
Burchard, Reverend Jedediah, 153, 231
Burgoyne, General John, 53–54, 57, 97, 115
Burling, land owner, 31
Burlington, 4, 91, 109, 124, 127, 133, 136, 137, 152, 158, 160, 207, 211, 214–22
airport, 278
fight for selection as capital city, 203–07
Grasse Mount, 214–22

Burlington, *Continued*
  purchase of site, 34
Burlington and Rutland Railroad,
  158–61, 279
Burt, Craig, 249
Business and politics, 201–02

Cabot, 119, 141, 260
Cady, Dan, 241–42
Calais, 118, 141
  school, 223–24
Camel's Hump, 16, 90, 162, 242, 269
Cameron, Secretary Simon, 164
Canada, loss by the French, 28
  trade with, 134
Canadian National Railways, 192
Canal, Lake Champlain to the St.
  Lawrence, project of I.
  Allen, 110
"Canoe place," 24
Capital city. *See* Montpelier
Capitol, State, at Montpelier, 176,
  203–04
  beauty of, 206
  fire in, 203
Carleton, General Sir Guy, 46, 47
Carnot, Lazare Nicolas Margue-
  rite, 92, 101
Central Railroad of Vermont. *See*
  Vermont Central Railroad
Champlain, Samuel de, 6–8
Champlain, Lake. *See* Lake Cham-
  plain
Champlain Canal, 156
Champlain Valley Exposition, 277–
  78
Chittenden, Martin, 274
Chittenden, Governor Thomas
  ("One-Eyed"), 59, 65, 70–
  72, 78–81, 83, 96, 98, 273,
  274–75
Civil War, 164–65
  Confederate raid on St. Albans,
  207

Clinton, Sir Henry, 63–73
Clothespins, manufacture of, 260,
  261
Coates, Walter, *Driftwind—from
  the North Hills,* 242–44
Cockburn, William, 35–36
Colburn, Zerah, 150–52
Colchester, 84, 88, 109, 112, 115,
  171, 258
Colchester jar, 271
Colchester Point, 52, 128, 279
Cold storage, tale of bodies kept
  in, 168–70
Colleges. *See* Education; *also*
  names of colleges
Colony of Vermont, proposed, 42–
  43
Colony, Free, for free love, 171–74
Confederate raid on St. Albans,
  207
Connecticut, land claimed by Penn-
  sylvania, 82
  land owners, 21, 23
  land war with New York, 28
Connecticut River, 3, 4, 6, 9, 13,
  15, 59
Conservation, soil, 273–74
Coolidge, President Calvin, 192
  birthplace, Plymouth, 197
Cork, 159
Council of Safety, 56, 57, 80
Country life, 253–55
Course of the river, 6
Covered bridges, 259
Craig, Burt, 251
Crane, Charles Edward, 240
Crown Point, 25, 26, 50, 52, 54,
  147
Current of the river, 24, 25, 270
Custer, General George A., 165

Dairying, 260
Dams. *See* Floods
Dartmouth College, 59–60

Davenport, Tom, and his electromagnetic machine, 146–49

Davis, Colonel Jacob, 120–21, 124–26, 134

Dawn Valcour Agricultural and Horticultural Association, 171–74

Day of Judgment, awaiting of, 153–55

Daye, Stephen, Press, 262

"Dead" kept in cold storage, 168–70

De Boer, Joseph A., 210

Deer hunting, 271

Deerfield, Massachusetts, massacre, and trek of survivors to Canada, 9–13, 15

Democrats and Federalists, 134–36

Depth of the river, 24

Dewey, Admiral George, 208–09, 225

Dewey, John, 222, 239–40

Diamond Dyes, 220–21

Dispute over jurisdiction, 4

Dog River, 118, 157, 225, 240, 263

Dow, Lorenzo ("Crazy"), 140–45

Dow, Mrs. Peggy, and her hymn book, 144–45

Driftwind—from the North Hills, by W. Coates, 242–44

Drownings in the river, 121. See also Floods

Dublin, 159

Dundas, Henry, 69, 70

Dwight, Timothy, 231, 239

East Barre, 176, 192, 195

Edison, Thomas A., on monopoly, 201

Education, 223–34

Edward Augustus, Prince (Duke of Kent), visit of, 124–26, 156

Electric Railway, Mount Mansfield, 167

Electromagnetic machine of Davenport, 146–49

Embargo Act, 127

Emerson, Ralph Waldo, visit of, 239

Emily S., repentance of, 154

English, the, Abnaki hatred of, 8

England and French warfare, 4, 14, 28

Episcopal school at Rock Point, 228

Epitaphs, 262

Erosion, soil, 273–74

Essex, 24, 78, 109, 166

Essex Junction, 276–77

verses on, by E. J. Phelps, 277

Ethan Allen Park, 278

Ethan Allen Players, 229

Exposition, Champlain Valley, 277–78

Factory girl, life of, 255–58

Fair, Champlain Valley Exposition, 277–78

Fairbanks, Governor Erastus, 164

Falls of the river, 4, 16, 21–25, 29, 33, 51, 52, 79, 83, 115, 122, 270, 271

Famous Vermonters, 207

Fanny Allen Hospital, 228, 229

Fassett, Captain Jonathan, 52, 53

"Father of Vermont." See Allen, Ira

Fauna, 263

Federal and State governments, conflict over control of water power, 199–202

Federal Power Commission, 197

Federalists and Democrats, 134–36

First Vermont Cavalry, 164–65

Fish in the river, 25, 121, 270

Fisher, Dorothy Canfield, 240

Fiske, Reverend Perrin B., 242
Flood control project, 192–202
Floods, 83, 185–202, 272
  great, of 1927, 185–93
Ford, Henry, 272
Forest, Vermont Research, 275
Fort Anne, 65
Fort Ethan Allen, 229, 278
Fort Frederick, 33
Fort George, 65–66
Fort William Henry, 28
Four-H Camp, 276
Free Colony, for free love, 171–74
"Freedom and Unity," State motto, 209
French, William, shooting of, 42
French and English warfare, 4, 14, 28
French and Indian War, 28
French River (name of the Winooski), 139
Frontier hardships, 113–14
Fur trade, 14

Gale, Ed, 251
Gale, Jenny, 248–52
Gantlet, running the, 18
Gates, General Horatio, 52, 53, 59
Gay, Leon, 211
General store at Moretown, 245–48
Geology of the river country, 5–6
George III, 40–41, 124, 126
Germain, Lord George, 63, 64, 70, 97
Gibson, Senator Ernest, Sr., 197
Glidden, Joseph and Mark, 176, 183
Goddard College, 227–28
"Gods of the hills," remark made by E. Allen, 29
Gold, 166–67
Gold Brook, 166–67

Gorge, Winooski, 278
  described by I. Allen, 24
Governors, simplicity of life, 209
Granite. See Quarries
Granite structures, 183
"Grants," land, 14
Grants, New Hampshire. See New Hampshire Grants
Grasse Mount, Burlington, 214–22
Gray Lock, Chief, 7–8, 15–19, 54
"Greatwood," 227
Greeley, Horace, 236
Green Mount Cemetery, 90
Green Mountain Boys, 35, 36, 38, 42, 44–48, 50, 51, 56, 68, 74
  capture of Ticonderoga, 43, 44, 56
  election of Warner as colonel, 45
  rewards offered for arrest, 39
Green Mountain Parkway dispute, 211–23
Green Mountain Power Corporation, 195–97
Green Mountains, 3, 5, 6, 7
Greylock, Mount, 18

Haldimand, General Frederick, 64–73
Hanging, first in the State, 132
Hanover, New Hampshire, 59–60
Hardships, pioneers', 113–14
Harrington, Luke, 271–72
Hasbrook, Philip, 274–75
Hastings, Dr. Thomas, on the Wright expedition, 15–16
Hermits, 263–64
Herrick's Rangers, 56
Hiking, 269
Historical Society, 211, 261–62
Holden, Captain Joseph, 123–24
Hoover, Herbert, 192
Hope Cemetery, 184
Horses, Morgan, 162–65

Hospital, Fanny Allen, 228, 229
Hospital for mental cases, 26
Houghton, Richard, 116–17
Howells, William Dean, praise of
    view over Lake Champlain,
    221
Hubbel's Falls, 24, 115
Hunting, 271
Huntington River, 271
Hurricane of 1928, 200
Hydroelectric power. *See* Power
Hymn book, Peggy Dow's, 145

Immigrants, from Ireland, 159
Italian quarry workers, 183–84
quarry workers, 180–81
Scottish quarry workers, 176–
    80
Independent Vermont, by C. M.
    Thompson, 70
Indians, Abnaki, 4, 7, 15, 54;
    eclipse of prestige, 19;
    hatred of the English, 8
Algonquin, 3, 4, 6–8, 10, 14, 15,
    28; eclipse of prestige, 18
atrocities, 18; inflicted on Deer-
    field survivors, 9–13; run-
    ning the gantlet, 18
Iroquois, 3, 6, 8, 14, 15; friends
    of the English, 8
letter to, by E. Allen, 46
Maine, 8
pottery, 270–71
raids, 15, 17, 115–17; Deerfield,
    Massachusetts, 9–13, 15
St. Francis, 4, 8, 10, 15, 18, 119
war trail, 4
Waranoke, 15
warfare, 6–8
Inventor on the Winooski, 146–49
Irish immigrants, 159
Iron, 28
Iroquois, 3, 6, 8, 14, 15
Italian immigrants, 183–84

Jackson, Andrew, 216
Jackson, Lieutenant Governor Hol-
    lister, death in flood, 186
Jar, Colchester, 271
Jefferson, Thomas, 52, 109, 110,
    127
Jericho, 24, 52, 115, 117, 122
John, Chief, 120
Jones, Secretary William, 133
Joy's Landing, 129
Judd, Edward, 263–64
Judgment Day, 153–55
Jurisdiction, dispute over, 4
Justin Morgan, horse, 162–65

Kent, Duke of (Prince Edward Au-
    gustus), visit of, 124–26,
    156
Kent, Atwater, 222
King, Rufus, 95, 96
Kingsbury's Branch, 118
Kipling, Rudyard, 239

Lafayette, visit of, 209, 210, 215,
    232
Lake Champlain, 3–7
Battle of, 54
view praised by W. D. Howells,
    221
Lake Mansfield, 252
Landslides, 263
"Last Day," 153–55
Laws of the Republic of Vermont,
    55
"Laws, blue," 251–52
"Lay of the Lost Traveler," by E.
    J. Phelps, 277
Learned, Winnie Bell, 234
Leavenworth, Henry, 216
Legend of Woksis and Moqua, and
    the discovery of maple
    syrup, 7
Legislature, 206–07
Length of the river, 3

Liberty, 83
Life in the country, 253–55
Lincoln, Abraham, 164
Lion Couchant (Camel's Hump),
    242
Liquor, battle against, 153
Little North Branch, 121, 210, 243
Lucioni, Luigi, 237
Lumbering, 24, 83, 91, 127, 216,
    219, 220, 246, 263
Lyceum, 193
Lyon, Lieutenant Matthew, 52, 53,
    96, 115

Macdonough, Lieutenant Thomas,
    133, 136–38
Mad River, 245, 263, 264
Mad River Glen, 263
Madison, James, 109, 134–36, 215
Manchester, 56
Mansfield. *See* Stowe
Mansfield, Mount. *See* Mount
    Mansfield
Manufactures, 219, 259
Maple syrup, legend of discovery,
    7
Maple tree and its products, 275–
    76
"Marble, Winooski," 264
Marriott, Sir James, 95–99
Marsh, James, 121–23, 232
Marvin, Charles, 216, 219
Massachusetts, claim of Vermont
    lands, 60, 73
Mathematician, Zerah Colburn,
    150–52
McKinley, President William, 208
Medicines, patent, 259
Mental hospital, Waterbury, 187,
    265
Methodist Hill, 140
Middlebury, 165, 233
Middlebury College, 110, 231,
    233–34

Middlesex, 36, 121, 245, 263
Mill, woolen, work in, 255–58
Miller, William, and Millerism,
    153–55
Miller Brook, 252
Millstone Hill, 175–84, 264
Missisquoi Bay, 128
Missisquoi River, 7, 8, 17, 19,
    207
Molly's Pond, 119, 188
Monopoly, views of Edison, 201
Monroe, James, 109, 216
Montpelier, 4, 118, 120–22, 134,
    139, 140, 153, 157, 162,
    181, 203–13, 214, 260–63
    cemeteries, 262
    controversy with Burlington over
        selection as capital city,
        203–07
    description, 210–11
    Dewey, Admiral, city's most
        famous man, 208–09
    flood of 1927, 186
    State House. *See* Capitol, State
Montpelier Seminary, 228
Montreal, plan of Ethan Allen for
    capture, 45–47, 67
Moqua and Woksis, legend of, 7
Moretown, 245–48
Morgan, Justin, and the Morgan
    horse, 162–65
Motor, first electric, 146–49
Motto, State, "Freedom and
    Unity," 209
"Mount Discovery," 16
Mount Mansfield, 90, 134, 166,
    242, 249, 269
    Electric Railway, 167
Mount St. Mary's Academy, 228
Mountain News, 249
Musicians, 269
Muxawuxal, 119

Names of the river, 3, 21, 139

Napoleon I, 92, 106, 146, 152
Narrows, Bolton, 5, 158, 159, 270
   looking down, test of nerves, 30
Navigability of the river, 5, 29,
      156, 201
Negotiations with English over
      possible alienation of Ver-
      mont, 63–73
Negro slavery, abolition of, 219
Neptune, 107
New Hampshire, 40
   claim on Vermont, 60
   land war with New York, 28
   relinquishment of land claims,
      73
   towns' movement to join Ver-
      mont, 59–60; return of
      towns to Vermont, 72
New Hampshire Grants, 23, 28,
      29, 31, 35, 38, 40, 42, 53,
      54, 97
New York, attempt to survey
      river land, 21–23
   land claims, 34, 36–43, 54, 60;
      relinquishment, 73
   land war with New Hampshire,
      28
   land owners in Vermont, 31
   town's return by Vermont, 72
Nicholl, Doctor, 96, 98
Non-Intercourse Act, 134
North Branch, 193
Northfield, 117, 157–59, 185, 225
Norwich University, 152, 225–26

Olive Branch, 93–95
Oneida Colony, 172
Onion River (name of the Winoo-
      ski), 21
Onion River Falls, 83
Onion River Land Company, 34,
      41, 43–45, 51, 54, 57, 59,
      60, 64, 68, 73, 79, 92–94,
      97–100, 107, 108, 216

Onion River Navigation and Tow
      Path Company, 156
Otter Creek, 38, 53, 84, 136, 149,
      198, 231

Paine, Governor Charles, 156–61
Paine, Judge Elijah, 125–26, 156,
      214–15
Paine, Tom, 101
   The Age of Reason, 140
Paine's Celery Compound, 220
Painters, 235–37
"Pardon Jones, the Mystery Man
      of Calais," 243–44
Parkway, Green Mountain, dispute
      over, 211–13
Partridge, Captain Alden, 225–26
Patent, first American, 127
Patent medicines, 259
"Peggy Dow's Hymn Book," 145
Pennsylvania land claim on Con-
      necticut, 82
Periere, de la, family, 14
Perkins, Doctor Nathan, 79, 89,
      239
Phelps, Edward J., "The Lay of
      the Lost Traveler," 277
Pickering, Timothy, 95
Pindar, Peter, 126
Pioneers, hardships of, 113–14
Pittsford, 25–27
Place, Captain de la, 44
Plainfield, 35, 141, 226–27, 262
Plymouth, birthplace of President
      Coolidge, 197
Poem by E. J. Phelps, 277
Poem by T. Rowley, 73
Poem, "Song of the Vermonters,"
      by Whittier, 238–39
Poetry, writers of, 238–44
Poetry Society, 269
Politics, State, 134–36, 194, 211
   and business, 201–08
Potash, smuggling of, 127–32

Potash Brook, 186
Pottery, Indian, 270–71
Power from flood-control dams,
    controversy over, 196–202
Power Commission, Federal, 197
Prescott, General, 47, 48, 95
Proctor, Secretary Redfield, 208

Quarries, granite, 175–84, 264
    silicosis, 184
    working method, 182–83
Quebec, attack on, 51
"Queen City." See Burlington
Quinlan, Gordon, 272–73

Railroad, coming of, 156–61
    "Sky Route," 180
        See also names of railroads
Ranch Camp, 251
Randolph, 116, 162
Rankin, John, 199–201
Rapids, 5, 115. See also Falls
Reason the Only Oracle of Man,
    by E. Allen, 140
Reid, Colonel John, 36–38
Religion, 139–45, 153–55
Republic of Vermont, 55–56, 78
    laws, 55
Revere, Paul, 218
Revolt of troops, 52–53
Revolution, American, 43, 63
Richelieu River, 46, 91
Richmond, 271, 272
Ripley, George, 263
Robinson, Reverend Amminidab,
    85
Robinson, Colonel Beverly, 65
Robinson, Rowland, 241
Rock of Ages quarry, 182
Rock Point Episcopal School,
    228
Rockwell, Norman, 237
Rocky River Farm, 252
Rogers, Robert, 17

Roosevelt, President Franklin Del-
    ano, 196, 198, 201
    visit, 194–95
Round Church, Richmond, 272
Rowley, T., poem by, 73
Royal Savage, 54
Ruschp, Sepp, 249
Russell, Byron, 253
Rutland, 158
Rutland and Burlington Railroad,
    158–61, 279

Sabbath, observance, 139, 252
Saddle Mountain (Camel's Hump),
    242
St. Albans, Confederate raid on,
    207
St. Albans Bay, 128
St. Francis Indians, 4, 8, 10, 15,
    18, 119
St. Lawrence River, 4
St. Michael's College, 228–29
Salisbury, Connecticut, 20, 28, 33,
    59, 74, 79
Sanborn, Nancy, 167
Saratoga, surrender of Burgoyne,
    57
Saxe, John G., 241
School at Calais, 223–24
Schools. See Education
Schuyler, General Philip John, 46,
    48, 50–53
Scottish immigrants, 176–80
Seigneuries, 14
Seymour, Senator Horatio, 216
Shays, Captain Daniel, and his
    Rebellion, 84
Sheep raising, 260
Sherwood, Captain Justus, 66–70
Shipman, Orren, 171–74
Shipway, Lake Champlain to the
    St. Lawrence, 91
Shipyard, first on the river, 83
Silicosis, 184

Skene, Colonel Philip, 42, 43
Skenesborough, 54, 71, 122
Skiing, 248–52, 263
"Sky Route," 180
Slavery, abolition of, 219
Smith, Governor Charles, 195
Smith, Joseph, 183
Smuggler's Notch, 134, 167–68, 269
Smuggling, 127–32
Society of St. Edmund, 228
Soil erosion, 273–74
"Song of the Vermonters," poem by Whittier, 238–39
Sources of the river, 119
Spanish-American War, 208
Stark, John, 56, 57
State House. See Capitol
Statehood, admission to the Union, 73
  eligibility for, 57
  fight for, 59–62
States' rights issue in flood control, 196–202
Stephen Daye Press, 262
Sterling Mountain and Pond, 269
Stevens, Captain, survey of river land; conflict with I. Allen, 21–23
Stevens, Benjamin, 32, 34–35
Stevens, Elbert, 168–70
Stevens Branch, 35, 36, 118, 146, 175, 184, 260
Stiles, Ezra, 89
Stimson, Secretary Henry L., 198, 199
Store at Moretown, 245–48
Storm, great, of 1928, 200
"Stovepipe City" (Barre), 181
Stowe (formerly Mansfield), 137, 149, 166, 167, 249, 250, 262, 263, 266
Stowe-Mansfield Association, 248, 250

Suez Canal, project of I. Allen, 102
Summer visitors, 276
Sunday observance, 139, 252
Swiss visitors, 252
Symphony Orchestra, 269

Talc, 264–65
Talleyrand, 101, 105, 106, 109
Telegraph, first, 148
Temperance movement, 153
Thompson, Charles Miner, Independent Vermont, 70
Tichenor, Isaac, 95, 98, 107, 108, 131, 135
Ticonderoga, 43, 46, 50, 54, 67
  taking by Green Mountain Boys, 43, 44, 56
Toomalek, 119–20
Trapp, Baron Georg von, and the Trapp Singers, 267–69
Treasure, buried, 166
Trees, 275
Tributaries of the river, 118, 122, 157, 175, 193, 195, 210, 231, 245, 252, 260, 263, 264, 266, 271
Tyler, Royall, 239

Union Village, 197, 198
Unitarian Church, Burlington, 218–19
University of Vermont, 108, 110, 214, 221, 230–35
  founding by I. Allen, 91, 103

Valcour Community, 171–74
Valley of the river, 6
Van Ness, Governor Cornelius, 215–16, 221
Varin, Lucette, 255–58
Vergennes shipyard, 136
Vermont Central Railroad, 156–61, 190, 192, 194, 249, 265, 266

Vermont Historical Society, 211, 261–62
Vermont Junior College, 228
Vermont Musical Festival, 269
Vermont Poetry Society, 269
Vermont Research Forest, 275
Vermont Symphony Orchestra, 269
Vermonters, famous, 207
Visitors, summer, 276

Wallace, Matthew, 135
War, English and French, 4, 14, 28
War of 1812, 133–38, 230
Waranoke Indians, 15
Ward, Burton, 245–48
Ward, Mr. and Mrs. Merlin, 246
Warner, Seth, 36, 38, 42, 45, 56
Washington, George, 44, 68, 70, 119, 127
  letter to Chittenden, 72
  on capture of E. Allen, 48
  on E. Allen, 58
Waterbury, 25, 36, 121, 123, 137, 192, 193, 250, 263–65
Waterbury mental hospital, 187
Waterbury River, 122, 195, 252, 266–67, 269
  Dam, 193–96, 198, 201
Watershed, 3
Weather Bureau, United States, 226
Weeks, Governor John E., 191–92
Wells, Edward, 220–21
Wells, Captain Thomas, expedition of, 16
Wells & Richardson Company, 220–21
Wentworth, Governor Benning, 23, 40–43, 54
Wheelock, Eleazar, 59–60
Wheelock, Dr. John, 151

Whiston, John, 23–24, 40
White, H. Augusta, 172–74
White River, 13, 15
Whittier, John Greenleaf, "Song of the Vermonters," 238–39
Wildersburg, 123–24
Willard, Bartley, 240–41
Willard, Emma, 231
Willcox, John, 171–74
Williams, Eunice (daughter of John), story of, 10, 18
Williams, Reverend John, 9–13
Williamstown, 146, 147, 149, 156
Williston, 53, 79, 83, 123, 234
Winooski (town), 160, 219, 256
Winooski Canal, 156
Winooski Gorge, 278
"Winooski marble," 264
Winooski Park, 228–30
Winooski River Soil Conservation Project, 273–74
Witches, 167
Woksis and Moqua, legend of, 7
Women, colleges for, 231, 233
Wood, Thomas Waterman, 235–36
Woodbury (horse), 164
Woodbury, (town), 118
Woodhouse (free love colonist), 172–74
Woodworth, Reverend Ziba, 135
Woolen mill, work in, 255–58
Wright, Captain Benjamin, expeditions of, 15–16
Wright, Reverend Chester, 135, 139
Wright, Medad, 193
Wrightsville, 192, 195
Writers, 238–44

Young, Reverend Joshua, 218–19
"Young Ladies' and Gentlemen's Lyceum," 193